First World War
and Army of Occupation
War Diary
France, Belgium and Germany

24 DIVISION
72 Infantry Brigade
Prince of Wales's (North Staffordshire Regiment)
1st Battalion
1 November 1915 - 31 May 1919

WO95/2213/1

The Naval & Military Press Ltd
www.nmarchive.com
Published in association with The National Archives

Published by

The Naval & Military Press Ltd

Unit 10 Ridgewood Industrial Park,

Uckfield, East Sussex,

TN22 5QE England

Tel: +44 (0) 1825 749494

www.naval-military-press.com

www.nmarchive.com

This diary has been reprinted in facsimile from the original. Any imperfections are inevitably reproduced and the quality may fall short of modern type and cartographic standards.

© **Crown Copyright**
Images reproduced by permission of The National Archives, London, England, 2015.

Contents

Document type	Place/Title	Date From	Date To
Heading	WO95/2213/1		
Heading	1st Battalion North Staffordshire Regiment November 1915.- May 1919		
War Diary		01/11/1915	30/11/1915
Miscellaneous	Div Routine Order by major gun I.B. Corps. C.B	09/11/1915	09/11/1915
Heading	1st Battalion North Staffordshire Regiment December 1915.		
War Diary		01/12/1915	06/01/1916
Heading	1st Battalion North Staffordshire Regiment January 1916		
Heading			
War Diary		06/01/1916	31/01/1916
Heading	1st Battalion North Staffordshire Regiment February 1916		
War Diary		30/01/1916	02/03/1916
Heading	1st Battalion North Staffordshire Regiment. March 1916		
War Diary		01/03/1916	01/04/1916
Heading	1st Battalion North Staffordshire Regiment April 1916		
War Diary		02/04/1916	03/05/1916
Miscellaneous	A Form. Messages And Signals.	29/05/1916	29/05/1916
Miscellaneous	A Form. Messages And Signals.	30/05/1916	30/05/1916
Miscellaneous	Special Order		
Miscellaneous	A Form. Messages And Signals.		
Heading	1st Battalion North Staffordshire Regiment. May 1916		
War Diary		01/05/1916	31/05/1916
Miscellaneous	Appendix D. The Distinguished Service Order.	22/05/1916	22/05/1916
Heading	1st Battalion North Staffordshire Regiment June 1916		
War Diary		01/06/1916	30/06/1916
Heading	1st Battn. The North Staffordshire Regiment. July 1916		
War Diary		01/07/1916	31/07/1916
Heading	1st Battalion North Staffordshire Regiment August 1916		
Heading	War Diary of 1st Bn North Staffordshire Regt. from 1-8-16 To 31-8-16		
War Diary		01/08/1916	31/08/1916
Miscellaneous	Appendix A. War Diary period 1st Aug.-31st. Aug. 1916.		
Miscellaneous	Appendix B, War Diary 1st.-31st. Aug. 1916.		
Miscellaneous	Appendix C, War Diary. Period 1st.-31st. Aug. 1916.		
Miscellaneous	Appendix D, War Diary. Period 1st.-31st. Aug. 1916.	30/08/1916	30/08/1916
Miscellaneous	Appendix E. War Diary, period 1st.-31st. August, 1916.	31/08/1916	31/08/1916
Miscellaneous	Appendix F. War Diary period 1st.-31st. Aug. 1916.		
Miscellaneous	Appendix G. War Diary period 1st. Aug.-31st. Aug. 1916.	11/09/1916	11/09/1916
Heading	1st Battalion North Staffordshire Regiment September 1916		
War Diary		01/09/1916	30/09/1916
Miscellaneous	Appendix A. War Diary period 1st. to 31st. Sept. 16.		
Miscellaneous	G. 24C. Division.	10/09/1916	10/09/1916
Miscellaneous	72nd Infy Bde	10/09/1916	10/09/1916

Heading	1st Battalion North Staffordshire Regiment October 1916		
War Diary		01/10/1916	31/10/1916
Miscellaneous	Appendix A. War Diary, period 1st. to 31st. October 1916.	02/10/1916	02/10/1916
Miscellaneous	Appendix B. War Diary Period 1st Oct 16 to 31st Oct. 16		
Heading	1st Battalion North Staffordshire Regiment November 1916		
War Diary		01/11/1916	30/11/1916
Miscellaneous	Appendix A. War Diary period 1st.-30th. Nov.		
Miscellaneous	if anything unusual occurred.	28/11/1916	28/11/1916
Heading	1st Battalion North Staffordshire Regiment December 1916		
War Diary		01/12/1916	31/01/1917
Heading	War Diary 1st Battn North Staffordshire Regt. Month of February 1917.		
War Diary	Philosophe	01/02/1917	03/02/1917
War Diary	Hulluch Right Sub-Section	04/02/1917	13/02/1917
War Diary	Noeux-Les-mines	13/02/1917	13/02/1917
War Diary	Busnettes	14/02/1917	28/02/1917
Miscellaneous	Attempted German Raid on the Battn. Trenches.	10/02/1917	10/02/1917
Miscellaneous	1st Battalion North Staffordshire Regiment.		
Heading	War Diary for month of March 1917.		
War Diary	Busnettes	01/03/1917	04/03/1917
War Diary	Fouquereuil	05/03/1917	05/03/1917
War Diary	Bully Grenay	06/03/1917	08/03/1917
War Diary	Moroc Left Sub Section Calonne Defenses	04/03/1917	14/03/1917
War Diary	Calonne	15/03/1917	26/03/1917
War Diary	Bully Grenay	27/03/1917	31/03/1917
Heading	1st Battn. N. Staff. Regiment 72nd Infantry Brigade 24th Division April 1917		
Heading	War Diary for month of April 1917.		
War Diary	Bully Grenay	01/04/1917	01/04/1917
War Diary	Maroc	02/04/1917	07/04/1917
War Diary	Calonne	08/04/1917	15/04/1917
War Diary	Cite St Pierre	16/04/1917	20/04/1917
War Diary	Allouagne	21/04/1917	22/04/1917
War Diary	Westrehem	23/04/1917	25/04/1917
War Diary	Reclinghem	26/04/1917	30/04/1917
Heading	War Diary for May 1917.		
War Diary	Reclinghem	01/05/1917	08/05/1917
War Diary	Ligny-Lez Aire	09/05/1917	09/05/1917
War Diary	Boeseghem	10/05/1917	11/05/1917
War Diary	Near Abeele	12/05/1917	13/05/1917
War Diary	Brandhoek	14/05/1917	14/05/1917
War Diary	Zillebeke Sector	15/05/1917	29/05/1917
War Diary	Hopoutre (S.W. Poperinghe)	30/05/1917	31/05/1917
Miscellaneous	1st Bn. North Staffordshire Regt. Programme of Training.		
Miscellaneous	1st Bn. North Staffordshire Regiment Programme of Training.		
Heading	War Diary month of June 1917.		
War Diary	Nr Abeele	01/06/1917	03/06/1917
War Diary	Hopoutre	04/06/1917	04/06/1917
War Diary	Duminion Camp	05/06/1917	06/06/1917

Type	Location	From	To
War Diary	Micmac Camp	07/06/1917	07/06/1917
War Diary	Railway Dugouts on Men in Ry near Ypres	08/06/1917	09/06/1917
War Diary	Mount Sorrel Trenches	10/06/1917	12/06/1917
War Diary	Dickebusch	13/06/1917	17/06/1917
War Diary	Mount Sorrel Trenches	18/06/1917	19/06/1917
War Diary	Micmac Camp	20/06/1917	23/06/1917
War Diary	Battle Wood Support	24/06/1917	29/06/1917
War Diary	Micmac Camp	30/06/1917	30/06/1917
War Diary	War Diary of 1st Bn North Staffordshire Regt. from 1/7/17-31/7/17		
War Diary	Senninghem	01/07/1917	18/07/1917
War Diary	Renescure	19/07/1917	19/07/1917
War Diary	Caestre	20/07/1917	20/07/1917
War Diary	Eecke	21/07/1917	21/07/1917
War Diary	Steenvorde	22/07/1917	23/07/1917
War Diary	Micmac Camp	24/07/1917	29/07/1917
War Diary	Trenches.	30/07/1917	31/07/1917
Miscellaneous	Action or 1st North Staffordshire Regt in Third Battle of Ypres commencing 31st July 1917	04/08/1917	04/08/1917
Miscellaneous	Report On The Operations Of 31st July, 1917	04/08/1917	04/08/1917
Heading	War Diary Of 1st. Battalion North Staffordshire Regiment. From 1st. to 31st. August 1917.		
War Diary	Mount Sorrel	01/08/1917	01/08/1917
War Diary	Micmac Camp	02/08/1917	11/08/1917
War Diary	Micmac	11/08/1917	11/08/1917
War Diary	Dickebusch	12/08/1917	15/08/1917
War Diary	Line	16/08/1917	19/08/1917
War Diary	Micmac Camp	20/08/1917	23/08/1917
War Diary	Dickebusch	24/08/1917	27/08/1917
War Diary	Front Line	28/08/1917	31/08/1917
Heading	War Diary 1st Battn. North Staffordshire Regt. September		
War Diary	Micmac Camp	01/09/1917	03/09/1917
War Diary	Dickebusch	04/09/1917	06/09/1917
War Diary	Trenches	07/09/1917	11/09/1917
War Diary	Micmac Camp	12/09/1917	13/09/1917
War Diary	Strazeele	14/09/1917	20/09/1917
War Diary	Le. Transloy	21/09/1917	24/09/1917
War Diary	Haut Allaine	25/09/1917	26/09/1917
War Diary	Bernes	27/09/1917	27/09/1917
War Diary	Trenches	28/09/1917	30/09/1917
Heading	War Diary 1st Battn. North Staffordshire Regiment October 1917		
War Diary	In the Trenches	01/10/1917	04/10/1917
War Diary	Support Line	05/10/1917	10/10/1917
War Diary	In the Trenches	11/10/1917	15/10/1917
War Diary	Support Line	16/10/1917	21/10/1917
War Diary	Trenches	22/10/1917	26/10/1917
War Diary	Vendelles	27/10/1917	31/10/1917
Heading	War Diary of 1st Battn. North Staffordshire Regt 1st-30th November 1917.		
War Diary	Front Line	01/11/1917	06/11/1917
War Diary	Support Line	07/11/1917	12/11/1917
War Diary	Front Line	13/11/1917	17/11/1917
War Diary	Support Line	18/11/1917	19/11/1917
War Diary	Vendelles	20/11/1917	24/11/1917

War Diary	Trenches	25/11/1917	30/11/1917
Heading	War Diary 1st Bn. North Staffordshire Regt. 1st-31st December 1917		
War Diary	Trenches	01/12/1917	03/12/1917
War Diary	Vendelles	04/12/1917	07/12/1917
War Diary	Cote Wood	08/12/1917	08/12/1917
War Diary	Trenches	09/12/1917	14/12/1917
War Diary	Cote Wood	15/12/1917	21/12/1917
War Diary	Vraignes	22/12/1917	31/12/1917
Miscellaneous	Reference the attached Training Programme.	20/12/1917	20/12/1917
Miscellaneous	1st Batt. North Staffordshire Regiment Programme Of Training		
Miscellaneous	Training Programme	06/12/1917	06/12/1917
Miscellaneous		07/12/1917	07/12/1917
Operation(al) Order(s)	Operation Order No. 201, 1st Battalion North Staffordshire Regiment.	08/12/1917	08/12/1917
Operation(al) Order(s)	Operation Order No. 202. 1st Battalion North Staffordshire Regiment.	08/12/1917	08/12/1917
Operation(al) Order(s)	Operation Order No. 203. 1st Battalion North Staffordshire Regiment.	13/12/1917	13/12/1917
Operation(al) Order(s)	Operation Order No. 204. 1st Battalion North Staffordshire Regiment.	19/12/1917	19/12/1917
Heading	I. O.		
Operation(al) Order(s)	Operation Order No 204 1st Battalion North Staffordshire Regiment.	19/12/1917	19/12/1917
Miscellaneous	Addendum To Operation Order No. 204. 1st Battalion North Staffordshire Regiment.	20/12/1917	20/12/1917
Map			
Miscellaneous			
Heading	War Diary 1st Battn. North Staffordshire Regt. month of January 1918.		
War Diary	Vraignes	01/01/1918	01/01/1918
War Diary	Montigny	02/01/1918	04/01/1918
War Diary	Line	05/01/1918	08/01/1918
War Diary	Support	09/01/1918	12/01/1918
War Diary	Vendelles	13/01/1918	29/01/1918
War Diary	Support	30/01/1918	31/01/1918
Operation(al) Order(s)	Operation Order No. 205. 1st Battalion North Staffordshire Regiment.	30/12/1917	30/12/1917
Operation(al) Order(s)	Operation Order No. 206. 1st Battalion North Staffordshire Regiment.	03/01/1918	03/01/1918
Operation(al) Order(s)	Operation Order No. 207. 1st Battalion North Staffordshire Regiment.	07/01/1918	07/01/1918
Operation(al) Order(s)	Operation Order No. 208. 1st Battalion North Staffordshire Regiment.	11/01/1918	11/01/1918
Operation(al) Order(s)	Operation Order No. 209 1st Battn. North Staffordshire Regiment.	24/01/1918	24/01/1918
Operation(al) Order(s)	Operation Order No. 210 1st Battalion North Staffordshire Regiment.	28/01/1918	28/01/1918
Heading	War Diary 1st Battn. North Staffordshire Regiment Period- February 1918		
War Diary	Support Templeux Quarries	01/02/1918	02/02/1918
War Diary	Front Line	03/02/1918	04/02/1918
War Diary	Line	04/02/1918	06/02/1918
War Diary	Vraignes	07/02/1918	14/02/1918
War Diary	Front Line	15/02/1918	18/02/1918

War Diary	Montigny	19/02/1918	22/02/1918
War Diary	Support	23/02/1918	26/02/1918
War Diary	Bernes	27/02/1918	27/02/1918
War Diary	Corbie	28/02/1918	28/02/1918
Operation(al) Order(s)	Operation Order No. 210 1st Battalion North Staffordshire Regiment.	01/02/1918	01/02/1918
Miscellaneous	Addendum To Operation Order No. 210.	02/02/1918	02/02/1918
Operation(al) Order(s)	Operation Order No. 211 1st Battalion North Staffordshire Regiment.	05/02/1918	05/02/1918
Operation(al) Order(s)	Operation Order No. 212 1st Battalion North Staffordshire Regiment.	05/02/1918	05/02/1918
Operation(al) Order(s)	Operation Order No. 213. 1st Battalion North Staffordshire Regiment.	13/02/1918	13/02/1918
Operation(al) Order(s)	Operation Order No. 214. 1st Battalion North Staffordshire Regiment.	17/02/1918	17/02/1918
Operation(al) Order(s)	Operation Order No. 215 1st Battalion North Staffordshire Regiment.	20/02/1918	20/02/1918
Operation(al) Order(s)	Operation Order No. 216. 1st Battalion North Staffordshire Regiment.	21/02/1918	21/02/1918
Operation(al) Order(s)	Operation Order No. 217 1st Battalion North Staffordshire Regt.	25/02/1918	25/02/1918
Heading	1st Battalion North Staffordshire Regiment March 1918		
Heading	War Diary Of 1st Battn. North Staffordshire Regt. 1st March 1918 Volume V		
War Diary	Corbie	01/03/1918	01/03/1918
War Diary	Devise	02/03/1918	11/03/1918
War Diary	Vermand	11/03/1918	21/03/1918
Heading	Cover for Documents. Nature of Enclosures. Details obtained from 2/1t. a. Peacock 21.3.18-6.4.-18.		
Miscellaneous			
Miscellaneous	Copy of letter from Capt. W.D. Stamer, M.C.		
Heading	1st Battalion North Staffordshire Regiment April 1918		
War Diary	Niebas	08/04/1918	19/04/1918
War Diary	Huclier	20/04/1918	30/04/1918
Miscellaneous			
Operation(al) Order(s)	Operation Order No. 1 1st North Staffordshire Regt.	16/04/1918	16/04/1918
Heading	War Diary 1st Bn. North Staffordshire Regt Month of May 1918		
War Diary		01/05/1918	31/05/1918
Operation(al) Order(s)	Operation Order No. 4. 1st Bn North Staffordshire Regiment.	07/05/1918	07/05/1918
Operation(al) Order(s)	Operation Order No. 5. 1st Bn. North Staffordshire Regt.	15/05/1918	15/05/1918
Operation(al) Order(s)	Operation Order No. 6 by Lieut. Colonel H.V.R. Hodson, Commanding 1st. Bn. North Staffordshire Regiment.	22/05/1918	22/05/1918
Operation(al) Order(s)	Operation Order No. 8. By, Lieut. Col. H.V.R. Hodson, Comdg. 1st. Bn. North Staffordshire Regt.	28/05/1918	28/05/1918
Heading	War Diary 1st to 30th June 1918. 1st Bn. North Staffordshire Regt.		
War Diary		01/06/1918	30/06/1918
Operation(al) Order(s)	Operation Order No. 9 by Lieut. Colonel E.V.R. Hodson. Commanding, 1st. Battalion, North Staffordshire Regiment.	02/06/1918	02/06/1918
Operation(al) Order(s)	Operation Order No. 10 By. Lieut. Colonel H.V.R. Hodson, Comdg. 1st. Bn. North Staffordshire Regiment.	08/06/1918	08/06/1918

Type	Description	Start	End
Operation(al) Order(s)	Operation Order No. 11. By Lieut. Col. H.V.R. Hodson Commanding 1st. Battalion North Staffordshire Regiment.	14/06/1918	14/06/1918
Operation(al) Order(s)	Operation Order No. 12. By Lieut. Col. H.V.R. Hodson Commanding 1st. Battalion North Staffordshire Regiment.	14/06/1918	14/06/1918
Miscellaneous	Orders In Continuation Of Operation Order No. 12. By Lieut Col. H.V.R. Hodson. Commanding 1st. Battalion North Staffordshire Regiment		
Operation(al) Order(s)	Operation Order No. 13. By Major G.O. Way. D.S.O. Commanding 1st. Battalion North Staffordshire Regiment.	20/06/1918	20/06/1918
Operation(al) Order(s)	Operation Order No. 14 by, Lieut. Col. H.V.R. Hodson. Comdg. 1st. Bn North Staffordshire Regiment.	25/06/1918	25/06/1918
Heading	War Diary Of 1st Bn. North Staffordshire Regiment. From July 1st To July 31st. 1918.		
War Diary	Cite St. Pierre	01/07/1918	01/07/1918
War Diary	Front Line	02/07/1918	07/07/1918
War Diary	Bully Grenay	08/07/1918	14/07/1918
War Diary	Cite St. Pierre	15/07/1918	20/07/1918
War Diary	Front Line	21/07/1918	26/07/1918
War Diary	Bully Grenay	27/07/1918	31/07/1918
Operation(al) Order(s)	Operation Orders No. 15 by Lieut. Colonel H.V.R. Hodson, Commanding, 1st. Battalion North Staffordshire Regiment.	02/07/1918	02/07/1918
Operation(al) Order(s)	1st. Battalion North Staffordshire Regt. Operation Order No. 16.	05/07/1918	05/07/1918
Operation(al) Order(s)	1st. Battalion North Staffordshire Regiment. Operation Order No. 17.	07/07/1918	07/07/1918
Operation(al) Order(s)	1st. Battalion North Staffordshire Regiment. Operation Order No. 18.	14/07/1918	14/07/1918
Operation(al) Order(s)	Operation Order No. 19 1st. Battalion North Staffordshire Regiment.	19/07/1918	19/07/1918
Operation(al) Order(s)	Operation Order No. 20 1st. Bn. North Staffordshire Regiment.	23/07/1918	23/07/1918
Operation(al) Order(s)	Operation Order No. 21 1st. Bn. North Staffordshire Regiment.	26/07/1918	26/07/1918
Heading	War Diary of 1st. Bn. North Staffordshire Regiment. From August 1st. 1918 To August 31st. 1918. Vol.		
War Diary	Bully Grenay	01/08/1918	01/08/1918
War Diary	Support Cite St Pierre	02/08/1918	06/08/1918
War Diary	Front Line	07/08/1918	13/08/1918
War Diary	Bully Grenay	14/08/1918	19/08/1918
War Diary	Right Sub Section	20/08/1918	22/08/1918
War Diary	Front Line	23/08/1918	28/08/1918
War Diary	Right Sub Section	29/08/1918	31/08/1918
Operation(al) Order(s)	1st. Bn. North Staffordshire Regiment. Operation Order No. 22	31/07/1918	31/07/1918
Operation(al) Order(s)	Operation Order No. 23. 1st. Bn. North Staffordshire Regiment.	06/08/1918	06/08/1918
Miscellaneous			
Operation(al) Order(s)	Operation Order No. 24. 1st. Battalion North Staffordshire Regiment.	10/08/1918	10/08/1918
Operation(al) Order(s)	Operation Order No. 25. 1st. Battalion North Staffordshire Regiment.	13/08/1918	13/08/1918

Operation(al) Order(s)	Operation Order No. 26. 1st. Bn. North Staffordshire Regiment.	19/08/1918	19/08/1918
Miscellaneous			
Operation(al) Order(s)	Operation Order No. 27. 1st. Bn. North Staffordshire Regiment.	25/08/1918	25/08/1918
Miscellaneous			
Operation(al) Order(s)	1st Bn. North Staffordshire Regt. Operation Order No. 28	29/08/1918	29/08/1918
Operation(al) Order(s)	Operation Order No. 29 1st. Bn. North Staffordshire Regiment.	31/08/1918	31/08/1918
Heading	War Diary of 1st Bn. North Staffordshire Rgt. September 1918		
War Diary	Bully Grenay	01/09/1918	06/09/1918
War Diary	Left Sub Section Cite St Pierre	07/09/1918	14/09/1918
War Diary	Left Sub Section	14/09/1918	19/09/1918
War Diary	Reserve Bully Grenay	20/09/1918	23/09/1918
War Diary	Left Sub Section	24/09/1918	30/09/1918
Operation(al) Order(s)	1st. Bn. North Staffordshire Regt. Operation Order No. 31.	12/09/1918	12/09/1918
Operation(al) Order(s)	1st. Bn. North Staffordshire Regiment. Operation Order No. 32.	15/09/1918	15/09/1918
Operation(al) Order(s)	1st. Bn. North Staffordshire Regiment. Operation Order No. 33	17/09/1918	17/09/1918
Operation(al) Order(s)	1st. Bn. North Staffordshire Regt. Operation Order No. 34.	23/09/1918	23/09/1918
Operation(al) Order(s)	1st Bn. North Staffordshire Regt. Operation Order No. 35.	28/09/1918	28/09/1918
Miscellaneous	Herewith War Diary for the month of September.		
Heading	1st Bn North Staffordshire Regiment. War Diary:- Month ending 31st October 1918		
War Diary	Sus St Ledger	01/10/1918	06/10/1918
War Diary	Graincourt	07/10/1918	07/10/1918
War Diary	Cantaing	08/10/1918	08/10/1918
War Diary	Neirgnies	09/10/1918	10/10/1918
War Diary	Gagnocles	11/10/1918	11/10/1918
War Diary	Rly Embarkment SW of Avesnes Lez Aubert	12/10/1918	12/10/1918
War Diary	St. Aubert	13/10/1918	13/10/1918
War Diary	Montrecourt Wood	14/10/1918	16/10/1918
War Diary	Montrecourt	17/10/1918	17/10/1918
War Diary	St Aubert	18/10/1918	18/10/1918
War Diary	Cambrai	19/10/1918	25/10/1918
War Diary	Avesnes Lez Aubert	26/10/1918	31/10/1918
Heading	1st Battn North Staffordshire Regiment. War Diary. Month ending 30th November 1918.		
War Diary	Avesnes Le Aubert	01/11/1918	02/11/1918
War Diary	Haussy	03/11/1918	04/11/1918
War Diary	Sepmeries	05/11/1918	05/11/1918
War Diary	Wargnies Le Grand	06/11/1918	07/11/1918
War Diary	Bavay	08/11/1918	08/11/1918
War Diary	Bois De La Laniere	08/11/1918	11/11/1918
War Diary	Front Of Feignies	09/11/1918	09/11/1918
War Diary	FBG De. Mons	10/11/1918	10/11/1918
War Diary	Feignies	11/11/1918	11/11/1918
War Diary	Bouvignies	12/11/1918	12/11/1918
War Diary	St. Waast	13/11/1918	17/11/1918
War Diary	Maresches	18/11/1918	18/11/1918

War Diary	Cite Bessemer	19/11/1918	19/11/1918
War Diary	Ecaillon	20/11/1918	25/11/1918
War Diary	Landas	26/11/1918	26/11/1918
War Diary	Nomain	27/11/1918	30/11/1918
Operation(al) Order(s)	1st Battn. North Stafford Regiment Operation Order No. 36.	01/11/1918	01/11/1918
Operation(al) Order(s)	1st. Bn. North Staffordshire Regiment. Operation Order No. 38.	10/11/1918	10/11/1918
Operation(al) Order(s)	1st. Bn. North Staffordshire Regiment. Operation Order No. 40.	16/11/1918	16/11/1918
Operation(al) Order(s)	1st. Bn. North Staffordshire Regt. Operation Order No. 41.	17/11/1918	17/11/1918
Operation(al) Order(s)	1st Bn. North Staffordshire Regt. Operation Order No. 42.	18/11/1918	18/11/1918
Operation(al) Order(s)	1st Bn North Staffordshire Regiment. Operation Order No. 43.		
Operation(al) Order(s)	1st Bn North Staffordshire Regiment. Operation Order No 44.	25/11/1918	25/11/1918
Heading	1st Bn North Staffordshire Regiment. War Diary Month of December 1918		
War Diary	Nomain	01/12/1918	18/12/1918
War Diary	Tournai	18/12/1918	31/12/1918
Operation(al) Order(s)	1st Bn North Staffordshire Regiment. Operation Order No 45.	17/12/1918	17/12/1918
Heading	Herewith copy of "War Diary" for month of December 1918.		
War Diary	War Diary For Month Of January 1919		
War Diary	Tournai	01/01/1919	31/01/1919
Heading	War Diary For February 1919		
War Diary	Tournai	01/02/1919	28/02/1919
Heading	War Diary For March 1919		
War Diary	Tournai	01/03/1919	20/03/1919
War Diary	Tournai Camphin	21/03/1919	21/03/1919
War Diary	Camphin	22/03/1919	31/03/1919
Operation(al) Order(s)	1st Battalion North Staffordshire Regt. Operation Order No 46	20/03/1919	20/03/1919
Miscellaneous	Headquarters 72nd Infantry Brigade.		
Heading	War Diary April 1919		
War Diary	Camphin	01/04/1919	30/04/1919
Heading	War Diary May 1919		
War Diary	Camphin	01/05/1919	31/05/1919
Heading	1st Bn Nth Staffs Nov 1915-May 1919		

Woys / 22/3/1

72nd Brigade.

24th Division.

Came from 6th Division with 17th
Brigade 14. 10.15. Joined 72nd
Brigade 18.10.15.

1st BATTALION

NORTH STAFFORDSHIRE REGIMENT

NOVEMBER 1915.

May 1919

Army Form C. 2118.

WAR DIARY
or
INTELLIGENCE SUMMARY.

(Erase heading not required.)

1st Bn. The North Staffordshire Regt.

November 1915

Place	Date	Hour	Summary of Events and Information	Remarks and references to Appendices
	1st Nov.			
	2nd Nov.			
	3rd Nov.			
	4th Nov.			

Instructions regarding War Diaries and Intelligence Summaries are contained in F. S. Regs., Part II. and the Staff Manual respectively. Title pages will be prepared in manuscript.

Army Form C. 2118

WAR DIARY
or
INTELLIGENCE SUMMARY
(Erase heading not required.)

Instructions regarding War Diaries and Intelligence Summaries are contained in F. S. Regs., Part II. and the Staff Manual respectively. Title Pages will be prepared in manuscript.

Place	Date	Hour	Summary of Events and Information	Remarks and references to Appendices
S	5th Nov		From O.C. Saddles measured about to go to Mendin [?] at returns of 8" mules R.	
	6th Nov		Relieved "Support Trenches" 2nd LEINSTERS. Trenches in very bad state or bad.	
	7th Nov		Rain men of 4. Inches (fallen — "C" Coy. in a bad way	
	8th Nov		have some bay guards	
	9th Nov		Still snow, rain, still has trench	
	10th Nov		Fine. Someone spent event [?] for up bag in flank.	
	11th Nov		Fine. Trench begin to dry up	
	12th Nov		Heavy rain. H.Q. at Talk gone on leave. Relieved by 8" Royal Irish Rif. Bn. march back to Bulls. Camp & in before C.H.M about h.r. now command. Rain would not think	
	13th Nov		Major Lush returns from leave and assumes command.	
	14th Nov		Fine. Lut. Col. H. Shaw belongs from 24th Div Sirs I.S. back	

1875   Wt. W 593/826   1,000,000   4/15   J.B.C. & A.   A.D.S.S./Forms/C. 2118.

WAR DIARY
or
INTELLIGENCE SUMMARY
(Erase heading not required.)

Army Form C. 2118

Instructions regarding War Diaries and Intelligence Summaries are contained in F. S. Regs., Part II. and the Staff Manual respectively. Title Pages will be prepared in manuscript.

Place	Date	Hour	Summary of Events and Information	Remarks and references to Appendices
	15th Nov		Fine very cold at night	
	16th Nov		Showery	
	17th Nov		Relieved 8" Regt West Kents. Showery day, very cold night.	
	18th Nov		Trenches very bad indeed, officer & man 'C' Coy sent to walking wounded field.	
	19th Nov		Nothing of any importance occurred. Have wish it be have in trenches.	
	20th Nov		Prisoner had used Jaysen stated that 2nd Batt 178 Regt is in front of us, a Freshly cases batt afraid of their shots after the war & other rumours. 3 wounds sent to field ambulance on French.	
	21st Nov		Relieved by B: 1st Hampshire & watch on Coy. holdthese & trenches on Coy 12" Coy Seath M.G. have had left out G RENINGHELST.	

WAR DIARY
or
INTELLIGENCE SUMMARY
(Erase heading not required.)

Army Form C. 2118

Instructions regarding War Diaries and Intelligence Summaries are contained in F. S. Regs., Part II. and the Staff Manual respectively. Title Pages will be prepared in manuscript.

Place	Date	Hour	Summary of Events and Information	Remarks and references to Appendices
	23rd Nov		Began march to Mer. Billets when Division will rest for about a month. Marched to RYVELD, a bad march throughout. New motors will but some will draw up to units this end. 12 men fell out.	
	24 Nov.		Rested at RYVELD. rained all day.	
	25 Nov		Marched to ROUBROUCK VIA OXELAERE nr WIGMAERS, a remonstrating. Beautiful day and men marched magnificently. 8 men fell out.	
	26 Nov		Marched to HELLEBROUCQ in the rain.	
	27 Nov		Marched to find our Billets C Coy in LA RECOUSSE, A & D in ZOUAFQUES & B Coy at St HPO at out about WOLPHUS. Billets fairly good, roads in boues but they settled.	
	28 Nov		Began training. dull day with occasional showers.	
	29 Nov		Tuesday. Began work on Range at Bruend Rd.	
	30 Nov		Coys & remainder to 83rd Performance Camp in villa Bruend Rd.	

Div. Routine Orders
By Maj. Gen. J.E. Capper. C.B.
Comdg 24th Div 9-11-15.

Special orders

541. Honours & Rewards

The Div Commander wishes to bring to the notice of all ranks the acts for which Lieut Chew. C.S.M. Gould. and Lce Cpl Loughman were recommended and for which they have been rewarded.

Lieut G.D. Chew.
Awarded the Military Cross

On Oct 30th 1915 at great personal risk and alone made a daylight reconnaissance of the new St Eloi craters in front of our lines, which enabled covering parties to occupy them after dark, & resulted in bomb posts being established and communications made, thus denying the craters to the enemy. Later with bombing parties he helped to repel three attacks.

No 8212
C.S.M. Gould. F.W.
Awarded the Military Cross.

On the night of Oct 30/31 1915, at the St Eloi craters by his promptness & dash in reorganising and leading was chiefly instrumental in repelling three German attacks. But for him the first attack might well have succeeded. He was wounded in the face but refused to leave until daylight when he went to the aid post, returning as soon as his wound was dressed.

His services and example throughout the campaign have been invaluable.

No 9414.
Lce Cpl A Loughnane.

Awarded the
D.C.M.

At St Eloi crater on the night of 30/31st Oct 1915, when in command of a covering party was conspicuous in repelling two German attacks and though incapacitated by d wound during the second attack continued to set a splendid example of courage and endurance.

Nov 9th, 1915.

(Sgd) J Doyle
Lieut-Colonel
A.A. & Q.M.G. 24th Div

72nd Brigade.
24th Division.

1st BATTALION

NORTH STAFFORDSHIRE REGIMENT

DECEMBER 1915.

Army Form C. 2118

WAR DIARY
or
INTELLIGENCE SUMMARY

(Erase heading not required.)

Instructions regarding War Diaries and Intelligence Summaries are contained in F. S. Regs., Part II. and the Staff Manual respectively. Title Pages will be prepared in manuscript.

Place	Date	Hour	Summary of Events and Information	Remarks and references to Appendices
	1st Dec		Fine day. Bn. training continued	
	2nd Dec		Fine day. Platoon programme begun	
	3rd Dec		Rainy day. Training with live grenades begins. C and D Coys. musketry A & B Drill	
	4th Dec		Raining day. "C" Coy on the Range. Accident with grenades occurred Lt Phillips wounded.	
	5th Dec		Fine day.	
	6th Dec		Stormy showery day.	
	7th Dec		Showery day. I go on leave. Lt. Trickson assumes command	

WAR DIARY
or
INTELLIGENCE SUMMARY

Army Form C. 2118

(Erase heading *not* required.)

Instructions regarding War Diaries and Intelligence Summaries are contained in F. S. Regs., Part II. and the Staff Manual respectively. Title Pages will be prepared in manuscript.

Place	Date	Hour	Summary of Events and Information	Remarks and references to Appendices
	7th Dec		Fine day 4P.	
	8th Dec		Fine day.	
	9 Dec		Rain.	
	10 Dec		Finishing Fullery rifle competition won by 'C' Coy (Inter-Coy).	
	11 Dec		Rain. (B.). Inspection of army Remounts whole in this march.	
	12 Dec		Whole Front. Inter-Coy Firearm bombing won by 'A' Coy.	
	13th Dec		Showers. 'C' Coy won Pl. inter Coy Shoot.	
	14 Dec		Fine. 'A' Coy won Inter Coy Footballs. competition won by 'D' Coy.	

1875 Wt. W593/826 1,800,000 4/15 J.B.C. & A. A.D.S.S./Forms/C. 2118.

WAR DIARY
or
INTELLIGENCE SUMMARY

(Erase heading not required.)

Army Form C. 2118

Place	Date	Hour	Summary of Events and Information	Remarks and references to Appendices
	15th Dec		Storm day. I return from leave	
	16" Dec		Dull day.	
	17" Dec		Lt. Col. G.W. de Falbe C.M.G., D.S.O., leaves the Regt on promotion to comd of Brigade & arrival and return of English to report to British Secretary of State for War. Major a.S. Loew continues in command. (N.B: The post is an experimental. Sente stokes guns officers, 4 etc. not attached.) Sgt. Signaller Abbott "buzz" messages successfully.	
	18" Dec		Dull day	
	19" Dec		Dull day	
	20" Dec		Misty, dull day	
	21st Dec		Showery day. "A" Coy trench "B" Coy in support.	
	22" Dec		Dull day. "A" Coy trench "B" Coy 8th Watches by 4 guns to rifle. Regt find fresh three in 65th Bde. Enemy Bombing line trench is lost in Sunken Place.	

WAR DIARY
or
INTELLIGENCE SUMMARY

(Erase heading not required.)

Army Form C. 2118

Place	Date	Hour	Summary of Events and Information	Remarks and references to Appendices
	23rd Dec		Fine day. 'A' Coy sent a Coy 3rd Rifle Bde in Serve. Gnd by 2 gun L nil. Prepare to move to hrs Divisional area.	
	23/4 Dec		Dull, showery. 'A' Coy Gone to Bearson Junction by 3 gms L nil in Trench. Divisional Order by Football. Heavy Shows more Pte WATTEN.	
	25 Dec		Dull day. Men have Xmas Dinner under more favourable conditions than last year.	V.C.
	26 Dec		Dull showery day. [illegible] none reported.	
	27 Dec		Showery day. Known "gale" B. Foulk. Wd to hosp. Informed G.O.C. i.c. Bn. was Bullets down after noon, but he did not arrive.	
	28 Dec		B. inspected 8 Several Coffrs emb. 24 Div. The C.O. is in hands for the afternoon of the B. Dull day. Gen'l Coffr himself in protests Capt. Blew.	
	29 Dec		Fine dull B. horse comp'n attack.	

Army Form C. 2118

WAR DIARY
or
INTELLIGENCE SUMMARY

(Erase heading not required.)

Instructions regarding War Diaries and Intelligence Summaries are contained in F. S. Regs., Part II. and the Staff Manual respectively. Title Pages will be prepared in manuscript.

Place	Date	Hour	Summary of Events and Information	Remarks and references to Appendices
	30th Dec		Fine day. O: worked wounded	
	31st Dec		Showery day. B": practice CwS in attack.	
	1st Jan 1916		Showery day. Heavy gale. B": attack Practice.	
	2 Jan		Raining heavily. Advanced Parties leave to take over new Area at Hooge.	
	3rd Jan		Fine day. B": practice Advanced Guard, out post Outposts.	
	4th Jan		Rainy, stormy day.	
	5th Jan		Fine day.	
	6th Jan		Dull day, some rain. Marched to AUDRUICQ and then entrained for	

24th Division
72nd Brigade.

1st BATTALION

NORTH STAFFORDSHIRE REGIMENT

JANUARY 1 9 1 6

Army Form C. 2118

WAR DIARY
or
INTELLIGENCE SUMMARY
(Erase heading not required.)

Instructions regarding War Diaries and Intelligence Summaries are contained in F. S. Regs., Part II. and the Staff Manual respectively. Title Pages will be prepared in manuscript.

Place	Date	Hour	Summary of Events and Information	Remarks and references to Appendices
QUINTON	6 Jun			
	7 Jun		Dull day, some rain. Relieved 7th East Surreys in ZILLEBEKE LAKE DUG-OUTS with 'B'; less 'D' Coy. 'D' Coy occupied CHATEAU BELGE.	
	8 Jun		Fine day. Trial worked Parties 300 men from 'A', 'B', 'C' Coys	
	9 Jun		Showery morning. Blowed up dump. 200 men working	
	10 Jun		Dull day. 200 men working	
	11 Jun		Dull day. 200 men working	
	12 Jun		Fine Dull day. 350 men working	
	13 Jun		Dull day. Relieved 9th East Surreys in HOOGE. Left Section. Trenches very bad indeed, and very much changed from when we left in August.	

Army Form C. 2118

WAR DIARY
or
INTELLIGENCE SUMMARY
(Erase heading not required.)

Instructions regarding War Diaries and Intelligence Summaries are contained in F. S. Regs., Part II. and the Staff Manual respectively. Title Pages will be prepared in manuscript.

Place	Date	Hour	Summary of Events and Information	Remarks and references to Appendices
	14th Jan		Dull fine day. Quiet, some "whizz-bangs". Bright harvest light night much sniping especially in front of BELLEVARDE LAKE.	
	15th Jan		Fine half day. Some whizz bangs during the day. One man wounded. Relieved by 2nd Lincolns Regt. and march back to Huts G.18.a. CAMP C. One man wounded during relief but night quiet & bright harvest light.	
	16th Jan		Fine day. Three Coys in Huts, one in tents. Served up much churned up but as below CAMP B.	
	17th Jan		Fine day. Coys start training according to C.O's Programme.	
	18th Jan		Fine day.	
	19th Jan		Fine day.	
	20th Jan		Dull day. Lt. Saund FANSHAWE, 5th Brig. Commander inspects lines.	
	21st Jan		Dull day. Cold wind. G.O.C. 24th Div. inspects lines.	

WAR DIARY
or
INTELLIGENCE SUMMARY

Army Form C. 2118

Place	Date	Hour	Summary of Events and Information	Remarks and references to Appendices
	22" Jan		Dull day. Relieved 1st Royal Fusiliers in RAILWAY WOOD, Y WOOD Section. Trenches practically non-existent, some knee-deep, some shoulder, some everything.	
	23rd Jan		Made 6 the line held & made series of disconnected posts. Fine day. One man sniped in H19. Otherwise situation quiet.	
	24" Jan		Fine day. G.O.C 24 Div and B.G.C. inspected trenches. Two Frenchmen deserters delivered by Ramparts.	
	25" Jan		Fine day. "C" Coy Lewis material at several shelters.	
	26" Jan		Fine day. Relieved by 9" E. SURREYS. GAS ALERT given out 15" stood to about 60 to coves from 4.30 a.m. till dawn. Situation quiet.	
	27" Jan		Dull day. Fatigue work. R.E's 300 men.	
	28" Jan		Dull day. Fatigue work. R.E's 150 men.	
	29" Jan		Dull day. Fatigue work. R.E's 150 men.	
	30 Jan		Fine day. Relieved 9" E. Surreys in Railway Wood Section.	
	31 Jan		Fine day. Situation Quiet.	

24th Division
72nd Brigade.

1st BATTALION

NORTH STAFFORDSHIRE REGIMENT

FEBRUARY 1916

WAR DIARY
or
INTELLIGENCE SUMMARY
(Erase heading not required.)

Army Form C. 2118

Instructions regarding War Diaries and Intelligence Summaries are contained in F. S. Regs., Part II. and the Staff Manual respectively. Title Pages will be prepared in manuscript.

Place	Date	Hour	Summary of Events and Information	Remarks and references to Appendices
	30 Jan		Fine day. Relieved 9th E. SURREYS in RAILWAY WOOD SECTION.	
	31st Jan		Fine day. Situation quiet.	
	1st Feb		Frosty, bad night. Situation quiet.	
	2nd Feb		Fine day. Germans shelled Y WOOD. Bombk. at G.F. No 1 house unsuccessful as retaliation.	
	3rd Feb		Fine day. Relieved by 9 E. SURREYS. Returned to Brigade Reserve in CAMP A.	
	4th Feb		Showery. Find 150 working parties.	
	5th Feb		Fine. Find 150 working parties.	
	6th Feb		Find 150 working parties.	

Army Form C. 2118.

WAR DIARY
or
INTELLIGENCE SUMMARY.
(Erase heading not required.)

Instructions regarding War Diaries and Intelligence Summaries are contained in F.S. Regs., Part II. and the Staff Manual respectively. Title pages will be prepared in manuscript.

Hour, Date, Place	Summary of Events and Information	Remarks and references to Appendices
7th Feb.	Fine day. 72 I.B. move into Divisional Reserve. We remain at CAMP A.	
8th Feb.	Fine day.	
9th Feb.	Fine day.	
10th Feb.	Fine day.	
11th Feb.	Stormy day. Found working party of 400 men for Wiring under R.E.	
12th Feb.	Dull cold day. Found wiring party 120 men for R.E. Heavy bombardment on left of line. GAS ALERT ordered. Sent to received at 5.10 p.m., cancelled 6.10 h.m. Enemy attempt demanded Hazile 14 at 6 Div. with another Brench. No infantry attack.	
13th Feb.	Fine day. POPERINGHE shelled and bombed by German aeroplanes.	

WAR DIARY
or
INTELLIGENCE SUMMARY.
(Erase heading not required.)

Army Form C. 2118.

Hour, Date, Place	Summary of Events and Information	Remarks and references to Appendices
14th Feb.	Fine day. Heavy bombardment N.E. of HOOGE Section. Enemy mine exploded under H 14, 15, 16 and MUDDY LANE. No Infantry attack. Stood to at about 5 p.m. Remained in a state of readiness all night. Heavy bombardment in vicinity of BLUFF going on.	
15th Feb.	Enemy 15" mine G. two shells to recover 2.50 a.m. Slow G. shell 3.40 a.m. Enemy exploded two large 2 minutes at BLUFF at north works. Remained in state of readiness all day. Relieved 3rd Rifle Brigade in ZILLEBEKE LAKE DUGOUTS on night 15/16 inst.	
16th Feb.	Wet, windy day. Lengthening entry. Relieved 8 & 9 E. SURREYS in ZILLEBEKE DUG-OUTS. Moved at 6 p.m. & in 1st R. FUSILIERS in LEFT SECTION RIGHT SECTOR, HOOGE. Relief complete 2.30 a.m.	
17th Feb.	Dull morning, clearing in afternoon. Bn. H.Q. shelled during afternoon. 6 whiz bangs blown in but no serious damage done. Inspection in trenches carried out by General CAPPER at Brigadier MITFORD with him.	
18th Feb.	Several shots by skeffs-shells G. but no int activities apart from the usual.	

Army Form C. 2118.

WAR DIARY
of
INTELLIGENCE SUMMARY.
(Erase heading not required.)

Instructions regarding War Diaries and Intelligence Summaries are contained in F. S. Regs., Part II. and the Staff Manual respectively. Title pages will be prepared in manuscript.

Hour, Date, Place	Summary of Events and Information	Remarks and references to Appendices
19th Feb.	Showery day. Afternoon went with R.E. & to check 6 W. Gradian H.12.	
20th Feb.	Dull day. Relieved 8 & 9th E. SURREYS. Moved back to ZILLEBEKE DUG-OUTS. Relief complete 2.30 a.m. 21st inst.	
21st Feb.	Dull wet day. ZILLEBEKE LAKE DUG-OUTS at BELGIAN CHATEAU shelled. 'A' Coy lost 3 killed & 15 wounded by one shell.	his men at parapet shirt 6 bombs which exploded & 6's killed.
22nd Feb.	In morning enemy shell ZILLEBEKE DUG-OUTS with heavy mortar shells killing an ad wounding two. Much discomfort in afternoon due to [..] mg & shell but no permanent damage.	Dug-outs were shelled heavily too. few hours with one shell burst.
23rd Feb.	Gas by our own. Enemy shell DUG-OUTS lightly in charge. 9am Relieve 9 E.SURREYS in HOOGE.	
24th Feb.	Fine wet day. Situation quiet	

WAR DIARY
or
INTELLIGENCE SUMMARY.
(Erase heading not required.)

Army Form C. 2118.

Hour, Date, Place	Summary of Events and Information	Remarks and references to Appendices
25'. Feb.	Fine all day. Frost nightly. Situation quiet.	
26". Feb.	Fine day. Thaw begins.	
27". Feb.	Fair day, cold wind. Thaw slightly. Relieved 8 & E. SURREYS. Relief complete 5.30 a.m. Hours in 2 ILLEBENE [?] DUG OUTS.	
28". Feb.	Dull showery day. Fired 320 rounds into Ridge.	
29". Feb.	Fine day. Snow showers evening. Fired 310 rounds into Ridge. O.Whit-code [?] kn [?] "incised". Line call ? letter ___ E.M.	
1". March.	Dull day. Fired smoke into Ridge armed to Bremerstein [?]	
2". March.	Fine day. Attack made on BLUFF. Bavarians who were on our front near HOOGE and shell ZILLEBEKE LAKE at evening observed a phenomenal attack which seems ful...[?]	

24th Division
72nd Brigade.

1st BATTALION

NORTH STAFFORDSHIRE REGIMENT.

MARCH 1916

Army Form C. 2118.

WAR DIARY
or
INTELLIGENCE SUMMARY.
(Erase heading not required.)

Place	Date	Hour	Summary of Events and Information	Remarks and references to Appendices
	1st March		Dull day. Find small working parties arising a Demonstration	
	2nd March		Fine day. Attack made on BLUFF Germans 10hrs.22min a trench mortar HOOGE and shell ZILLEBEKE LAKE and environs spasmodically during day. Attack reported successful. 200 prisoners taken. Relieve (continued next page)	

Copied from previous months diary

For
2.5.27

WAR DIARY
or
INTELLIGENCE SUMMARY.
(Erase heading not required.)

Army Form C. 2118.

Hour, Date, Place	Summary of Events and Information	Remarks and references to Appendices
3rd March	9 E. SURREYS in HOOGE Trenches. Strong gale from NORTH-WEST and LAKE down known and continued throughout the relief, but afforded no casualties.	
4th March	Cold day, snow. Enemy quiet.	
5th March	Less cold. Thaw. Relieved by 2nd LEINSTERS. Bn came back by train to billets in HOP FACTORY, POPERINGHE, opposite RAILWAY STATION. Billets twice shelled during night.	
6th March	Cold day. Snow. Billets very indifferent and unsafe. Overcrowded, much to worse. Find work party 50 men.	
7th March	C & O day. Snow. Bn. man with Bellers in the town itself - a great change for the better. Work party 158 men.	
8th March	Cold day. Snow. Work party 100 men.	
9th March	Good day. Show.	
10th March	Move to CAMP F in OUDER DOM - VLAMERTINGHE Road. Then Fine day. Work party.	

Army Form C. 2118.

WAR DIARY
or
INTELLIGENCE SUMMARY.
(Erase heading not required.)

Instructions regarding War Diaries and Intelligence Summaries are contained in F. S. Regs., Part II. and the Staff Manual respectively. Title pages will be prepared in manuscript.

Hour, Date, Place	Summary of Events and Information	Remarks and references to Appendices
11th March	Fine day. Hostile shelling 100 mm.	
12th March	Fine day.	
13th March	Fine day. Some enemy aeroplanes. Hostile shelling 100 mm.	
14th March	Fine day. Some rain during night.	
15th March	Fine day. Relieved 2nd Canadian in (Hooge). Relief complete 11:30	
16th March	a.m. Fine day. Enemy artillery active.	
17th March	Fine day. Reconnaissance of STAPLES at C.2 made by Lts White, Hythe and Coffin Pl.s.	
18th March	Puzzling time for the reconnaissance of STAPLES at C.2 made by Lts were thrown. Scheme for later act in France and employed is	

Army Form C. 2118.

WAR DIARY
or
INTELLIGENCE SUMMARY.
(Erase heading not required.)

Instructions regarding War Diaries and Intelligence Summaries are contained in F. S. Regs., Part II. and the Staff Manual respectively. Title pages will be prepared in manuscript.

Hour, Date, Place	Summary of Events and Information	Remarks and references to Appendices
19th March	Easter.	
20 March	Fine day. 8th White at Hogg out for the manoeuvres for 2 Bn relieved by 1st Guards in trenches P.P.1 S.7 Telegraphs. 1.30 a.m. B: returns to CAMP A & rain. Rain. Arctic for hour.	
21st March	Cold, drizzly day. B: moved to Billets near MT KOKEREELE	
22nd March	Raining heavy. Training, Program begun.	
23rd March	Fine day. Officers reconnaissance of Mt KEMMEL defences made. O/C 2nd Bn. VANCOUVER Scottish.	
24th March	Snow. Major DUCMORE, D.S.O. takes command of Battalion.	
25th March	Dull day, cold.	
26th March	Rainy day.	

WAR DIARY
or
INTELLIGENCE SUMMARY.
(Erase heading not required.)

Army Form C. 2118.

Instructions regarding War Diaries and Intelligence Summaries are contained in F. S. Regs., Part II. and the Staff Manual respectively. Title pages will be prepared in manuscript.

Hour, Date, Place	Summary of Events and Information	Remarks and references to Appendices
27th March	Fine day. Showers at night (rare). Reconnoitred new trenches with C.O. Trenches in poor state of drainage, found in this we made observations - no parades, plenty dug-outs, semi-boardwalks - but they are comfortable.	
28th March	Fine day. Bn. moved into Divisional Reserve in DRANOUTRE. This Coys in Billets, HQ & tpts. needed everyone's not very good. But at times the no washing places. Bn. relieves 4. CANADIAN Bn.	
29th March	Fine day. G.O.C. V Corps visits Area.	
30th March	Fine day. O.B.C. visits Billets	
31st March	Fine day	
1st April	Fine day	

24th Division
72nd Brigade

1st BATTALION

NORTH STAFFORDSHIRE REGIMENT

APRIL 1916

24 APRIL ~~MAY~~ ~~JUNE~~ ~~JULY~~

Army Form C. 2118

W Surreys Regt

WAR DIARY
or
INTELLIGENCE SUMMARY.
(Erase heading not required.)

Vols 1st - 5
                  7 6
                  # 7

Hour, Date, Place	Summary of Events and Information	Remarks and references to Appendices

2 April — Fine day. Relieved 1st E. SURREYS in trenches NORTH of WULVERGHEM. Quiet night.

3rd April — Fine, quiet day. Transport brought out day's letter. Enemy active on our front. S P 7 shelled.

4th April — Fine dull day. Enemy active with rifle grenades on 15. 1 killed 4 wounded. We retaliate.

5th April — Fine day. Enemy shell with R.F.A. (?) his own trenches (Sultan) at 14"9'S well abroad.

6th April — Fine day.

7th April — Showery day. situation quiet.

8th April — Fine day. Some heavy activity on SPANBROEKMOLEN. Relieved by 8th E. SURREYS. Relief complete at dawn.

WAR DIARY
or
INTELLIGENCE SUMMARY.
(Erase heading not required.)

Army Form C. 2118.

Instructions regarding War Diaries and Intelligence Summaries are contained in F. S. Regs., Part II. and the Staff Manual respectively. Title pages will be prepared in manuscript.

Hour, Date, Place	Summary of Events and Information	Remarks and references to Appendices
9th April	Battalion moved into Bde Reserve KANDAHAR FARM and AIRCRAFT FARM. Fine day	
10th April	Fine day. 300 men working at night.	
11th April	Rain.	
12th April	Rain. 300 men working at night.	
13th April	Fine day. 300 men working at night.	
14th April	Fine day. Battalion relieved 9th E. SURREYS, relief complete 9.15 p.m. Quiet night.	
15th April	Fine day. Some artillery and trench mortar activity. We retaliated in kind	
16th April	Fine day. 5 min rapid fire for general hostile reveille of enemy	
17th April	Fine day. Much artillery activity on both sides (enemy mortars)	

Army Form C. 2118.

WAR DIARY
or
INTELLIGENCE SUMMARY.
(Erase heading not required.)

Hour, Date, Place	Summary of Events and Information	Remarks and references to Appendices
18th April.	Fine day. Enemy trench mortar on D5a at 6 with new quick firing howitzer seems what seemed to me Stoke's gun in retaliation.	
19th April	Dull day. 3 cm mortar on D.5. during afternoon.	
20th April.	Showery day. heavy minnies on D5 & D4 during afternoon. 2 c.m. minnies and few trench mortar howitz. nearby by our heavy mortar. Relieved by 1 E. Surrey Regt. Relief complete 10 P.M. Horses wet through and Manure, DRAIN-OUTEE. GAS ALERT	
21st April	Showery day. Fund 200 men working. GAS ALERT cancelled 11 P.M.	
22nd April	Dull day.	
23rd April	Fine day.	

WAR DIARY
INTELLIGENCE SUMMARY
(Erase heading not required.)

Army Form C. 2118.

Hour, Date, Place	Summary of Events and Information	Remarks and references to Appendices
24th April	Fine day. Trench程序 normal.	
25th April	Fine day. Lewis Gun demonstration given before B.C.C. 7 J.O. GAS ALERT 11 h.m.	
26th April	Fine day. Relieved 9th E. SURREYS. relief compl. 1.45 a.m. 27th. Ins Ptes wounded by 5th Div. arbitrator that GAS attack is imminent on this sector	
27th April	4.54 a.m – enemy mounted on the B.s' detailed to attack however. 7 m dy. O.s shelled & 力 mnns can 12 casualties. Some heavy shrnes in every but we work. 12.15 a.m. Wind EAST unify after heavy. Both sides unduly much alarmed. 1. a.m. Wind N.E. mild. Wind SUIT ABLE to B.— as enemy enfilade Battery putting in saloons at 2 a.m. to pre-arranged. 1.25 a.m. Some trogen fire shown Always being singularly effete upon our time etc. 2.a.m. all quiet. Situation normal. 4.30 a.m. Situation normal.	Wind EAST and very light.
28th April		

Army Form C. 2118.

WAR DIARY
or
INTELLIGENCE SUMMARY.
(Erase heading not required.)

Hour, Date, Place	Summary of Events and Information	Remarks and references to Appendices
29th April	Fine day. Wild lie on w.B. Situation quiet during day. Orders have been told A. is attached received 10.10 p.m. The information communicated to Coys and posts sent out. Snipers worked.	
30th April	12.50 a.m. Fire from A Coy detect Germans working on wire. 12.55 a.m. Heavy rifle fire burst on RIGHT. Some ran to the cover from German trenches in front of D3, D4 & D6. Some German snipers came in & threw at our trenches in middle on their front line and supports. In spite of our attack. Some rifled chlorine, my own wire, whistle ended about 20 minutes. Wind blowing about 10 m.p.h. so that gas cannot be seen in to D4 (50 Y 2) in about 11 seconds at the distance bet D3 and D6 is about 20 seconds. This did not allow much time to adjust helmets a further 65 minutes of men were gassed in the LEFT (A) at RIGHT (D) Coys. 1.20 a.m. (approx) Germans began D4 assault. Enemy hill or wound all the men holding the front line salient and into the ground, others front 13 Coy who were holding the part of trenches temporarily carried by the withdrawal of the attack and the men that were. Those wounded	

WAR DIARY
or
INTELLIGENCE SUMMARY

Army Form C. 2118.

Hour, Date, Place	Summary of Events and Information	Remarks and references to Appendices

had two stretcher bearers killed, & 6 to the whole of the orderly to bring wounded in. It appears however was held up on the left by a heavy fire, and he did not press his attack home until the low in the night. An immediate counter-attack was organised by Captain CHEN who together with 2nd Lt YOUNGMAN 9th & Sussex Regt. (who had come up with a working party previous to the attack) succeeded in regaining most of the right-hand of the redoubt. Captain Potts then advanced and the two halves of the redoubt, comming in close contact with a small party of the enemy between the would be, the remaining trench - heads retired, and the two would countain anything more than a slight advance of the enemy. were were able to return to their own lines via the main road and set to work what they had caused. Sometime man after to have been employed in this work, the rest made their way back, taking one more prisoner, killed & wounded a fair number, and placed a lot of dying men drown a disused mining shaft.

Army Form C. 2118.

WAR DIARY
or
INTELLIGENCE SUMMARY.
(Erase heading not required.)

Instructions regarding War Diaries and Intelligence Summaries are contained in F. S. Regs., Part II. and the Staff Manual respectively. Title pages will be prepared in manuscript.

Hour, Date, Place	Summary of Events and Information	Remarks and references to Appendices
	What however this has not been is September.	
1st May	Our losses from G.S. fires were considerable chiefly to this 2nd unit which div (avoided) on the short distance between the trenches. Smoke helmets when slightly perforated in some parts meant effective. A large number of men suffered from the effects however it is 12 to 24 hours after this the gas had travelled hand of their cover, however, were very slight. The remainder of the day was very quiet. Fine day. Situation quiet.	Congratulatory Wire from G.O.C. 24 Div marked B. Special Orders marked C.
2nd May	From him a little enemy artillery activity. Otherwise —. buried by "G" & "C" Coy M.G. — however its B & Reserve. Fine day.	
3rd May	no workers Ruling. Fine day.	

"A" Form. Army Form C. 2121.

MESSAGES AND SIGNALS.

Prefix	Code	Words	Charge	This message is on a/c of:	Recd. at 11.10 m.
Office of Origin and Service Instructions. 25		Sent At ... in. To ... By ...		A. .... Service. (Signature of "Franking Officer.")	Date 29.4.1 From Z By Colch

TO —

Sender's Number.	Day of Month.	In reply to Number	AAA
* W 79	29th		

MGE from 76 IB reads just
AAA 2 dunbois have Trench
come in to E 0145 enemy will
AAA They any to-night or
attack with gas AAA this
early to morrow morning by a
information was sent spoken to
Company Commander who have
pro ment and he now
misunderstood when AAA Prisoners OK
on them was to
HQ AAA anti tank

From	25
Place	
Time	10.7 p.m.

The above may be forwarded as now corrected (Z)
Censor. Signature of Addressee or person authorised to telegraph in his name.
* This line should be erased if not required.

"A" Form. Army Form C. 2121.

MESSAGES AND SIGNALS.

Prefix: Code: KLAM Words: 23 Charge:
Office of Origin and Service Instructions.
YX

Sent At ___ m. To ___ By ___

This message is on a/c of:
B. Service.
(Signature of "Franking Officer.")

Recd. at ___ m. Date ___ From ___ By ___

TO { 1st NORTH STAFFORDS 722 B

*Sender's Number: G 63
Day of Month: 30
In reply to Number:
AAA

Glad you held your own

From: Gen CAPPER 24 Division
Place:
Time: 11.5 m

(Z) pure copy

Special Orders

The Squadron of the Second Cavalry
[illegible] under [illegible] the [illegible]
engaged in [illegible] the [illegible]
[illegible]
[illegible]
[illegible]
[illegible]
[illegible]

"A" Form.
MESSAGES AND SIGNALS.

Army Form C. 2121.

No. of Message

Prefix	Code	m.	Words	Charge			
Office of Origin and Service Instructions.					This message is on a/c of:	Recd. at	m.
			Sent			Date	
			At	m.	_____Service.		
			To			From	
			By		(Signature of "Franking Officer.")	By	

TO {

Sender's Number.	Day of Month	In reply to Number	
*			**A A A**

From			
Place			
Time			

The above may be forwarded as now corrected. **(Z)**

Censor.   Signature of Addressor or person authorised to telegraph in his name.

* This line should be erased if not required.

(688-9) —McC. & Co. Ltd., London.— W 14143/641. 225,000. 4/15. Forms C 2121/10.

24th Division
72nd Brigade.

1st BATTALION

NORTH STAFFORDSHIRE REGIMENT.

M A Y   1 9 1 6

24th Division
72nd Brigade.

Army Form C. 2118.

WAR DIARY
or
INTELLIGENCE SUMMARY.
(Erase heading not required.)

Instructions regarding War Diaries and Intelligence Summaries are contained in F. S. Regs., Part II. and the Staff Manual respectively. Title pages will be prepared in manuscript.

Place	Date	Hour	Summary of Events and Information	Remarks and references to Appendices
	1st May		Fine day. Situation quiet	
	2nd May		Fine day. A little enemy artillery activity. Battalion relieved by 9th E Surrey Regt. moved into Brigade Reserve	
	3 May		Fine day. No working parties	

Copies from diary F previous month

Ap. C. 21.5-2.)

Army Form C. 2118

WAR DIARY
or
INTELLIGENCE SUMMARY

(Erase heading not required.)

Instructions regarding War Diaries and Intelligence Summaries are contained in F. S. Regs., Part II. and the Staff Manual respectively. Title Pages will be prepared in manuscript.

Place	Date	Hour	Summary of Events and Information	Remarks and references to Appendices
	4th June		Fine day. 40 mm water in trench.	
	5th June		Fine day. B. H.Q's shelled and of Bus Farm. One O.R. wounded. 2 G.O. been wounded	
	6th June		Showery. 'C' Coy shelled and of Sticks nr KANDAHAR FARM. Shell wound	
			280 mm water in trench.	
	7th June		Showery. 230 mm water in trench.	
	8th June		Showery. Relief of "C" Coy in trenches.	
	9th June		Rain. Quiet day. Some heavies in front line.	
	10th June		Fine day. Enemy shelled other line. 6 intertines reported immediate reply	
	11th June		Fine day. Some shell burst.	

1875 Wt. W593/826 1,000,000 4/15 J.B.C. & A. A.D.S.S./F.arms/C. 2118.

Army Form C. 2118

WAR DIARY
or
INTELLIGENCE SUMMARY
(Erase heading not required.)

Instructions regarding War Diaries and Intelligence Summaries are contained in F. S. Regs., Part II. and the Staff Manual respectively. Title Pages will be prepared in manuscript.

Place	Date	Hour	Summary of Events and Information	Remarks and references to Appendices
	12 May		Fine day. Some enemy shelling. Men toward on out-post lines and bathrooms.	
	13 May		Rain. ~~[struck through]~~ Much shelling of reserve dug-out and mills.	
	14 May		Rain. Some artillery but less shelling. Battalion relieved by 9th E. Surreys. Moved to Divisional Reserve, DRANOUTRE.	
	15 May		Dull day. Tried Lewis Gun ration amounting to 270 rounds during divisional "Rest". Remainder 70 frd through Brawn at Lewis Gun courses.	
	16 May		Fine day. Usual fatigues.	
	17 May		Fine day. Usual fatigues. C. in C. grants awards as in Appendix D for gallantry. See App. D during Bn attack on 30 April 1916.	
	18 May		Fine day. Usual fatigues.	
	19 May		Fine day. Brigadier General MITFORD C.B., D.S.O., personally interviewed and con-gratulated the N.C.O's and men, chiefly by C. C. Battn. relieved by 7 E. Surreys	

WAR DIARY
or
INTELLIGENCE SUMMARY

Army Form C. 2118

(Erase heading not required.)

Instructions regarding War Diaries and Intelligence Summaries are contained in F. S. Regs., Part II. and the Staff Manual respectively. Title Pages will be prepared in manuscript.

Place	Date	Hour	Summary of Events and Information	Remarks and references to Appendices
	19th May		in WOLVERGHEM Trenches. Relief completed 10.45 p.m.	
	20th May		Fine day. Some shelling of reserve dugouts & our ridge. Enemy sniping active in my Bn.	
	21st May		Fine day. Quiet. Enemy galleries opposite D4 blown in by our miners.	
	22nd May		Fine day. O's HEQ's at Dranoutre. 8th shelled. No damage done	
	23rd May		Fine day. Our gas chamber exploded in N.30.a by our R.A. Our T.M.R. exploded Two gas cylinders south from D4 SOUTHWARDS at exploded	
			opposite D3.	
	24th May		Fine day, drizzling [illegible] etc. H.A.R. sends every 3 minutes from O4 NORTHWARDS. No apparent result. O's relieved by 3rd E. Surrey Regt. Relief complete 11 p.m. have into Bde Reserve.	
	25th May		Fine day. 2nd works Parties 195 strong.	

Army Form C. 2118

WAR DIARY
or
INTELLIGENCE SUMMARY
(Erase heading not required.)

Instructions regarding War Diaries and Intelligence Summaries are contained in F.S. Regs., Part II. and the Staff Manual respectively. Title Pages will be prepared in manuscript.

Place	Date	Hour	Summary of Events and Information	Remarks and references to Appendices
	26th May		Fine day. Working Parties.	
	27th May		Fine day. Usual working parties.	
	28th May		Fine day. Army Commander, General Sir Herbert Plumer, presented ribbons to officers and men of the 7 & 9 D.S. following officers and men of the Regiment decorated :— Capt. L.L. Pyke D.S.O., R. Sgt-Major Brough D.C.M., C. Sgt. Major Sewell M.C., D.C.M., C.Q.M.S. McEvoy D.C.M., Cpl. Swinson D.C.M., 2nd Cpl. Emerton D.C.M., 2nd Cpl. Bellamy D.C.M., held at Halot :— Pte. Brennan, 2nd Bn. Honours. Usual working parties.	
	29th May		Usual working parties (a.m.). Some rain at night.	
	30th May		Friday. Battalion relieved 9th E. Surrey Regt. Relief completed 10.40 p.m.	
	31st May		Fine day. Quiet.	

APPENDIX D.

The Distinguished Service Order.

Captain and Adjutant V.V. Pope.

The Distinguished Conduct Medal.

No. 8151 Corp. Bray

No. 8975 Corp. Simpson (attached 72/2 Trench Mortar Battery).

No. 7951 Loe/Corp. Emberton.

No. 12365 Pte. Gallimore.

The Military Medal.

No. 11932 Pte. Brammer.

No. 9027 Loe/Corp. Norman.

No. 7598 Pte. Kenney.

The Military Cross.

2Lt. Youngman 9th. East Surrey Regiment.

Captain and Adjutant
1st. North Stafford Regiment.

22/5/16.

24th Division
72nd Brigade

1st BATTALION

NORTH STAFFORDSHIRE REGIMENT

JUNE 1916

WAR DIARY or INTELLIGENCE SUMMARY

Army Form C. 2118

June 1916   J B Clapp[?]

(Erase heading not required.)

Instructions regarding War Diaries and Intelligence Summaries are contained in F. S. Regs., Part II. and the Staff Manual respectively. Title Pages will be prepared in manuscript.

Place	Date	Hour	Summary of Events and Information	Remarks and references to Appendices
	1st June		Fine day.	
	2nd June		Fine day.	
	3rd June		Fine day.	
	4th June		Fine day. E. KENTS attempt mine alteration on our right. We demonstrate with rent-mines, rifle-fire etc., drawing very heavy shell-fire. Enterprise a failure. Our casualties 34 killed & wounded. Cpl. Patterson killed.	
	5th June		Fine day. Battalion relieved 8:" & 7:" E Surrey. Have in Co. Divisional Reserve DRAN-OUTRE.	
	6th June		Fine day. Field works. Rates 250 daily.	
	7th June		Fine day.	
	8th June		Fine day.	

Army Form C. 2118

WAR DIARY or INTELLIGENCE SUMMARY

(Erase heading not required.)

1st Stafford   June 1916

Place	Date	Hour	Summary of Events and Information	Remarks and references to Appendices
	9. June		Fine day. Work on usual.	
	10. "		Fine day " " "	
	11. "		Showery day " " "	
	12. "		Showery do " " "	
	13. "		Showery day. Relieve 9th E.S. wervey relief completed 2 a.m.	
	14. June		Fine day. Quiet. at 11 h.m. whistles put on to 12 midnight in accordance with DAYLIGHT SAVING.	
	15. "		Fine day. Quiet.	
	16. "		Fine day. Sus alert. Wind N.N.E. but very unsuitable return to N 5 wet.	6094
	17. "		Everyone for attack at 12.20 a.m. Two waves to go at about interval. That was partially cured by gas but been shown from NORTH. My in 1st 5	

War Diary or Intelligence Summary

Army Form C. 2118

Place	Date	Hour	Summary of Events and Information	Remarks and references to Appendices
	18th June		followed. Our casualties heavy amount. to 2 & 3 O.R. and 4 officers killed wounded and gassed. Some had shell effects and others do while wounded effected this shellfire general and in excess of those decisions. Enemy attacks will have attained after movement etc. Enemy battle headache on line or area was made out clear.	
	19th June		This day B'ns relieved by 4th & 7th E. Surrey Regt. Bns - 16 Brig. de Reserve.	
	20th June		This day. Two almost G.H.Q. at about 3.30 a.m. Working Parties 150 found.	
	21st June		Quiet day. Working Parties 150 found.	
	22nd June		From day. Working Parties 150 strong. 6 ward Chambers inspected and allowed report as to the 24 Div. & dept of the opr. fight with the Division; between them his or attacks within 7 weeks. General letter is speed fright that he was affecting prowess of the D in which he had been before. Two day. Working Parties 150 strong.	
	23rd June		Two day. Working Parties 150 strong.	
	24th June		From day. Battalion parties. Fird. 50 men to help to make D4, heavy downfall. Pretty miserable. Battalion night enduring of the conditions.	

1875 Wt. W593/386 1,000,000 4/15 J.B.C. & A. A.D.S.S./Forms/C. 2118.

WAR DIARY or INTELLIGENCE SUMMARY

Army Form C. 2118

(Erase heading not required.)

Instructions regarding War Diaries and Intelligence Summaries are contained in F. S. Regs., Part II. and the Staff Manual respectively. Title Pages will be prepared in manuscript.

Place	Date	Hour	Summary of Events and Information	Remarks and references to Appendices
	25th June		Trenches. 7 and 2 & 4 in coys gas attacks into trenches.	
	26th June		Shown do. HdQrs shelled with field guns at 5-9. Two direct hits from either coast of HdQrs moved to ancestral devour. Huntingdon's comp. 15 cm.	
	27th June		Shown do. Company relieves 23 L. army for eight hrs.	
	28th June		Trenches. Gas attack by us on Bayer front followed by Trench Raid by 8th Inniskillings. Battalion moves into dugouts and trenches from 11 p.m. to 6½ a.m. 1 man hit by stray bullet.	
	29th June		Trenches. Battalion relieved when 9th E.S. swung to trenches. Heavy bombardment of Bayer front about 6.30 p.m. Battalion ordered to Stand To and later to move to Battle Positions. At 11 p.m. when to move on unrelief received, move to Battle Positions. Two man stabbed, dangerously. Some casualties from S marines rifle specialty. Relief complete 3.15 a.m.	
	30th June		Trenches. Two & quiet. Enemy intermittent shelling. Supports knocked down	

72nd Inf.Bde.
24th Div.

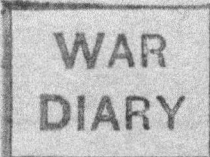

WAR DIARY

1st BATTN. THE NORTH STAFFORDSHIRE REGIMENT.

J U L Y

1 9 1 6

WAR DIARY or INTELLIGENCE SUMMARY

Army Form C. 2118

72/24

Place	Date	Hour	Summary of Events and Information	Remarks and references to Appendices
SD	June		dry	
	1st July		Fine dry. [struck through] Relieved 88: Buffs. Relief complete 1.15 a.m. Huenville Bth Hampers. Doncaster Huts, Locre. B. Apt	6/0/ 8/3
	2nd July		Fine dry. Move to hutments on plain. B" Coy on plain.	
	3rd July		Showery day. Inspection by General.	
	4 July		Fine dry. Fuse dy 16 Trainer	
	5 July		Fine dry. Fuse 250 mm worth	
	6 July		Showery. Fuse 270 mm worth. Draft of 960 O.R. arrivers	
	7 July		Showery day. Fuse 150 mm worth. In but draft, rifles on different ch especially these from 11th O. ad 7/5.	

Army Form C. 2118.

WAR DIARY
or
INTELLIGENCE SUMMARY
(Erase heading not required.)

Instructions regarding War Diaries and Intelligence Summaries are contained in F. S. Regs., Part II. and the Staff Manual respectively. Title Pages will be prepared in manuscript.

Place	Date	Hour	Summary of Events and Information	Remarks and references to Appendices
	July 7th (cont).		Division returns at 10.30 p.m. to billets we were here from 6th Australian Infantry in Pradelinghe.	
"	8		This day. Remainder moved up here in the morning. Took over NORTH of river DOUVE up to WULVERGHEM—MESSINES ROAD. On his relief hut in Support in Grand Bois. Relieve 6th Australian 13th relief complete 1.40 a.m. quiet.	6/1F 1/5
"	9		This day. Everything very quiet except for a few 4 inch mortars on our right.	
"	10		This day. Situation quiet.	
"	11		This day. Readjustment of B.N. front, we had now here Front line Trenches at this matters & E. Surreys at the our Supports Picks. from 8th Devons. all quiet.	
"	12		This day. Situation quiet.	

WAR DIARY or INTELLIGENCE SUMMARY

(Erase heading not required.)

Place	Date	Hour	Summary of Events and Information	Remarks and references to Appendices
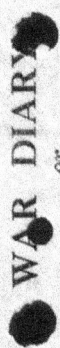	13th July		Fine day. Situation quiet.	
	14th July		Fine day. Situation quiet.	
	15th July		Fine day. Situation quiet.	
	16th July		Fine day. Installed gas cylinders in Trenches 159, 140.	
	17th July		Fine day. Installed more cylinders in Trench 140.	
	18th July		Fine day. Run from to demonstrate wells, gas etc to cows & gaslime was left at 11 h.m. Wind unfavourable, no demonstration.	
	19th July		Fine day. Relieved by 8th Regt Inf Indr Bgd. Marched to KORTEPYP.	
	20th July		Fine day. Division relieved at 9 a.m. Bn marched to KORTEPYP, entrained at 2 h.m. to Billets at LA ROUKHOSHILLE.	

Army Form C. 2118

WAR DIARY or INTELLIGENCE SUMMARY

(Erase heading not required.)

Instructions regarding War Diaries and Intelligence Summaries are contained in F. S. Regs., Part II. and the Staff Manual respectively. Title Pages will be prepared in manuscript.

Place	Date	Hour	Summary of Events and Information	Remarks and references to Appendices
	21st July		Fine day. Began training	
	22" July		Fine day. Training	
	23" July		Fine day. Training	
	24th July		Fine day. March to BAILLEUL in train 8.22 a.m. Detrain LONGUEAU about 6 p.m. March through AMIENS WESTWARDS. Bivouac in outskirts of AMIENS.	
	25" July		Fine day. March to FOURDRINOY arriving about 9 a.m. Battalion billetted in village.	
	26" July		Fine day. Began Battalion training in area BOIS DU CAVILLON.	
	27" July		Fine day. Company walks & musketry attack etc.	

WAR DIARY or INTELLIGENCE SUMMARY

Army Form C. 2118

Place	Date	Hour	Summary of Events and Information	Remarks and references to Appendices
	28th July		Fine day. Training. Division Route March & chanks of nudes, very hot and dusty, several men [ill met].	
	29th			
	30th July		Fine day. "Sunday Rest".	
	31st July		Fine day. March to AILLY Station opposite as per orders at 1.45 p.m. Train due 2 p.m. Gunners companies detrained 6 p.m. De Gaine MERICOURT L'ABBÉ about 8 p.m. March to MORLANCOURT arriving about 10 p.m. Billets in village.	1. Rgr Capt and adjt [signature] March 8 Suffolk Rgt

31/7/16

24th Division
72nd Brigade.

1st BATTALION

NORTH STAFFORDSHIRE REGIMENT

AUGUST 1 9 1 6

Vol 18

Confidential

War Diary of
1st Bn North Staffordshire Regt.

From 1-8-16   To 31-8-16

WAR DIARY or INTELLIGENCE SUMMARY

Army Form C. 2118

Place	Date	Hour	Summary of Events and Information	Remarks and references to Appendices
	1st August		Fine day. March to SANDPIT SOUTH of MEAULTE arriving about 7.30 p.m. Uneventful	
	2nd August		Fine day. Began training.	
	3rd August		Fine day. Visit FRICOURT. German trenches badly mauled by our R.A. but not so much mauled as their trenches at HOOGE in Aug '15. Many dug-outs still in tact.	
	4th August		Training continued. Further known walk. Aeroplane chevy morning, not very successful. Anniversary @ attack in the morning. Practice B. attack in attack. Major Somervel Coffin e.B. etc.	The Officers A.
	5th August		Fine day. Training going. Battln. practised attack in afternoon, attacked the Battalion it.	
	6th August		Fine day "Sunday rest". Battln watched by Officers only, turn dug out (?) lifted.	
	7th August		Fine day. Train up industrial.	
	8th August		Fine day. Orders received at 1 a.m. to be ? to move of 12 m d on railhead Q.5. J.B. bdes rendld at 4 p.m.	

WAR DIARY or INTELLIGENCE SUMMARY

Army Form C. 2118

(Erase heading not required.)

Place	Date	Hour	Summary of Events and Information	Remarks and references to Appendices
	9th August		Fine hot day. Orders received 1.30 p.m. Battalion to move at 4.30 p.m. to Billon Copse district. Orders cancelled 2.30 p.m. Orders received Bde letter nos. him in front (GUILLEMONT) night 10/11th August.	
	10th August		Dull day, some rain. Battalion moves up to LA BRIQUETERIE relieving 1/10th LIVERPOOLS (LIVERPOOL SCOTTISH) in a series of front line and trenches. This Battalion was one of those relieved us at St ELOI 22 June 15. Casualties during relief one wounded. Relief complete 9.15 p.m.	
	11th August		Fine hazy day. A few shells in support trenches, enemy seems quiet. 7 a.m. working party B.C.D Coys to dig new trench 200 yds in front to front line, A Coy to in from TEALE TRENCH. At 8.45 p.m orders received to not have all working parties like to the new trench an attack being made on our right at 9.30 p.m. B.C.D Coys started, A Coy had already left to [...] at TEALE TRENCH before this could be worked, so stayed in support, and new trench handed, being it [...] and however, or however, received about 11.15 p.m. that work would be carried on from midnight on however details C,11 Coy moved up at [...] with B Coy. Moved up and [...] at work, D'Coy did not go up [...] to carry on each dawn. Work from TEALE TRENCH night and. 12,0 gets extended Junction from GUILLEMONT — TRONES WOOD ROAD NORTHWARDS.	

Army Form C. 2118

WAR DIARY
or
INTELLIGENCE SUMMARY
(Erase heading not required.)

Instructions regarding War Diaries and Intelligence Summaries are contained in F.S. Regs, Part II. and the Staff Manual respectively. Title Pages will be prepared in manuscript.

Place	Date	Hour	Summary of Events and Information	Remarks and references to Appendices
	12th August		Trench duty. This day's casualties 14 men killed 5 wounded. When relieved at 11 a.m. that R.W. Kents were coming up 12th ult. Relief begun at about 4.30 p.m. almost immediately with allied attack on our whole right — Which we had not been warned. Relief compl'd 9.30 p.m. (approx) a few casualties in general. Enemy bombardment on front line, and communic'd HOLLOW ROAD 9.30 p.m. to 10.30 p.m., 11 p.m. to midnight, 1 a.m. to 2 a.m. intense bombardment of HOLLOW ROAD and front line from 3.45 a.m. to 5.30 a.m. During shelling which held not shown enemy bombardment. Casualties 12 noon 7 O.R. killed 20 wounded. Middle held at front lines and HOLLOW ROAD 9.30 p.m. — 10.30 p.m. Remainder of night shelling heavy.	Shelling tremendous any night could save.
	13th August		Fine with occasional showers. Desultory shelling of HOLLOW ROAD during morning, casualties 6, 12 noon 4 O.R. killed 19 wounded. Quiet day on the whole, a few shells in support at front lines during afternoon and night. Communication trenches completed in a third on almost. Peaceful and allocated.	Two C.T. dug to advance line still it seems for is not to begin.
	14th August		Quiet day. Quiet morning. Casualties 6 to 12 noon. 1. O.R. killed 6 wounded. 5 men in polic' wounds, one of whom being found of this; hardly wounded on head. Relief attempted by daylight but 4.45 p.m. by 8. Royal West Kent Regt. Seen 8 men who shelled GUILLEMONT ROAD at C.T. hardly filed about 7 p.m. Relief helped up after dark. Enemy aeroplanes active during day.	
	15th August			

1875 Wt. W593/826 1,000,000 4/15 J.B.C. & A. A.D.S.S./Forms/C. 2118.

WAR DIARY or INTELLIGENCE SUMMARY

Army Form C. 2118

Place	Date	Hour	Summary of Events and Information	Remarks and references to Appendices
	16th August		Flying low in a very strong manner. Postponed relief to-gen 9 h.m. Bazentin shelled. South of TRONES WOOD, and HOLLOW ROAD 9.15 h.m. enemy bombarded the trenches Bty Empla- about 11h.m. 15A men in BRIQUETERIE Area. Eventually Germans advanced Compy down when B.G.C. authorised relief to proceed. Afternoon and night could not move too far. 7th Batt. detailed for rank and stood to Hand 6 attacks on GUILLEMONT. Div. was now composed of 1 of 2nd 7 q.O.R. 6 pm to day. 2 a.m. This dull day, British received first Australian unit to be relieved by 13th MIDDLESEX knowing day 16". md. further received 1 h.m. (USA Battalion with orders to relieve MONTAUBAN Defences before 5 h.m. (6 a.m.). D and D Coys led the way. Remains to Battalion to man to CRATERS A.B. & h. a relief. Found to 12 noon 13.O.R. wounded. Total wounded by dropping in 18. O.R. killed, 60 wounded, 15 missing. MONTAUBAN relief completed 5 h.m 7 E. SURREYS attack near Arrow head S.E. & ARROW HEAD COPSE S.40 h.m attack failed owing to wire uncut bombardment of enemy machine guns. Relief cancelled. Return to brought up from CRATERS to BRIQUETERIE awaiting 3 a m 17th inst. Remainder 50 men to act as bearers to help to assist wounded from SCOTTISH TRENCH.	
	17th August		This Comp(Wil) a Cornwallis 6.12 noon 9.O.R. wounded (6 accidentally wounded while detonating bombs on 16th inst.). Informed 2.30 h.m. that Battalion would be relieved by 9th ROYAL SUSSEX REGT that afternoon, guide to be at Brd. H.Q. 3 h m at about 7 h m. SLYP. Officer 72.9.B. 2nd C Sgents took to Battalion on relieving had been seen of the Sussex and at 8.45 h.m. Brit. his 3rd and SELF comments. 73.9.B. relieved the Battn. to move without down. relieved. Battn. moved by 6th CRATERS AREA A.8.6., h. 12 Coys in MONTAUBAN	

WAR DIARY or INTELLIGENCE SUMMARY

Army Form C. 2118

Place	Date	Hour	Summary of Events and Information	Remarks and references to Appendices
	18th August		Before relieved by 9th E. Surrey Regt. Battalion completed move at about 11 h.m. the "Belles" being old British trenches without any shelter whatsoever. Happy it did not rain. Immediately after Bn. HQrs left the BRIQUETERIE b.p. a Lieut. R.A.M.C. was killed by a stray shell. This officer had served with the Battalion since Nov. 1914 and, I am told, about turned to run in July 16 had never left it. His hall has a gruesome fate. A shoulder to shell, and the Battalion M.O. known to me when he was killed. Friday. 6 other ranks wounded list of Battalion now mounted when 6 B.G.C. 73 O.R. for 48 hrs. attack on GUILLEMONT. Battalion in shelters in trenches in Ravine, north of Quarry by BRIQUETERIE. Casualties to 12 noon 1 officer killed 4 O.R. wounded. Whereupon 1.30 p.m. Battalion to move to BRIQUETERIE. at 2.15 p.m. Battalion arrived BRIQUETERIE 3.30 p.m. extra S.A.A. bombs and sets of tools and issued. Rations arrived 4.30 p.m. & are served. Upon state 2nd Battalion had two pontoons sent up to the RIGHT where STRONG POINT SOUTH WEST of ARROWHEAD COPSE has held attack up. Their important role is to form situation and follow. 7th NORTHANTS took back 6 the QUARRY between hold up on our right. 15th MIDDLESEX were cut to pieces by own artillery, not even a mother on ambush. One boy 2nd LEINSTERS attempted to copy 6th attack and was cut up at own machine guns fire from STRONG POINT. 9th SUSSEX attempted to open fire	

1875 Wt. W593/826 1,000,000 4/15 J.B.C. & A. A.D.S.S./Forms/C. 2118.

Place	Date	Hour	Summary of Events and Information	Remarks and references to Appendices
	19. August		NORTHANTS will move by what starts As Gaols. The whole Brigade was therefore held in support ready by about 5 P.M. While the N.F. captd. 1 mm before 1/ the NORTHANTS who still held the QUARRIES and goin' up will 179B. on this left. this first diphni. About 5.30 P.M. Battalion received orders from B.B.E. 73 B.B. to move up to ARROW HEAD COPSE Junch to relieve 2nd LEINSTERS. Who cancelled 5.45 P.M. orders had been sent to LEINSTERS to let them know to go on & attack. Orders received 8.15 P.M. Battalion to move up to relieve LEINSTERS and attack at 1 A.M. 19th inst. Orders for attack cancelled 9.30 P.M. relief to continue "attack will not take place before 1 A.M. 14th." 24 DIV moves on dates "attack will not be proceeded with to-morrow." Relief completed about 3 A.M. Trenches badly knocked about in the greatest possible state of disorder. Shell shaving some showers. Casualties 6.12mm Major (U-HOLE) wounded. 7.O.R. killed, 14 wounded & missing. Our Field guns dropped several shells short during morning, some in our front line trenches, some in our front line support. About 12 mm Brigade Major 72 B.B. (72 J.B. had one from 73 J.B. during morning) informed us that this Battalion would not attack but would be relieved that night. Our own artillery kept up field shells on German dumps this afternoon, the enemy's trenches his home at 8.40. P.M. shelling our front. At 8.15 P.M. the enemy had and most more on our left at an enemy shelling our front. Their barrage died away towards 9.15 P.M.	

WAR DIARY or INTELLIGENCE SUMMARY

Army Form C. 2118

Place	Date	Hour	Summary of Events and Information	Remarks and references to Appendices
	20th August		16th CHESHIRE REGT. relieved Battalion which being completed at 3.20.a.m. moved back to CRATERS AREA. At 11 a.m orders came from Bde. that the Battalion and Cy Reserve (Details) would take part in an attack on the enemy in rear informed that Battalion would proceed in Brigade Reserve at about 12.30 p.m. this BRIQUETERIE	
	21st August		6.12 noon. 1 officer (Capt. H. G. P. Akerbled (compound #24 Aug) Barnsley, his and his platoon of 40 at 7 S.O.R. company at 4.a.m. at 5.30 a.m. it was reported that B.40 hrs. drawn from reinforcements at Tunnel Trench Day. Bound to 5 to 12 noon 3.O.R. wounded. Battalion in Bde. Reserve to attack on HULL STREET at moment all 8th QUEENS at 4.30 p.m.	1 (H.H.H.) wounded O.R. 1 killed, 4 wounded
	22nd August		A.m. orders to move to the BRIQUETERIE were received at 10.15 A.M. and to move to the BRIQUETERIE were received, with a view to commencing the 8th QUEENS in the QUARRY LINE. On arrival at BRIQUETERIE received Orders to Queens. Battalion made up of 4 coys. Killed compH'd 5. 10. a.m. Heavy shelling of EDWARD TRENCH at 8th Hd QPS, GUILLEMONT ROAD, St. James and morning. By 8 a.m. QUARRY LINE trench-mortared, LIEUT. LEES being killed. High morning, near hit ex-O.R. 2 killed 10 wounded R.F.A. who shell QUARRY. Bound 5 to 12 noon. 10 officers killed, 10 wounded 4 morning relieved wounded. Battalion relieved by 11th KINGS ROYAL RIFLE CORPS, relief commenced 12 m X midnight. On relief Battalion moved to CITADEL.	
	23rd August		Fini whole day. bound 5 to 12 noon. 3.O.R. wounded. Fed 100 men whilest. 4. p. m. whole whole party to work here ——— service returned to camp on completion of its work	

WAR DIARY or INTELLIGENCE SUMMARY

Army Form C. 2118

Place	Date	Hour	Summary of Events and Information	Remarks and references to Appendices
	24th August		At about 2 a.m. 24th inst. Fine day. Issued Coy'n C.B. reports all depths over 1' avg. Relief a men tot. Strength this from the SHROPSHIRES.	
	25th August		Dull hot day, some heavy showers. Bern at 9 a.m. to two recces between DERN-ACOURT & MELLENCOURT. Bad mud, many shelts from the front. Enemy about 3.45 h.m. almost rained (rained) walk on enemy shell which burst on AMIENS - ALBERT ROAD. Ran very back and not in good marching line.	
	26th August		Dull day. Some showers. Arrived Pd/S visit DELVILLE WOOD Trenches with a view to taking them over shortly. Trenches in poor condition. Communication trenches very narrow.	
	27th August		Showery day. General Goffe C.B. inspected addresses 4/7 2.J.B. at 9.30 a.m. (see Appendix c). (Battalion moves in to close Bill's on RIREMONT 2.15. h.m. accommodation very inadequate but officers some shelter from the rain. Coy commanders recce DELVILLE WOOD section known at 5.30 a.m.	
	28th August		Showery day. Two officers C & D Coys and guides visit DELVILLE WOOD sector. Training continued.	

WAR DIARY
or
INTELLIGENCE SUMMARY

Army Form C. 2118

Place	Date	Hour	Summary of Events and Information	Remarks and references to Appendices
	29 August		Quiet day. Two officers and parties A & B Coys, Sig. Sergt. and Major CONWAY, D.S.O. visit DELVILLE WOOD trenches. 24 Division in Corps Reserve to attack of 4" Army 72 I.D. m.g. be moved at 4 hours notice. Subsequent orders received to the effect that within 6pm we am prepared 48 hours and that 24 Div will relieve 14 Div. and 33 Div. on night 30/31st August.	
	30 August		Cold rainy day. 35 m.g. cutting S.W. wind. Frequent heavy showers. Left RIDGEMONT 6.10 a.m. March 6 Coys in F.B.d. covering lorries about 9.15 a.m. in camp Kinfield. Os moved off to relieve 9 Rifle Brigade in DELVILLE WOOD at 5.30 h.m. arrive at BERNAFAY QUARRY 7.30 h.m. Wood shelled at intervals. Coy dispositions as follows:— C Coy held from ALE ALLEY exclusive to about S.18.b. 7.9. BHQ with HQs advanced posts; D Coy from S.18.b.7.9 to Junction of cocoa lane — INNER TRENCH exclusive with advanced posts on BEER TRENCH; B Coy held DEVIL'S TRENCH; A Coy were in reserve in YORK AVENUE.	See Map A.
	31 August		Relief complete 4.45 a.m. dull day. Enemy shells Wood at intervals during [?] Hun from 11 a.m. — 3 h.m. about 12 noon enemy made frontal attack on 1st SOUTH STAFFORDS Regt in our dells on our RIGHT. This was repulsed by machine gun fire, as was a second frontal attack. A third bombing attack was made down HOP ALLEY which reached the SOUTH STAFFORDS and of this trenches NORTH HOP ALLEY, a plug the ALE ALLEY BARRIER and in the confusion seizing about 40 YARDS of the trench	

1875 Wt. W593/826 1,000,000 4/15 J.B.C. & A. A.D.S.S./Forms/C. 2118.

RIGHT & EDGE TRENCH. As one of our Lewis guns at a large number of bombs had been lost to the SOUTH STAFFORDS at ??? of the S.S.STAFFORDS which been down our front the attack was ??? ??? for this it ??? ??? have been our RIGHT now was complete in this air and the whole of the position in front day of being turned. Lt/Col. 2Lt S.S. WORSLEY, M.C., managed to rally ??? of the SOUTH STAFFORDS in the WOOD and LIEUT BISTOCK threw out a line a as a defensive flank to his right ???, while 2Lt I.A. WHITE mg galleries ??? led the enemy's advance down in the Trench. When the enemy was ??? briskly. Such units as ??? left in our RIGHT Coy at ???thdrew. Some were ??? fighting (that with the SOUTH STAFFORDS have been lost while the will had been put out of action by bombs. 9Cmd of ??? therefore considered to bomb in further gun ??? S.A.A. at least before any further attack could be attempted. Heavy shelling on this ??? front ??? during the day, the SOUTH W SOUTH-EAST edges of the WOOD ??? continuing ??? but to left no actual attack was made & ??? our front but on the 8 ROYAL WEST KENTS at ??? ??? this front line in BEER TRENCH at the STRING POINT in COCOA LANE in ??? of the bombardment, the enemy advanced

Meanwhile was unfortunately be held ???

down COCOA LANE and received the STRONG POINT. C.W. LEFT POST won the complete in the air on its left and the N.C.O i/c aware the SOUTH STAFFORDS returning to his regt. were directed to withdraw to the WOOD. This he did establishing himself in EDGE TRENCH about — 50 yards EAST of its junction with COCOA LANE, no making a defensive flank for the remaining H.Q.5. The N.C.O. i/c No 2 POST seeing what had happened and his men wounded to No 3 POST to discover I got away had reorganised on a front that the had not done so there was remaining there and held this POST on their own. News of this information had been received at "B" H.Q.S. and the first intimation of an attack was brought by CAPT. PRESTON commanding Junior Banks Batter 6 of 7" DIV. who informs that this 3 STAFFORDS had been driven out of HOP ALLEY and ALE ALLEY and were retiring through the WOOD. MAJOR DUDMORE then ordered A Coy from YORK ALLEY to move up to protect our RIGHT flank and now under guidance of CAPT. PRESTON (who a home was present at 8.30 h.m., but unfounded of Coy who went forward). The information counted this Hell-bombers was sent to reinforce CAPT. PRESTON took B Coy in DEVIL'S Wood. the remaining two platoons going to their billets.

WAR DIARY
or
INTELLIGENCE SUMMARY
(Erase heading not required.)

Army Form C. 2118

Place	Date	Hour	Summary of Events and Information	Remarks and references to Appendices
			No further attacks were made during the remainder of the day or night, but a heavy bombing was kept up all night in DELVILLE WOOD. Ops 2nd QUEENS relieved the 1st SOUTH STAFFORDS during the night, and the 8th QUEENS relieved the 8th ROYAL WEST KENTS now LEFT. C. Pyne Capt & adjt Middx 8/15/15	See Appendices E for ops Reports. Appendix F for messages nos 1 to 72 & to additional orders and other movements.

Appendix A. War Diary period 1st. Aug.-31st. Aug: 1916.

On the 4th. August 1916 the Divisional Commander addressed the Battalion preparatory to its being engaged in the Battle of the Somme in the following terms:-

He expressed his approval of the good work done by the Battalion ever since it had come under his Command in situations that were always trying and often of great severity and stated that the Higher Command knew and appreciated that work. Nothing was harder and more distasteful to troops than to sit still and take punishment without being able to retaliate, and that had been our lot for a long time. But our turn had come now and he felt assured that we should wipe off all scores in a manner equally satisfactory to ourselves as it would be unpleasant for the enemy. We were likely, however, to go into the trenches first of all to hold the line, but we must remember that even so we must always be on the offensive, seeking to gain ground wherever possible and patroling 'No Man's Land' daily and nightly.

Finally he wished to impress upon all ranks three things that had been proved to be of the first importance; water, ammunition communications. Water was a great problem in this country and men must learn to economise and hoard it. They would often be thirsty, but they must resist the temptation to drink as long as possible and then they must drink as sparingly as possible. Ammunition too must be husbanded. Trench warfare had taught men to be very extravagant with their S.A.A., but they must 'unlearn' that lesson. The supply of S.A.A. and water in the field was one of the greatest difficulties the Staff had to confront. Communications were of vital importance and everyone must do his utmost to get information back to the various Headquarters. Terrible mistakes had occurred through failure to keep those in rear informed of the progress of those in front. Too much stress could not be laid on the importance of these three points in any instruction that might be given the troops.

Appendix 5, War Diary: 1st.—31st. Aug. 1916.

        The following Officers moved up to the Forward Area on the 15th August 1916.

Bn. Hd. Qrs.

Major. W.P.E.R. Dugmore, D.S.O. R. of O.

Major. K.S. Conway, D.S.O., 1st. N.S.R.

Capt. and Adjt. V.V. Pope, D.S.O., 1st. N.S.R.

Capt. C.H.L. Coney, Signal Officer, 3rd. N.S.R.

Lieut. J. Bostock, Intelligence Officer, 1st. N.S.R.

CAPT. A.J. WAUGH. R.A.M.C. MEDICAL OFFICER.   Killed in Action. 17.8.'16

'A' Coy.

Capt. G.O. Way. 4. N.S.R.

Lieut. M. Lees. 1st. N.S.R.   Killed in action. 22.8.16.

2Lt. O.V. Hole. 10th. N.S.R.   Wounded. 18.8.16.

2Lt. E.R.G. Wood. 1st. N.S.R.

'B' Coy.

Capt. G.C. Thomson. 3rd. N.S.R.

Lieut. R.E. Hodgson. 1st. N.S.R.

2Lt. H.B. Ryley. 4th. N.S.R.

2Lt. E.J. Swallow. 1. N.S.R.

'C' Coy.

Capt. G.P. Hill. 4th. N.S.R.   Killed in Action. 19.8.16.

2Lt. S.J. Worsley. 4th. N.S.R.

2Lt. A.H. Allen. 10th. N.S.R.

2Lt. C.C. Harris. 4th. N.S.R.

'D' Coy.

Capt. A.L. Tillinson. 4th. N.S.R.

2Lt. M.M. Robertson. 9th. N.S.R.

Lieut. G.R.A. Syfret. 3rd. N.S.R.

2Lt. F.E. Schadhorst. 4th. N.S.R.

Appendix C, War Diary. Period 1st.--31st. Aug. 1916.

On the 27th. August, 1916, the Divisional Commander addressed the 72 Infantry Brigade, after he had inspected it, as follows

He congratulated General Mitford on commanding such a fine body of men and said that General Mitford must be as proud as he himself was of the 72 Infantry Brigade. He was especially pleased with the Brigade's smart and soldierly appearance on parade that morning, since it showed that our recent experiences in the Battle had not affected the men's spirits in any way. Our experiences in the attack on GUILLEMONT, the first attack made by the Division since the Battle of LOOS, had been rough, but our efforts had met with considerable success and we had seized a vantage-point of much importance.

A few days ago he had been sent for by the Commander-in-Chief and had been congratulated on the way in which the Division had handled the spade prior to and during the attack on GUILLEMONT. None of the work we had done then had been wasted. We had suffered casualties, but nothing like as heavy as they must have been, had that spade-work been neglected.

Now we might again be called upon to make an attack shortly and that at no very distant date, but he felt confident that whatever task was allotted us the 72 Infantry Brigade would carry it through with satisfaction to themselves and honour to the Division.

Appendix D, War Diary. Period 1st.--31st. Aug. 1916.

@@@@@@@@@@@@@@@@@@@

The following Officers moved up to the Forward Area with the Battalion on the 30th August. 1916.

Bn.Hd.Qrs.

Major W.F.B.R.Dugmore, D.S.O. R.of O.

~~Major A.S.Conway, D.S.O. 1st.N.S.R.~~

Captain and Adjutant V.V.Pope, D.S.O. 1st.N.S.R.

~~Lieut. Keene, R.A.M.C. T.C.~~
CAPTAIN. N. McLEOD. R.A.M.C. T.C.

'A' Coy.

Captain P.Washington. 3.N.S.R.   Wounded 1.9.16.

Lieut.D.Sear. 3.N.S.R.

Lieut.R.Ritson. 7.N.S.R.

2Lt.E.R.G.Wood. 1st.N.S.R.

'B' Coy.

Captain G.G.Thomson. 3.N.S.R.

Lieut.R.E.Hodgson. 1st.N.S.R.   Killed in Action 31.8.16.

LIEUT. D.W. RENWICK 3.N.S.R

~~2Lt.I.A.While. 4.N.S.R.~~

2Lt.L.J.Swallow. 1st.N.S.R.

'C' Coy.

Lieut.J.K.Bostock. 1st.N.S.R.   Wounded 31.8.16.
2Lt. I.A. WHILE 4.N.S.R   Wounded and Missing. 31.8.16.

2Lt.S.J.Worsley. 4.N.S.R.

~~2Lt.A.H.Allen. 10.N.S.R.~~

2Lt.C.C.Harris. 4.N.S.R.

'D' Coy.

Captain G.D.Chew. 4.N.S.R.

2Lt.M.M.Robertson. 9.N.S.R.   Killed in Action 31.8.16.

Lieut.G.R.A.Syfret. 3.N.S.R.   Wounded 31.8.16.

2Lt.F.E.Schadhorst. 4.N.S.R.   Wounded 31.8.16.

30.8.16

Appendix E. War Diary, period 1st.-31st. August, 1916.

Messages sent to Bn.Hd.Qrs. by o.c. Coys during and after Attack on DELVILLE WOOD on 31st. Aug. 1916.

No. 1. To O.C. 1st. North Stafford Regt.

    German bombardment has now lasted nearly 5 hours. We have suffered heavy casualties. Our guns do not seem to be replying much. We have for certain 12 killed and about 25 wounded already.

11.45.a.m.   sd. G.D.Chew Capt.
31.8.16.   O.C. 'D'Coy.

Endorsed as follows:-

    O.C. 'D'Coy.

BROWNSETT is wounded and in my trench. MOORCROFT has volunteered to take this message.

Also endorsed:-

    I have sent Lieut. RENWICK & 20 men to reinforce 'D'Coy.

                                          sd. G.THOMSON Capt.
31.8.16.   O.C. 'B'Coy.

Received at Bn.Hd.Qrs. 2.45.p.m. by Pte.MOORCROFT.

xxxxxxxxxxxxxxx

No. 2.

Adj. 1st. North Staffords.   31.8.16.

After fairly heavy bombardment and very heavy shelling on our left as a diversion the Germans attacked the S.Staffords barrier bombing up to the barricade, but were driven back by bombs and Lewis gun. Our Stokes Guns barraged the sap.

C Coy casualties about

6 buried)
10 wounded)
nil killed)

Have reinforced D Coy with 1 officer & 20 men.

My Lewis Gun is now in action again; have taken three men of B Coys team to replace casualties & am keeping gun in trench in reserve as S Staffords have lost a gun & may need assistance.

                                              sd. J.K.BOSTOCK Lieut. O.C.C
2.45.p.m.   Coy.
Endorsed:- received 4.p.m.

Appendix E (cont.).

No. 3.

To O.C. 1st. North Stafford Regt.

Situation Report

D Coy's trench is at present held by the remainder of D Coy and 20 men and 1 officer from B Coy. C Coy have pushed to the left a few yards. The Lewis Gun in INNER TRENCH (D COY) is out of action. The left forward post in BEER TRENCH has been driven in to near the edge of the wood. I have no news from the right post under 2Lt. ROBERTSON.

Several parties of Germans have been seen at long distances. At present the Germans are reported to be massing in dead ground about 500 yds. E. of edge of wood.

We are in touch with C Coy on the right & the W. KENTS on the left.

2.25.p.m.   sd. G.D.CHEW Capt.
31.9.16.   O.C. D Coy.

Endorsed:- received 4.50 p.m.

No. 4.

From O.C. 'B'Coy.
To The Adjutant.

    6.15.p.m.

Estimated casualties:-

Killed officers 1 (Lieut.R.E.HODGSON shell fire. 31.8.16.)

Killed O.R. 14.

Wounded O.R. 10.

We are at present being heavily shelled in what is left of DEVIL'S TRENCH.

The Front Line appears fairly quiet.

I have got an officer & 20 men with 'D'Coy. A party of 16 men are carrying bombs for 'C'Coy. I have lent 'D'Coy our stretchers and 6 men for their wounded.

I will send Corp. FLOWERS with gun to CAPT.CHEW.
Detailed casualty report will follow.

                                           sd.G.G.THOMSON Capt.
                                             O.C. 'B'Coy.

31.6.16.

Appendix E.(cont.).

No.5.

      Adjutant.   12 midnight.

Situation now quiet. We have now blocked trench about 120 yds. N. of Coy. Hd.Qrs.

We hold sap to BEER TRENCH and I have dug in about 30 yds. to protect rear.

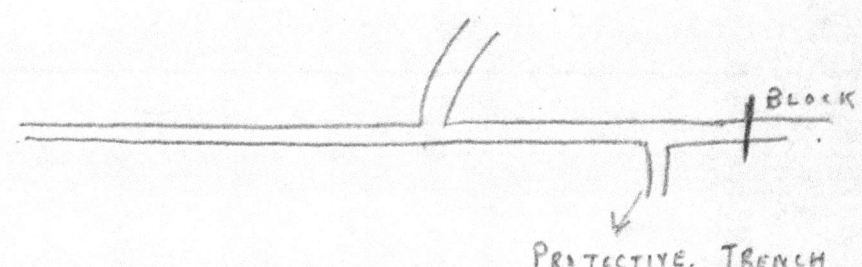

We were held up through want of bombs and fresh bombers. I have asked 'B' Coy for 20 men & an officer if possible & we must have more bombs in case of futher enemy attack.

        sd.S.J.WORSLEY 2/Lt.

No.6.

   Adjt. 1.N.S.R.

    Capt: PRESTON says that he has heard from a QUEENS officer that 2 Coys had been sent to relieve the S.STAFFORDS.

    ½ Coy just moving off.

9.30.p.m.

        P.WASHINGTON Capt.

Appendix F. War Diary period 1st.-31st.Aug.1916.

@@@@@@@@@@@@@@@@@@

Messages sent to 72 Infantry Brigade and other units and replies received.

No.1.

    PRIORITY.

               TO BLOCK.

    N.S.471 31 AAA

    Enemy bombardment still as intense as ever.

    From BUCKLE.

    Time 3.45.p.m.

No.2.

    TO BLOCK.

    N.S.472 31 AAA

    RIGHT Coy reports enemy attacked ALE TRENCH BARRIER about 1.p.m.AAA were repulsedAAA NO attack on BN. FRONT up to 2.45.p.m.

    From BUCKLE.

    Time 4.10.p.m.

No.3.

    PRIORITY.   TO BLOCK

    N.S.473. 31 AAA

    LEFT COY reports enemy said to be massing in dead ground about 500 yd EAST of WOOD AAA timed 3.25.p.m. AAA enemy fire has slackened

    From BUCKLE

    Time 5.p.m.

No.4.

    PRIORITY.   TO BLOCK

    N.S.474. 31 AAA

    Trench Mortar Officer 7th.DIV. reports Germans now occupy Trench on EAST EDGE of DELVILLE WOOD WEST of HOP ALLEY from ALE ALLEY to SOUTH STREET probably AAA Enemy moving SOUTH when last seen AAA NO reports from our Front AAA Am moving reserve Coy under guidance of Capt.PREST 7 DIV. T.M.Bty. to junction of PILSEN LANE-DIAGONAL TRENCH S.18.b.7.0 (approx). with orders to protect my flank.

                                  sd.V.POPE Capt. and Adjt.

5.30.p.m.   1st. North Stafford Regiment.

Appendix F.(cont.).

No.5.

O.C. 1st. SOUTH STAFFORDS

N.S.475. 31 AAA

CAPT.PRESTON T.M.Bty. 7 DIV. reports enemy now occupying Trench on EAST edge of DELVILLE WOOD AAA When last seen were moving SOUTH AAA Our Front appears to hold fast AAA NO reports yet received from our RIGHT Coy AAA Wounded state all is well with us AAA Am moving 2 platoons up from YORK TRENCH to junction of PILSEN TRENCH and DIAGONAL TRENCH S.18.b.7.0. to protect our flank, join up with our RIGHT Coy and if necessary counter-attack AAA Garrisons of HOP ALLEY and ALE XXX BARRICADE retired into WOOD AAA When CAPT& PRESTON left your Coy officers were trying to rally them in WOOD AAA There appear to be none of your men on our RIGHT now from this report AAA Please let me know your situation and any contemplated movements.

sd. V.POPE Capt.and Adjt.

8.45.p.m.   1st. North Stafford Regiment.

No.6.

O.C. 1st. North Staffords

KEEL 31-8-16 AAA

Will you please inform me position on your front. Enemy heavily attacking on our front repulsed twice, again attacking. Please inform me of your position.

O.C. 1st. South Staffords

(untimed- probably received about 8.p.m.(?)).

No.7.

VERY URGENT.   O.C. North Staffords. A.23. 31-8-16. AAA

Following situation of 1st. South Staffords AAA B Coy fallen back from HOP ALLEY towards centre of wood in line with HAYMARKET. A Coy fallen back from BEER TR towards S.E. corner of DELVILLE WOOD AAA C Coy is immediately behind them AAA D Coy has gone back to MONT-AUBAN AAA Position of 2nd. The Queens supporting us C.B.D.Coys sent up to DIAGONAL TR. to support and reinforce the SOUTH STAFFORDS with orders to get in touch on left and extend their right. Please try and get touch with these Coys and assist in rejoining line AAA Send up a large supply of bombs AAA

From O.C. 1st. South Staffords

Time 9.22.p.m.

Appendix F.(cont.)

No.8.

Adjt. 8th.QUEENS

N.S.476 31 AAA

S.O.S. rockets received AAA Situation now appers to be enemy have captured Trench along EAST edge of DELVILLE WOOD AAA Message from O.C 1st SOUTH STAFFORDS timed 9.22.p.m. begins AAA B Coy fallen back from HOP ALLEY towards centre of Wood in line with HAYMARKET A Coy fallen back from BEER TRENCH towards S.E. corner of DELVILLE WOOd AAA C Coy is immediately behind them AAA D Coy has gone back to MONTAUBAN AAA Position of 2 QUEENS supporting us AAA C,B,D, Coys sent up to DIAGONA TRENCH to support and reinforce the SOUTH STAFFORDS with orders to get touch on left and extend their right AAA ends AAA SOUTH STAFFORDS are in want of bombs and S.A.A. AAA NO reports from our Front which appears quiet AAA Please send this information on to 72 I.B. priority AAA Propose sending bombs and S.A.A. being brought up by your parties to aid SOUTH STAFFORDS.

        sd. V.POPE Capt.and Adjt.

9.45.p.m.   1st. North Stafford Regiment.

No.9.

O.C. 1st. SOUTH STAFFORDS

N.S.477 31 A31 AAA

8th.QUEENS are bringing up 30 boxes bombs 30 boxes S.A.A. for us AAA If you really require these of course we will give them to you AAA Please say whether you would like them to be delivered to your Hd.Qrs AAA Guide should be sent here to await them.

        sd. V.POPE Capt.and Adjt.
        1st North Stafford Regiment.

No.10.

BLOCK

N.S.479. 31

Enemy appear to have taken part of RIGHT COY TRENCH AAA Counter-attact being made AAA Situation obscure AAA Have sent down for details AAA O.C.Coy reported killed.

From BUCKLE.

Time 11.p.m.

No.11.

O.C. N.S.R.

Appendix F.(cont.).

No.11.

O.C. N.S.R.

A.25. 1/9 AAA

One of my officers has just arrived from DEVILS TR. just South of HOP ALLEY and reworts that enemy after heavy shelling followed by INF attack succeeded in driving part of my left coy back AAA I sent one of my coys to make a counter-attack supported by 3 coys of the 2nd. Queens & I hope our line is now reestablished but I am anxious that you should ascertain whether your right is in touch with left of my Battalion AAA If you could kindly push forward yr right it would/help to re establish our original line which must be done before daybreak.

12.15.   sd. R.M.Ovens Lt.Col.

No.12.

O.C. 1st. SOUTH STAFFORDS.

N.S.481. 1. A.25. AAA

We sent orderly up to find out situation at 10.30.p.m. but he has NOT yet returned from RIGHT Coy. AAA Believe Coy commander killed AAA Will inform you immediately I hear from my RIGHT Coy.

sd. V.POPE Capt.and Adjt.
1st. North Stafford Regiment.

No.13.

BLOCK.

N.S.483. 1. AAA

Situation now reported by SOUTH STAFFORDS to be as follows AAA Enemy holds SOUTH EAST corner of WOOD namely Hd.Qrs. of NORTH STAFFORDS RIGHT TRENCH (EDGE TRENCH) and SOUTH STAFFORDS TRENCH down to HOP XXX ALLEY AAA S.STAFFORDS bombed down HOP ALLEY but could NOT hold it owing to M.G. fire from ALE ALLEY AAA Believe S.STAFFORDS hold SOUTH- ERN EDGE of WOOD from HOP ALLEY AAA situation on our Front quiet AAA Small groups of enemy have been seen walking about slope EAST of WOOD about 800 to 1000 YDS from INNER TRENCH.

sd. V.POPE Capt.and Adjt

8.40.a.m.   1st North Stafford Regiment.

Appendix G. War Diary period 1st. Aug.-31st. Aug. 1916.

Report from 2/Lt. S.J. WORSLEY, M.C. with regard to the German Attack on
DELVILLE WOOD on the 31st. Aug. '16.

To Adjt. 1st. North Stafford Regiment.

Note. Owing to the necessity of sending this through the post I have omitted names of places, dates, etc.

On the morning of our first day in the trenches (31st. Aug.) about 8.30.a.m. a heavy bombardment began on a considerable front, less heavy on 'C' Coy's right platoon front where our lines approached fairly closely to those of the enemy.

About 12 noon the bombardment slackened considerably in our sector & the enemy made a bombing attack on the strong point held by the regiment on our right (1st. SOUTH STAFFORDS). This attack was beaten off but our own store of bombs, which was never great, was seriously diminished.

We also lent a L. Gun which remained in or near the S. Point (ALE ALLEY Strong Point).

Artillery fire again became intense about 7.p.m. & half an hour later before dark the enemy again attacked. This time he avoided S.P. & attacked frontally the continuation of our own trench. The garrison of this trench used bombs instead of rifles & so lost this position.

The occupants of S.P. seeing themselves about to be cut off then rushed into our trench causing considerable confusion. They had abandoned all stores.

It was this temporary confusion which prevented our making a firm stand at the outset. The enemy now began to bomb our trench.

Lt. BOSTOCK was soon hit but not until he had established a line of riflemen in rear of our parados.

2/Lt. WHILE fought most gallantly & following his example the men stood firm. This officer was then reported wounded and missing but the enemy was held completely by this time.

2/Lt. WYNDHAM, 72 T.M.B. now took charge of the the bombing squad & proceeded to strengthen the barricade & reorganise the bombing squads-- a difficult task considering the exhausted condition of the men.

This officer fought his gun until he had no more ammunition & showed great courage & coolness throughout. In my opinion his services deserve recognition.

About 11.p.m. the situation became farly quiet & the enemy occupied about 30 yds. of our trench.

I am confident that had there been a plentiful supply of bombs we could have cleared our trench by a sharp counter-attack, but for well over 12 hours we could not muster 70 grenades. in our trench. Hence I decided to strengthen my present position.

About 3.p.m.(1st.inst.) I decided to push a small party beyond our barrier, This party discovered that a considerable portion of the trench was unoccupied.

I was unwilling to begin a battle but I ordered another barricade to be made which would give us another 20 yds. of trench & also Coy Hd.Qrs.

As a result of this move we recovered one Stokes Gun & several trench maps, papers etc., which the enemy had carefully packed for removal.

Before dusk we were relieved.

(sd.) S.J.WORSLEY 2/Lt.
N. Stafford Regt.

Sept.11.1916.

24th Division
72nd Brigade

1st BATTALION

NORTH STAFFORDSHIRE REGIMENT

SEPTEMBER 1 9 1 6

WAR DIARY or INTELLIGENCE SUMMARY

Army Form C. 2118

Place	Date	Hour	Summary of Events and Information	Remarks and references to Appendices
1st Bn H.Q.			From 5 a.m. - 7 a.m. there was a lull in the enemy shelling & opportunity was seized to take the troops up to DELVILLE WOOD. Shortly after this was completed heavy enemy shelling & artillery began about 8 a.m. and was kept up throughout the morning. MAJOR OTTLEY ROYAL FUSILIERS, transferred two Coys 9th E. SURREYS to positions (one in..) two Coys were put in VICAR TRENCH. Soon the bombardment increased until the 9th E. SURREYS were relieved. At 9 pm 9th E. SURREYS WOOD which the 1st was held. Bombardment was until 4.45 & continued as afternoon before. A counter attack was made at 4.17 & 7.3.6. was left when counter attack started. I will take the rest & the enemy brought the wood down & for the name of the attacks at night.	[signature]
2nd S.H.			May be complete about 9 a.m. the Col. platoons managed in MONTAUBAN & ate Gd. (St. hours)) to 10 a.m. The E. SURREYS did not retire, one LEFT & LEFT CENTRE POST on RIGHT POST at BEER TRENCH two to the front. & they had some Lewis guns with them but they were thought to have no return at half their cost or 2nd 30 hours in wire. Th Gutlal was thought Show to a quire of wounds (and two ROSSIGNOL & FRIZOUT most preserved to DELVILLE WOOD but initially enemy bombard with flash followed by another bombard)	

WAR DIARY or INTELLIGENCE SUMMARY

Place	Date	Hour	Summary of Events and Information	Remarks and references to Appendices
	3rd Sept		out and march up) had been for month (the weather the rain having rendered difficulties on the roads.	
			Issued Gummy Rifle left station up to E. SURREYS at 4.30 a.m. Enemy Aeroplane E. SURREYS co-operate with 7 Div in attack on captured Trenches in DELVILLE WOOD, Enemy hull Lt. Col. DELAFONTAINE killed C.O., MAJOR OTTLEY Second in command. MAJOR DUGMORE D.S.O. assumed 6th (Late 2nd in command of Bn) 2i/c. RIGHT SECTION and moved up to DELVILLE WOOD about 5.30 h. A18 Coys moved up to the (now E. SURREYS at G.H.Q., Q.A.O.S.S. remained at MONTAUBAN with CAPT. A.O.T. POPE, D.S.O., M.C. A ty moved into DEVIL'S TRENCH, a ground from through the L Bay Incorps B Coy moved to YORK TRENCH. CAPT G.G. THOMSON took command of the Trench line in the E. SURREY Coys had its main offence left.	
	4th Sept		Due to LEFT HALF Bn concerned refire of Relief 4.30 a.m. at 10 a.m. having been relieved ~~~~~~~~~~~~~~~~~~~ RIGHT HALF BN had general clear up clay in DELVILLE WOOD. Preparel relief found the continents	

Place	Date	Hour	Summary of Events and Information	Remarks and references to Appendices
5th Sept			Dull day. LEFT HALF B[attalio]n occupied valleys (or RIGHT HALF between 4.30 a.m. and 7 a.m. to consolidate from enemy fire. LEFT HALF B[attalio]n relieved by 1/10 LIVERPOOL SCOTTISH at about 6 p.m. RIGHT HALF relieved by 1/5 LOYAL NORTH LANCASHIRE Regt. Relief carried out during night. Relief carrying out in place by attack not completed by 7 Div. Our troops on right of attack were not in position when B[attalio]n left trenches immediately in rear of attack on C DEVILS TRENCH. Lt. RYLEY with two Platoons B Coy had moved up to Platoon dump and gave them the attack was ordered not to push out. 7 Div attack failed but on other 2 QUEENS. 7th B[attalio]n moved gradually out although 7 Div had been unaware that we could give them assistance. Immediately Lt. RYLEY attacks the enemy front machine gun fire on his 15 men and half platoon fell. Lt. RYLEY was immediately killed and though a few men reached the German trench and entered it the [?] ... not sufficient to hold it and were captured by the 2 QUEENS. when other attempts also failed when the enemy barrage prevented them the rely carried. Finally relief in full. about 1 am B" returned to support in FRICOURT trench.	A[ppendix] A communique MAJOR GENERAL CAPPER'S message to 4th Bn 5 S. Staffs.
6th Sept				

Army Form C. 2118

WAR DIARY
or
INTELLIGENCE SUMMARY
(Erase heading not required.)

Place	Date	Hour	Summary of Events and Information	Remarks and references to Appendices
	7th Sept		Casualties from 30th Aug – 5th Sept inclusive. Killed officers 3. O.R. 49. Wounded officers 4. O.R. 155. Missing officers 1 (wounded) O.R. 9. Total 221. During the afternoon the Battalion moved to camp near DERNACOURT. E.B.a. 9.d. & c.d. Continuing on in the Commander in Chief who slipt in on his arrival to the small car the Regiment most heartily cheered in the strongly Française.	
	8th Sept		Brigade ordered to be ready at 4 p.m. to support EDGEHILL (BERNACOURT) 1 h.h. Bn moved to 4 h.m. forward LONGUÉ 11 h.m. trucks & B.Co BELLANCOURT. The men's parts [illegible] carried by transport. Regt transport marched to BELLANCOURT by route march leaving DERNACOURT 1 a.m.	
	9th Sept		Reconnaissance BELLANCOURT 2 c.m. Regt B & C Cos led by mounted officers. Transport arrived about 5 p.m.	
	10th Sept		Day of Quiet Training	
			Day of Ordinary Training	

Army Form C. 2118.

WAR DIARY
or
INTELLIGENCE SUMMARY.
(Erase heading not required.)

Instructions regarding War Diaries and Intelligence Summaries are contained in F. S. Regs., Part II. and the Staff Manual respectively. Title pages will be prepared in manuscript.

Hour, Date, Place	Summary of Events and Information	Remarks and references to Appendices
11th Sept.	Training continued.	
12th Sept.	Training continued. Jonal fatigue as men unloading barges early from 11 A.M. to 11 A.M. 13.9.16.	
13th Sept.	Training continued. Howitzer battery of ours MAJOR A.S. CONWAY D.S.O. Half bns. sent to Aust. Retirement for	
14th Sept.	Training continued. Remainder of bns. sent to Aust.	
15th Sept.	Training continued.	
16th Sept.	Training in trenches.	
17th Sept.	Training - Revd. Barnard Roy joined.	
18th Sept.	Training in trenches.	

Army Form C. 2118

WAR DIARY
or
INTELLIGENCE SUMMARY
(Erase heading not required.)

Instructions regarding War Diaries and Intelligence Summaries are contained in F.S. Regs., Part II. and the Staff Manual respectively. Title Pages will be prepared in manuscript.

Place	Date	Hour	Summary of Events and Information	Remarks and references to Appendices
	19th Sept.		Battalion marches ABBEVILLE and entrain there for BRYAS marching thence to HESTRUS, the 24 Division now coming under orders of FIRST ARMY.	
	20th Sept.		Training continued.	
	21st Sept.		Training continued.	
	22nd Sept.		Training continued.	
	23rd Sept.		Training continued.	
	24th Sept.		Battalion marches to BRUAY, billeted in the town.	
	25th Sept.		Training continued.	
	26th Sept.		Battalion marches to VILLERS AU BOIS ul CAMBLAIN L'ABBÉ. A & B Coys Army billeted in CAMBLAIN L'ABBÉ, 13th Coy Au Bois, 72 B. hors lines Brivin ui ?	

1875 Wt. W593/826 1,000,000 4/15 J.B.C. & A. A.D.S.S./Forms/C. 2118.

WAR DIARY
or
INTELLIGENCE SUMMARY

(Erase heading not required.)

Army Form C. 2118

Place	Date	Hour	Summary of Events and Information	Remarks and references to Appendices
	27th Sept.		Training continued. Average 80 men per day leave for Belgium while B.s	
	28th Sept.		Training continued. Fatigue of One Officer and 50 men sent to work for R.A.	
	29th Sept.		Training continued.	
	30th Sept.		Training continued.	

Appendix A.   War Diary period 1st. to 31st. Sept. '16.

General Capper's message to the Battalion on the 5th. Sept. 1916.

Following message was forwarded to companies in DELVILLE WOOD on the 5th. Sept. '16., by Major W.F.B.R. Dugmore, D.S.O., commanding Composite Battalion in DELVILLE WOOD.-

The G.O.C. Division has been up to Battalion Headquarters for the express purpose of asking the Commanding Officer to convey to all ranks his great admiration for the way the men have behaved.   He realises what a tremendous strain it has been and fully sympathises with all.

It has been a great gratification to him to know that you have been able to stick it.

B3435

G. 24th Division,

The Divisional Commander directed me verbally to obtain & send in a report on the circumstances under which Lieut. Rugby was called upon by the Bn. on our right to cooperate in an attack on the post in ALE ALLEY on night of 5th Aug.

10 Sept: 16.

B. .... Br. General,
Comdg: 72 .... Bde.

GX 166.
11/9/16

72nd Infy Bde

On the 5th inst., owing to my being unable to obtain any information of a definite character from the Battn on my right (8th Devons), & knowing the precarious position of my right, I instructed Lt Ryley to take up a supporting position in rear of my right, with ½ Coy (22 rifles) & 1 L.G.

I explained to him that as far as I could ascertain the Battn on my right were holding DIAGONAL TR. & towards HOP ALLEY., but that I could not find out anything about their contact with the enemy at the S.E corner of DELVILLE WOOD:

It would be an easy matter for the enemy to work round the rear of EDGE TR, & I wished him to prevent this, & to take up position accordingly: that an offensive was intended on our right, but that we were so weak, that all we could do was to co-operate by M.G. & L.G. fire.

After Lt Ryley had taken up his position in the Wood I received a wire instructing me to give up any ground required by the Battn on my right.

I sent this wire to that Battns HdQrs & asked what they wished in the matter. The reply was to the effect that it did not concern them. I wired a copy of their reply to you.

Meanwhile - an officer, accompanied by a Sergt & L'Cpl of the 2nd Queens - got in touch with Lt Ryley, & instructed him to co-operate with their offensive by attacking frontally, through the wood to the S.E. corner, & fixing a time, which as far as I can find out, was to be in ½ an hour from the time of meeting Lt Ryley - giving Lt Ryley no opportunity of informing me.

2

At the hour appointed 2/Lt Ryley ordered his men to fix bayonets, &, with his L.G. charged over the ground towards the S.E. corner. The L.G. was knocked out by a shell, & 2/Lt Ryley was killed a few yards after he had started. Sergt Little & some of the men got within bombing distance of the enemy, but were nearly all killed by M.G. fire.

At no time was I informed that the 2nd Queens was on my right, or that any relief (if any occurred) of the 8th Devons was contemplated.

Repeatedly I endeavoured to ascertain what the position was on my right, & what was contemplated, but absolutely no information of any use was given, nor was any effort made to keep me in touch with movements or orders.

The action of the 2nd Queens in taking my one weak support for an offensive, might have led to disaster & the loss of our whole front line.

The O.C. 2nd Queens never once communicated with me, & it was only by accident I heard of that batt'n being in the neighbourhood.

10 Sept 16

W.H.Dugmore Major
Comdg 1 North Staffords

24th Division
72nd Brigade

1st BATTALION

NORTH STAFFORDSHIRE REGIMENT

OCTOBER 1916

Army Form C. 2118.

WAR DIARY
or
INTELLIGENCE SUMMARY.
(Erase heading not required.)

Instructions regarding War Diaries and Intelligence Summaries are contained in F. S. Regs., Part II. and the Staff Manual respectively. Title pages will be prepared in manuscript.

Hour, Date, Place	Summary of Events and Information	Remarks and references to Appendices
1st Oct.	Dull day. Enemy continued	
2nd Oct.	Raid today. British relieve 12 ROYAL FUSILIERS in Support BERTHONVAL SECTION, which employed one Battn. R.A. 7 days Rats against.	See Appendix A in Report on 7 days Raid.
3rd Oct.	Some rain from officer and S.W. Battalion employed on R.E. work. Casualties 0. 12 men nil.	
4th Oct.	Same day. Casualties 0. 12 men nil.	
5th Oct.	Dull day. Casualties 0. 12 men nil.	
6th Oct.	Dull day. Casualties 0. 12 men nil.	
7th Oct.	Dull day. Casualties 0. 12 men nil.	

WAR DIARY
or
INTELLIGENCE SUMMARY.

Army Form C. 2118.

Hour, Date, Place	Summary of Events and Information	Remarks and references to Appendices
8th Oct.	Rainy day. Bouzincourt. 12 noon nil.	
9th Oct.	Dull day. Bouzincourt to 12 noon nil.	
10th Oct.	Fine day. Relieve 8th R.W. Kents in BERTHONVAL sector. Relief completed 3 p.m. Bouzincourt to 12 noon nil.	
11th Oct.	Fine day. Bouzincourt to 12 noon nil.	
12th Oct.	Fine day. Bouzincourt to 12 noon. 1. O.R. wounded. 1.O.R. killed (attached M.G. Coy.) 1. O.R. wounded. Some enemy heavy trench mortar bombs on the Chord.	
13th Oct.	Fine day. Bouzincourt to 12 noon. 1. O.R. killed.	
14th Oct.	Fine day. Bouzincourt to 12 noon 1.O.R. wounded.	
15th Oct.		
16th Oct.	Fine day. Bouzincourt to 12 noon nil.	

Army Form C. 2118.

WAR DIARY
or
INTELLIGENCE SUMMARY.
(Erase heading not required.)

Instructions regarding War Diaries and Intelligence Summaries are contained in F. S. Regs., Part II. and the Staff Manual respectively. Title pages will be prepared in manuscript.

Hour, Date, Place	Summary of Events and Information	Remarks and references to Appendices
17th Oct.	Quiet showery day. Special relative party under Lieut. BROWN and 2/Lt. HARRIS attempted to raid the enemy trench opposite OLD BOOT STREET SAP. Wire found to be uncut and alarm guns & enemy looking out. Scheme was therefore cancelled without casualties.	See appendices B & C.O.s Report.
18th Oct.	Quiet day. Battalion relieved by 2nd Lincolnshire Regt. Relief complete 9.35 p.m. Battalion moved into billets. Divisional Reserve. HQrs, A & B in CAMBLAIN L'ABBÉ. C & D Coys in VILLERS AU BOIS.	
19th Oct.	Quiet day. Training began. Working parties 50 men found for R.E.	
20th Oct.	Quiet day. Training continued, also work for R.E.	
21st Oct.	Quiet day. Training & work continued.	

Army Form C. 2118.

WAR DIARY
or
INTELLIGENCE SUMMARY.
(Erase heading not required.)

Instructions regarding War Diaries and Intelligence Summaries are contained in F. S. Regs., Part II. and the Staff Manual respectively. Title pages will be prepared in manuscript.

Hour, Date, Place	Summary of Events and Information	Remarks and references to Appendices
22nd Oct.	Cold day. Chalk Rd. Work with R.E. continued	
23rd Oct.	Cold raining day. Training continued	
24th Oct.	Showery day. Returned to Divisional Reserve for a Battle. 1st Guards D.G. March to Bully - Noeux les Mines.	
25th Oct.	Showery day. Relieved 13 E. Surreys in Brig de Reserve in PHILOSOPHÉ.	
26th Oct.	Fine day. Fnd 70 mm working under R.E.	
27th Oct.	Fine day. Fnd 70 mm working under R.E.	
28th Oct.	Showery day. Fnd 70 mm working under R.E.	
29th Oct.	Showery day. Church Parade, had a march.	[signature]

Army Form C. 2118.

WAR DIARY
or
INTELLIGENCE SUMMARY.
(Erase heading not required.)

Instructions regarding War Diaries and Intelligence
Summaries are contained in F. S. Regs., Part II.
and the Staff Manual respectively. Title pages
will be prepared in manuscript.

Hour, Date, Place	Summary of Events and Information	Remarks and references to Appendices
30th Oct.	Stormy day. Work as usual.	
31st Oct.	Stormy day. Battalion relief gd. Royal West Kents in HULLUCH SECTION, RIGHT SUB-SECTION. Relief complete 2.05 p.m. A few enemy trench mortars being enemy. Nil. S.m.	by B.per. Oct. recd (signed) Maj. E. Sufford Kent 31.10.16

Appendix A. War Diary, period 1st. to 31st. October 1916.

Report on Fatigue Party found by 1st.N.S.R. for 51st.Bde.R.F.A.

To O.C. 1st. North Staffords.

The working party sent to this brigade under Lieut. RODWELL have put in some very good work while they have been here. They are first-rate men with a spade & pick and I hope they have been comfortable.

(sd.) E.F.Hood Major

2.10.16.   cdg.51st. Bde. R.F.A.

APPENDIX B. War Diary, period 1st. Oct.'16 to 31st. Oct.'16.

Report on attempted Raid on German Trenches on 17/18th. Oct.'16.

TO 72nd. Infantry Brigade
N.S.649   17th.

The raiding party under Lt. Brown, 2/Lt. Harris, & 37 o.r. left OLD BOOT ST. SAP at 6.30.p.m. Conditions for raid almost perfect. The leading group under Lt. Brown went for 150 yards when the tape gave out, & about the same time a listening post, consealed in a shell-hole gave the alarm by blowing a whistle. Lt. Brown's party laid low for some time, & then he crawled forward to enemy wire, & found no opening. Very lights showed that on the whistle sounding the parapet was manned.

The Mound was reconnoitred, & Lt. Brown found a sap or old trench connected it with the enemy front line. After waiting some considerable time, and finding no opportunity, Lt. Brown decided to withdraw. The whole party returned to our lines at 7.50. without casualties.

Reasons of failure:- enemy evidently prepared & waiting alarm being given by the firing of our medium & Stokes mortars on this part of the line - quite a fresh target, as until to-day nothing except field guns could reach the frontage of this battalion, & consequently the wire was untouched.

2nd. Lack of reconnaissance - Many efforts had been made since the Battn. came into the line to reconnoitre the ground, but the bright moon has prevented our patrols getting sufficiently near.

3rd. The men entered throughly into the spirit & were all volunteers, but there had been no opportunity of practising them in their several roles.

4th. The distance to the wire proving to be greater than the length of the tape, & as the ground is very much broken up by old trenches without a tape direction is very difficult.

Note. If raids are to be made on this portion of the line, the wire must be systematically cut & repairs prevented. This wire-cutting should not take place just before a raid.

(sd.) W.F.B.R.Dugmore, Lt.Col.
Cmdg. 1st. North Staffords.

24th Division
72nd Brigade

1st BATTALION

NORTH STAFFORDSHIRE REGIMENT

NOVEMBER 1916

Army Form C. 2118.

WAR DIARY
or
INTELLIGENCE SUMMARY.
(Erase heading not required.)

Instructions regarding War Diaries and Intelligence Summaries are contained in F.S. Regs., Part II. and the Staff Manual respectively. Title pages will be prepared in manuscript.

Hour, Date, Place	Summary of Events and Information	Remarks and references to Appendices
1st Nov 1916.	Fair day. Wind S.S.W. Snow drifting hard - uncertain in front of support-line. Casualties 6 12 mm I.O.R. wounded (shell-shock). Our Stokes and rifles rd-held. Bombardment of enemy trenches carried out from 11.30 a.m. till 12 h.m. Showing slight damage. Enemy T.M's showed usual activity. Casualties 6 12 mm nil. Wind nil. 	
2nd Nov.	Fair day. Wind S.S.W. Casualties 6 12 mm nil.	
3rd Nov.	Dull day. Wind South. Enemy trench mortars active during afternoon. Our R.A. and Stokes retaliated. Casualties 6 12 mm 2 O.R. wounded	
4th Nov.	Dull day. Wind S.S.E. Usual T.M. activity. Casualties 6 12 mm 1 O.R. wounded	
5th Nov.		
6th Nov.	Showery day. Wind South. Usual T.M. activity. Rate Batten relieved 8th R.W. Kent. Have on relief to Brigade Reserve TENTH AVENUE. Relief complete 3 h.m.	

WAR DIARY or INTELLIGENCE SUMMARY

Army Form C. 2118

Place	Date	Hour	Summary of Events and Information	Remarks and references to Appendices
	7th Nov.		Bomballis to 12 noon 4. O.R.	
	8th Nov.		Working party. Bomballis to 12 noon, 1 O.R. wounded. 270 men working on fatigues etc.	
	9th Nov.		Raining hard. Bomballis to 12 noon NIL. 15 men working.	
	10th Nov.		Fine day. Bound to 6.11 mm NIL. 150 men working	
	11th Nov.		Fine day. Bomballis to 12 noon NIL. 148 men working.	
	12th Nov.		Dull day. Bomballis to 12 noon NIL. 140 men working	
	13th Nov.		Showery day. Relieve 8th R.W. KENTS. Relief completed 3.30 p.m. Trenches in a bad condition. Bomballis to 12 noon NIL.	
	14th Nov.		Fine day. Trench work - what a return. Bound lies to 12 noon NIL.	
	15th Nov.		Fine day. Bomballis to 12 noon NIL.	

Army Form C. 2118

WAR DIARY
or
INTELLIGENCE SUMMARY
(Erase heading not required.)

Instructions regarding War Diaries and Intelligence Summaries are contained in F. S. Regs., Part II. and the Staff Manual respectively. Title Pages will be prepared in manuscript.

Place	Date	Hour	Summary of Events and Information	Remarks and references to Appendices
	15th Nov.		Fine day. Usual T.M. activity. Consol. 5 to 12 noon. 1 O.R. killed.	
	16th Nov.		Fine day. Consol. 5 to 12 noon: Nil.	
	17th Nov.		Fine cold day. Consol. 5 to 12 noon. Nil.	
	18th Nov.		Showery day. Battalion relieved by 8th Royal War. Relief Regt. Relief complete 10.45. a.m. Move into Brigade Reserve. PHILOSOPHE, Cornaillie 6 12 noon. Nil.	
	19th Nov.		Dull day. Fnd 120 men working parties & fatigues.	
	20th Nov.		Dull day. Fnd. same fatigues. Sx6 giving lectures to men on "Bombs" from 5".	
	21st Nov.		Dull day. Usual fatigues.	
	22nd Nov.		Dull day. Usual fatigues. Aeropl. combat in evening.	

1875 Wt. W593/826 1,000,000 4/15 J.B.C. & A. A.D.S.S./Forms/C. 2118.

WAR DIARY
or
INTELLIGENCE SUMMARY
(Erase heading not required.)

Army Form C. 2118

Place	Date	Hour	Summary of Events and Information	Remarks and references to Appendices
	23rd Nov.		Fine day. Did usual fatigues.	
	24th Nov.		Fine day. Relieive 8th R.W. Relief complete 11.15 a.m. Enemy shell POSEN ALLEY slightly during relief. Casualties to 12 mn Nil.	
	25th Nov.		Showery day. Somewhat situation quiet - Casualties to 12 noon Nil.	
	26th Nov.		Fine day. Somewhat situation quiet. Casualties to 12 nn Nil. at 10.10 p.m. a STOKES mortar emplacement blew up killing 7 O.R. and wounding 4 mn of the Regiment, and killing 4 O.R. 72 T.M. Bty. The explosion appears to have been caused by a few bombs being left in the emplacement which was not occupied by the Battery from midday onwards. Over 150 rounds of STOKES ammunition blew up. C.S.M. REDFERN, who acted with great presence of mind and showed extreme personal courage, was amongst the killed.	
	27th Nov.		Dull day. Some T.M. activity during day on entire Coy at night by Enemy and our own in replies. Casualties to 12 noon. O.R. 5 killed, 1 missing (presumed killed), 9 wounded (7 serious).	See Appendix A for reports also re ???

1875. Wt. W593/826. 1,000,000. 4/15. J.B.C. & A. A.D.S.S./Forms/C. 2118.

WAR DIARY or INTELLIGENCE SUMMARY

Army Form C. 2118

Place	Date	Hour	Summary of Events and Information	Remarks and references to Appendices
	28th June		Dull day. Situation generally quiet. Casualties to 12 noon :- 1 O.R. wounded	
	29th June		Dull windy day. Situation quiet.	
	30th June		Dull day. Battalion relieved by 8th R.W.KENTS. Relief complete about 3 h.m. Move into Bn Support TENTH AVENUE. Casualties to 12 noon Nil	

J Ryle B/Major
[signature]

APPENDIX A. War Diary period 1st. - 30th. Nov.

Being reports, etc., in connection with explosion of STOKES Gun emplacement and ammunition Store on the night 26/27th. Nov.

I.

To the Adjutant, 1st. North Stafford Regt.
From O.C. 'D' Coy., 1st. North Stafford Regt.
Report on explosion of Stokes Gun dug-out and emplacement.

At 10 p.m. it was reported to me that the Stokes gun emplacement was on fire, and that Coy. Sergt-Major REDFERN, who was on duty at the time, was investigating the matter. I then went myself to investigate the see what could be done. At the moment that I left Coy. Hd. Qrs. the ammunition in the emplacement exploded. I hurried to the spot, passing several men of my company on the way, who informed me of what had taken place.

When I arrived on the spot I found five men buried in the Support Trench at the junction of BOYAU 68 and the Support Trench, their heads only were above ground, and they could speak. From them I got a rough idea of how many men were buried and where.

I immediately collected a working party of my company, and set to work to dig out those who were buried. I also sent to 'C' company for a working party. When the 'C' Company working party arrived I sent the men of my company back to their places in the company sector.

From information received I understand that when the sentries in the front line heard the explosion, they stood their platoons to. They understood that a mine had exploded in BOYAU 68, and the platoons on the left sent bombing parties down the Trenches to where they would be needed.

I also understand that Coy. Sergt. Major REDFERN who was on duty at the time, having been informed that a fire had broken out in the Stokes emplacement collected a party of about twelve men in the Support trench, and with Sergt. WILLIAMS and CORP. BARLOW went into investigate the fire. I understand that the three Stokes Gunners with their gas-helmets on had gone down into the emplacement to extinguish the fire. They were last seen piling sandbags on th ammunition in the emplacement. Coy. Sergt-Major REDFERN, Sergt. WILLIAMS, and Corp. BARLOW, were at the entrance to the emplacement in BOYAU 68 when the explosion took place. The other twelve men and one Stokes gunner were at the entrance in the Support trench at the head of BOYAU 68. All these men were buried.

I understand that the Stokes gunners had lit a fire in their emplacement in 68 and then gone off to their other dug-out by VENDIN ALLEY. They were informed when the emplacement in 68 caught fire, and leaving one man in VENDIN ALLEY the remaining three men and a corporal went to see what they could do.

We dug out seven men alive and none of them were badly injured. We also dug-out four dead men. There are seven men as yet unaccounted for.

I think that Coy Sergt-Major REDFERN in assembling his party in the Support Trench considered that they would be quite safe.

if anything unusual occurred.

          (sd.) W.D.Stamer Lieut.
27.11.16.   O.C. 'D' Coy. 1st. North Staffords.

II
 Futher report on explosion of Stokes Mortar dug-out and emplacement

  The positions of my N.C.O's as stated in previous report is now proved to have been as under.

  Coy. Sergt-Major REDFERN was about five steps down the dug-out. Sergt. WILLIAMS was at the junction of 68 and Support Trench. Corp. BARLOW was on top of the dug-out shovelling earth onto the fire.

  The following bodies have been recovered since the previous reports.

  Corp. BARLOW 1st. North Staffords.
  Pte. GREEN 8th. Royal West Kents attached 72 Trench Mortar Bty
  Pte. CATTLE 8th. Queen's attached 72 Trench Mortar Battery.

          (sd.) W.D.Stamer Lieut.
28.11.16.   O.C. 'D' Coy. 1st. North Staffords.

24th Division
72nd Brigade.

1st BATTALION

NORTH STAFFORDSHIRE REGIMENT

DECEMBER 1916

Army Form C. 2118.

1 N Stafford Regt
Vol 22

WAR DIARY
or
INTELLIGENCE SUMMARY.
(Erase heading not required.)

Instructions regarding War Diaries and Intelligence Summaries are contained in F. S. Regs., Part II and the Staff Manual respectively. Title pages will be prepared in manuscript.

Place	Date	Hour	Summary of Events and Information	Remarks and references to Appendices
	1st Dec		Find working parties for R.E. etc. church while in Brigade Support.	
	2 Dec		Usual Working Parties	
	3rd Dec		Find usual parties	
	4 Dec		Usual Parties	
	5 Dec		Usual Parties	
	6 Dec		Relieved 8th R.W. Kents in Hulluch Sector, Right Subsector. Relief complete about 3.30 p.m. Situation generally.	
	7 Dec			
	8 Dec		Situation generally quiet.	

Army Form C. 2118.

WAR DIARY
or
INTELLIGENCE SUMMARY.
(Erase heading not required.)

Instructions regarding War Diaries and Intelligence Summaries are contained in F. S. Regs., Part II and the Staff Manual respectively. Title pages will be prepared in manuscript.

Place	Date	Hour	Summary of Events and Information	Remarks and references to Appendices
	9th Dec		Situation normal.	
	10th Dec		Situation normal	
	11th Dec		Situation normal	
	12th Dec		Bn. relieved by 2nd R.W. Kents. Relief complete 11.30 a.m. Move to Brigade Reserve PHILOSOPHE.	
	13th Dec		Fund 130 men working daily whilst in Brigade Reserve	
	14th Dec		Move Ruta.	
	15th Dec		Move Ruta.	
	16th Dec		Move Ruta. Here marched to Auchy. Brigade broken. Found that one man on last company was broken.	
	17th Dec		Move Ruta. Church Parade.	

2353 Wt. W2544/1454 700,000 5/15 D. D. & L. A.D.S.S./Forms/C. 2118.

Army Form C. 2118.

WAR DIARY
or
INTELLIGENCE SUMMARY.
(Erase heading not required.)

Instructions regarding War Diaries and Intelligence Summaries are contained in F. S. Regs., Part II. and the Staff Manual respectively. Title pages will be prepared in manuscript.

Place	Date	Hour	Summary of Events and Information	Remarks and references to Appendices
	18th Dec		Relieved 8th R.W. Kents in HULLUCH Sector, RIGHT Subsector. Relief complete 11.30 a.m.	
	19th Dec		Dull. Situation generally quiet.	
	20th Dec		Bright cold day. Situation quiet. Some enemy activity	
	21st Dec		Dull day. Some shelling on Kent. Situation quiet.	
	22nd Dec		Dull day. Situation generally quiet.	
	23rd Dec		Enemy Winch-mortars often in action from upon whole Brigade Front at 8.30 a.m. Enemy artillery fire upon TENTH AVENUE at LE RUTOIRE PLAIN, field guns upon front of Suffolks, 5.9's upon DACKEY TRENCH. Our retaliation was kept up by this unit till about 3 p.m. Our counter-battery work and our shock in trench. Our casualties were not heavy amounting to 5 O.R. Willis and one other in trench.	

2333. Wt. W2344/1454 700,000 5/15 D.D.& L. ADSS/Forms/C. 2118.

WAR DIARY
INTELLIGENCE SUMMARY
(Erase heading not required.)

Army Form C. 2118.

Place	Date	Hour	Summary of Events and Information	Remarks and references to Appendices
	24th Dec		Killed... O.R. wounded - C.S.M WOODMAN was among the killed. At 4 h.m the fire had compelled Coys. and the left Coy was relieved. Small shell during Battn. relieved by 8th Royal Welsh Fus's. Relief complete 2.30 p.m. Marched to Bulgar Support TENTH AVENUE.	
	25th Dec		Dull day. Coy 6 ran Elly bombs at enemy trenches throughout the day and night S-VPs. 9 o'clock evening T.M. ammunition. Dull day. Fired 2.50 mm mortars.	
	26th Dec		Dull day. Intermittent work parties	
	27th Dec			
	28th Dec		Dull day. Issued working parties.	
	29th Dec		Rainy. Issued working parties.	
	30th Dec		Dull day. Relieved 8th R. W. Fus's in Front line. Relief complete 2.30 p.m. Trenches in appalling condition, mud to waist — knee-deep in mud in most places. Thigh-	

Army Form C. 2118.

WAR DIARY
or
INTELLIGENCE SUMMARY.
(Erase heading not required.)

Hour, Date, Place	Summary of Events and Information	Remarks and references to Appendices
31st Dec	deep in the remainder.	
	Dull day. Situation generally quiet.	

Army Form C. 2118.

1 N Staffords R 24

WAR DIARY
or
INTELLIGENCE SUMMARY.

(Erase heading not required.)

Instructions regarding War Diaries and Intelligence
Summaries are contained in F. S. Regs., Part II.
and the Staff Manual respectively. Title pages
will be prepared in manuscript.

Vol 23

Place	Date	Hour	Summary of Events and Information	Remarks and references to Appendices
	1st Jan 1917		Enemy activity in front line by trench mortars, minnies, snipers, machine gun fire etc. etc. Retaliated as usual.	
	2nd Jan 1917		Situation normal	
	3rd Jan		Situation normal	
	4th Jan		Situation normal	
	5th Jan		Battalion relieved by 8th R.W.Kents, moved into Bigors Horn PHILOSOPHE.	
	6th Jan		This was a day in Billets.	
	7th Jan		A.& B. Co'ys "Xmas" dinners held, Divisional Band and "Snipers" performance of winners.	
	8th Jan		C. & D. Co'ys Xmas dinners held, Divisional Band performed. Rev. MINNEAR, M.C.	

2333 Wt. W3344/1454 700,000 5/15 D,D.&L. A.D.S.S./Forms/C. 2118.

WAR DIARY
or
INTELLIGENCE SUMMARY.

Army Form C. 2118.

Place	Date	Hour	Summary of Events and Information	Remarks and references to Appendices
	9th Jan		Gave an order that night. Men showed a great reserve.	
	10th Jan		Went into the line.	
	11th Jan		Relieved 8th R.W. Kents in HULLUCH Section. Right Subsect. Relay emplt. shot - milling. Some trench mortar activity in NEW CUT and SUPPORT LINE Casualties 1 O.R. killed 3 wounded.	
	12th Jan		Situation normal	
	13th Jan		Situation normal	
	14th Jan		Situation normal	
	15th Jan		Situation normal. Battalion relieved & moved in and in Reserve trenches before dawn on 27th inst.	

Army Form C. 2118.

WAR DIARY
or
INTELLIGENCE SUMMARY.
(Erase heading not required.)

Place	Date	Hour	Summary of Events and Information	Remarks and references to Appendices
	16th Jan		Situation normal.	
	17th Jan		Situation normal. Situation relieved by 5th R.W. Kents, relief complete 5.p.m. hours into Brigade Support. TENTH AVENUE a relief.	
	18th Jan		Fine no man working during day. Snow and frost began	
	19th Jan		Usual work parties. cold day	
	20th Jan		Cold day, work parties. have work parties	
	21st Jan		Cold day. Work parties.	
	22nd Jan		Cold day. Usual parties.	
	23rd Jan		Cold day. relieve 5th R.W. Kents in line. Relief complete about noon	

2353 Wt. W2544/1454 700,000 5/15 D, D, & L. A.D.S.S./Forms/C. 2118.

WAR DIARY or INTELLIGENCE SUMMARY

Army Form C. 2118.

Place	Date	Hour	Summary of Events and Information	Remarks and references to Appendices
	24th Jan		Fair cold day. Quiet on situation generally.	
	25th Jan		Fair cold day. Quiet on left. 9th E. SURREYS patrol engaged enemy on LEFT. Some hostile trench mortar & bomb and trench activity generally quiet. Enemy were not out at proper points of entry without orders etc.	
	26th Jan		Fair mild day. Attempts at more active ambush but with small success. Owing to sound heard to frequent noise.	
	27th Jan		Fair mild day. Quiet everywhere generally. S.S. & 72 Dof. R.G	
	28th Jan		Fair mild day. Officers of 10th Yorkshire Regt came to take over trenches. Relief cancelled by wire at 6.30 p.m.	
	29th Jan		Fair cool day. Battln relieved by 6th R.W. Kents. Proceeded by relief.	

Place	Date	Hour	Summary of Events and Information	Remarks and references to Appendices
	30th Jan		W/T Brigade Runner, Philosopher. Relief complete about 11 a.m. Fine mild day. Tour with Roles M.G. army.	
	31st Jan		Fine mild day. Work with Indians.	

G R Brewhaus
Maud (Mtr) Col

CONFIDENTIAL.

WAR DIARY.

1ST BATTN NORTH STAFFORDSHIRE REGT.

MONTH OF FEBRUARY. 1917.

Army Form C. 2118.

WAR DIARY
or
INTELLIGENCE SUMMARY.
(Erase heading not required.)

Place	Date	Hour	Summary of Events and Information	Remarks and references to Appendices
Philosophe	1.2.17	10 a.m.	During a lecture by 2Lt ALLEN on the Mills Bomb a bomb accidentally exploded wounding 2Lt ALLEN and 8 other ranks. A Court of Inquiry found that the accident was due to the carelessness of No 6337 Sgt. W. COLLINS.	
		12 noon	Total casualties 2 Lt A. H. ALLEN and 8 other ranks wounded. Weather continued fine and frosty; wind East.	
Philosophe	2.2.17	12 noon	No casualties. Weather continued frosty; wind East.	
Philosophe	3.2.17	12 noon	No casualties. Hard frost. Wind East. Reinforcement of 59 other ranks joined the battalion.	
Hallreck Right Sub-Section	4.2.17	12 noon	Relieved the 8th Bn. Royal West Kent Regt in the front line trenches. No casualties. Weather fine and frosty. Wind South West. Capt. V.P. POPE goes to Brig. Hqrs.	
"	5.2.17	12 noon	Enemy trench mortars active during the night against the right and centre companies. Two other ranks wounded. Weather continues fine and frosty. Wind South West.	
"	6.2.17	12 noon	Total casualties 1 other rank wounded. Weather continued fine and frosty. Wind East.	
"	7.2.17	12 noon	Total casualties 1 other rank wounded. Weather continues frosty. Wind S.E.	

Army Form C. 2118.

WAR DIARY
or
INTELLIGENCE SUMMARY.

(Erase heading not required.)

Place	Date	Hour	Summary of Events and Information	Remarks and references to Appendices
Pollock Reght Sub Section	6.2.17	12 noon	Total Casualties nil. Weather fine and frosty. Wind North East.	
"	9.2.17	12 noon	Total Casualties 1 other rank killed; 1 other rank wounded. Weather fine and frosty. Wind North East.	
"	10.2.17	5 a.m.	The enemy attempted to raid our trenches at bayon 64. The raid was beaten off; 1 Officer and three other ranks were taken prisoner and four dead bodies were recovered from No Man's Land. Our Casualties were 3 other ranks wounded. An account of the hostile raid is attached.	A
"	10.2.17	12 noon	Total Casualties 4 other ranks wounded. Weather fine; Wind N.E.	
"	10.2.17	5 p.m.	The Battn. was relieved in the front line trenches by the 6th Royal West Kent Regt., and went into Brigade Support in 10th Avenue.	
"	11.2.17	-	Total Casualties nil. Weather fine and cold. Wind N.E.	
"	11.2.17	12 noon		
"	11.2.17	4 a.m.	At 4.11 a.m. a party (from under Lt G. W. Mappleback RENWICH consisting of two Officers (Lt Renwick and Lt Ryley) and 66 other ranks attempted to raid the enemy trenches opposite an unoccupied portion of our line between Bay aux 69 and 70. The attempt was unsuccessful and the raiding party withdrew after suffering	

WAR DIARY
or
INTELLIGENCE SUMMARY.

Army Form C. 2118.

Place	Date	Hour	Summary of Events and Information	Remarks and references to Appendices
Mallard Right S.A. Section	11.2.17	7.15 p.m.	The following Casualties :– 2 other ranks wounded, Lt RYLEY, Lt Ropley and 3 other ranks missing. A party of 103rd Field Coy R.E. who accompanied the raiders to blow up enemy dug-outs also suffered casualties :– 2 other ranks killed, 1 other rank wounded. On account of the attempted raid to attacked.	B
"	12.2.17	12 noon	Total casualties 2 other ranks killed, 14 other ranks wounded, Lt Ropley and 3 other ranks missing. Weather continuous frosty, hard westerly	RYLEY
"	13.2.17	12 noon	Total casualties nil. Weather warmer, wind south west.	
"	"	2 p.m.	The Battn. was relieved in Tenth Avenue by 10th Royal Fusiliers which completes the relief of the 24th Division by the 37th Division. On relief the Battn. marched	
Bivouacs to Butte	"	"	to Mallets in Roerue – Les – Bivouacs.	
Burnetts	14.2.17	12 noon	At 10 a.m. the Battn. marched out of Roerue – Les – Mines to Burnetts, the rest area. Total casualties nil. Wind north-west, weather cold.	
"	14.2.17	3.45 a.m.	The Battn. arrived in Burnetts.	
"	15.2.17	12 noon	Total casualties nil, weather cold, wind S.E. The battn. rested and a certain amount of re-organisation was done.	

Army Form C. 2118.

WAR DIARY
or
INTELLIGENCE SUMMARY.
(Erase heading not required.)

Instructions regarding War Diaries and Intelligence Summaries are contained in F.S. Regs., Part II and the Staff Manual respectively. Title pages will be prepared in manuscript.

Place	Date	Hour	Summary of Events and Information	Remarks and references to Appendices
Buanettes	16.2.17	12 noon	Total casualties nil. Weather warmer, wind south east. The work of re-organisation was continued. Lieut W.B. STAMER to ? Amb.	PSN
Buanettes	17.2.17	12 noon	Total Casualties nil. Weather warmer, wind southerly. The Battn. commenced carrying out the training programme for the next period	
Buanettes	18.2.17	12 noon	Total casualties nil. Weather singular, wind South. 11667 M.I.B. SHAW 2/Lt E.R. BYAS HALE 2/Lt E.C. [jones Bn]	
Buanettes	19.2.17	12 noon	Major W. Backhouse to ? Amb. Lt A.B. MARTIN returned from ? Amb. 8 O.R. reinforcements from Training Bn and 12 O.R. from Base joined Bn. Training in accordance with programme continued. Weather wet. Wind S.W. Re-organisation was completed. Casualties nil. BACKHOUSE P.D. HARRIS ALLEN	PSN
Busnettes	20.2.17	12 noon	Lieut H. Allen to ? Amb. Captn R. Harris is acting Adjutant vice Lt L.T. Swallow. Training in accordance with programme. Weather wet, wind S.W. & Casualties nil. SWALLOW	PSN
Busnettes	21.2.17	12 noon	Capt H.G. Robinson to ? Amb. Training continued in accordance with programme. Weather fine, casualties nil ROBINSON	PSN
Busnettes	22.2.17	12 noon	Training carried on in accordance with programme. Weather wet. Mean Tw. Casualties nil	PSN
Busnettes	23.2.17	12 noon	Training " " " " Weather Damp windest "	PSN
Busnettes	24.2.17	12 noon	10024 Pte Allen H. 28061 Pte Hall A. 81114 Pte Frost T. 36089 cpl Rous A. awarded military medal and 7598 L/cpl KENEY Kenney T. wounded bar to md. medal by Corps Commander. Training Programme continued Weather wet. windy.	PSN

Army Form C. 2118.

WAR DIARY
or
INTELLIGENCE SUMMARY.
(Erase heading not required.)

Place	Date	Hour	Summary of Events and Information	Remarks and references to Appendices
BUSNETTES	25-2-17	12 noon	6 other Ranks & improvements joined Bn from Base. Training Programme carried on as before. Weather cheerup W.n.w. S.w. Casualties nil	BSA
BUSNETTES	26-2-17	12 noon	Training Programme continued as before. Capt. G.S. THOMPSON admitted to hospital from Lewis school on Feby 17th. Weather fine. Wind S.W. Casualties nil	BSA
BUSNETTES	27-2-17	12 noon	Lieut. W.B. STAMER rejoined Battalion from Hospital. Training continues as per programme. Weather fine. Wind S.W. Casualties nil	BSA
BUSNETTES	28-2-17	12 noon	2/Lieut E.C. HALE went into hospital. Bn went into open to hidden Enemy. Training Programme continued as yesterday. Weather fine. Winter Casualties nil	BSA

BSJohns Captain & Adjutant for the Colonel
Comm'g 15th N'l Staffs Reg't
28/2/17

A.

Attempted German Raid on the Battn. Trenches.
10.2.17.

At 5 a.m today the enemy attempted to raid our trenches near Boyau 64. The attempt was preceded by a heavy trench mortar bombardment of all calibres lasting from 4.45 a.m to 5 a.m. As the intensity of the bombardment diminished one of our sentries noticed a party of the enemy advancing towards our lines. He gave the alarm to the Lewis gun post just south of Boyau 64 by throwing a bomb to his right. The Lewis Gunner allowed the enemy to get up to our wire and then opened fire. Most of the raiders ran back in confusion. Cries of "kamerad" were heard, and C.S.M. Middleton of "C" Coy. got over the parapet and brought in two of the enemy wounded. Soon after C.S.M. Middleton and Lt Wheatcroft went out beyond our wire and brought in 1 officer and 1 other rank prisoners, both unwounded. Four dead bodies were also brought in. Our total casualties were 3 other ranks slightly wounded.

When the prisoners were searched a map of our trenches and a plan of operations were found, and also a photograph of the raiding party taken some days before the raid. Copies of the photograph were taken, one is attached.

The G.O.C. 24th Division, and B.G.C. 72nd Inf. Brig. congratulated the battalion on the repulse of the raid saying that it "reflected credit on all concerned."

C.J Swallow Lt-a/ Adjutant,
1 North Stafford. Regt.
10.2.17.

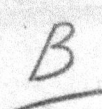

1ST BATTALION NORTH STAFFORDSHIRE REGIMENT.

Attempted raid by 1st North Stafford Regt. on German Trenches.

At 7-15 p.m., on the 11. 2. 17. the Battalion attempted to raid the German Trenches at a point opposite an unoccupied portion of the Front Line between LOTAD 69 and 70. Preparations for the raid had been in progress for some time. A party of 68 other ranks under Lieut. Mappleback and two other Officers, Lieut. Renwick and Lieut. D.A.C.B. Ryley, had been training at PHILOSOPHE for about a fortnight. For several days previous to the attempt our Artillery had cut a gap in the German wire at the point selected. This gap was kept open during the night by Lewis Gun fire and any new obstacle that appeared was removed by the 60 pounder Trench Mortar.

By way of a feint the enemy wire was also cut to the North of Rosen Crater.

The raiding party had also 7 men of the 103rd Field Company R. E. attached for the purpose of carrying over mobile charges and blowing up dug-outs.

The general scheme of the raid was that at zero the Artillery should open on the German Front Line and then immediately form a box barrage round the area to be raided. Meantime the leading parties were to double across No Man's Land through the gap and into the enemy trenches.

The raid proved a failure. The enemy were on the alert and apparently expecting the raid. No sooner had the raiding party started than the enemy Artillery opened on our trenches and heavy machine gun fire swept No Man's Land. A Stokes Smoke bomb falling short added to the confusion and the party retired as best it could.

Our casualties were 2 other ranks killed, 13 other ranks wounded, Lieut. Ryley and 3 other ranks missing. The 103rd Company, R. E. also had the following casualties :- 2 other ranks killed, 1 other rank wounded.

The Battalion was congratulated by the C. O. C. 24th Division on their gallant attempt to enter the enemy trenches.

L. J. Swallow Lt. a/Adjt.
.... for .... Lieut. Col.
Commdg. 1st Battalion North Staffordshire Regiment.

Vol 25 1st Battn North Staffordshire Regt.

War Diary for month of March 1917.

WAR DIARY or INTELLIGENCE SUMMARY

Army Form C. 2118.

Place	Date 1917 MARCH	Hour	Summary of Events and Information	Remarks and references to Appendices
Bushettes	1st	12 noon	Capt. H.G. Robinson returned from Field Ambulance, Lt. & Q.master E.T. Langridge returned from Divisional School. Training carried out with an overseas with programme. Weather fine. Wind S.W. Casualties nil.	PSN
Bushettes	2	12 noon	Lt. W.H. Orrom joined Battalion from England. Training as yesterday. Weather fine as yesterday. Casualties nil.	PSN
Bushettes	3	10 noon	Training in programme. Battalion baths utilised. Weather fine. Casualties nil.	PSN
Bushettes	4	10 noon	Battalion marched to Fouquereuil (relieving the 8th R.W.Kents in billets) and remained the night. Weather fine. Wind N.W. Casualties nil.	PSN
Fouquereuil	5th	10 noon	Battalion marched to Bully Grenay and relieved the 11th Canadian Battalion there in Brigade Reserve. Officers to reconnoitre Bougues front in Calonne Sector. Weather Snowed. Wind N.W. Casualties nil.	PSN
Bully Grenay	6th	12 noon	Lt. W.H. Orrom transferred to 8th N. Staffs Regt. 4 officers reconnoitred front as yesterday. Men training as before. Wind N.W. Weather fine. Casualties nil.	PSN
Bully Grenay	7th	12 noon	Lts. J. Bourn and A.E. Hodge joined Battalion from England also S.O.R. joined. Training as before. 9/Lt. W.H. Wheatcroft killed in action. Weather cold. Wind N.E. Casualties 1 officer killed. O.R. nil.	PSN
Bully Grenay	8th	12 noon	Relieved 8th R.W.Kent Regt. in left subsection of Calonne Defences. Weather cold & snow. Wind S.E. Casualties nil.	PSN

Army Form C. 2118.

WAR DIARY
or
INTELLIGENCE SUMMARY.

(Erase heading not required.)

Instructions regarding War Diaries and Intelligence Summaries are contained in F. S. Regs., Part II. and the Staff Manual respectively. Title pages will be prepared in manuscript.

Place	Date 1917 MARCH	Hour	Summary of Events and Information	Remarks and references to Appendices
MOROC Left Sub Section CALONNE Defences	9th	Noon	Occupied trenches and held front line with (A Coy & C Coy) two companies from front line and two in Support Bays & Donjon. Winds S.W. Wet. Casualties nil.	PSN
"	10th	"	As yesterday. Casualties nil. Enemy active with minnies.	PSN
"	11th	"	As yesterday. Wind S.W. weather wet. Total Casualties 3 O.R. wounded.	PSN
"	12th	"	As yesterday. weather wet. Wind S.W. Condition of trenches in very bad condition. Casualties nil	PSN
"	13th	"	As yesterday. weather wet. Wind S.W. Enemy very active with minnies. 1 O.R. wounded { S/ W H Ryan awarded ITALIAN BRONZE MEDAL for valour in the field	PSN
"	14th	"	Relieved by 8th R. West Kent Regt. in above mentioned trenches. Moved to CALONNE in Brigade Support. weather wet wind S.W. Casualties nil.	PSN
CALONNE	15th	12 Noon	9/m E.S. GORE and 2/Lt D.J.C. CRUICKSHANK joined the Battalion from England. Training Platoon under Lt L.T. Sumner moved to ALLOUAGNE for training purposes. Total number 2 off 68 OR	PSN
CALONNE	15th	12 noon	Battalion in Brigade Support in Calonne. Weather fine. Wind S.W. Casualties nil	PSN
"	16th	12 noon	As yesterday. Very many working parties. Wind S.W. weather fine. Casualties nil.	PSN
"	17th	12 noon	As yesterday. Wind S.W. weather fine. Wind S.S.W. Casualties nil.	PSN
"	18th	12 noon	As yesterday. Capt. G.G. THOMSON rejoined from 7A. 6 O.R. joined Battalion from Base. weather fine Wind W. Casualties nil.	PSN

Army Form C. 2118.

WAR DIARY
or
INTELLIGENCE SUMMARY.
(Erase heading not required.)

Instructions regarding War Diaries and Intelligence Summaries are contained in F.S. Regs., Part II. and the Staff Manual respectively. Title pages will be prepared in manuscript.

Place	Date 1917 MARCH	Hour	Summary of Events and Information	Remarks and references to Appendices
CALONNE	19th	12 noon	Battalion in Brigade Support moving working parties, weather wet wind NW. Casualties nil.	BSN
"	20th	12 noon	As yesterday. [crossed out] Battalion relieved by 9th East Surrey Regt in CATONNE and relieved 8th R.W. Kent Regr in MOROC trenches ENTRENCHING BATTALION weather wet wind NW. 2 O.R. joined Battalion from 3[crossed out]. Weather wet wind SW. Casualties nil.	BSN
"	21st	12 noon	Battalion holds Left Subsector CATONNE DEFENSES. B & D Coys in front line. A & C Coys in Support MOROC. Wind NW weather cold. Casualties nil.	BSN
"	22	"	As yesterday. Enemy quiet little shelling. Weather Snowed. Wind NW. Total casualties 1 O.R. killed.	BSN
"	23	"	As yesterday. Enemy active with T.M's. to our DOUBLE CRASSIER. 9/Lt C.H. RODWELL to 7.A. wind NW. Weather Cold. Casualties Nil.	BSN
"	24th	"	As yesterday. Enemy still active with T.M's. Weather snowed wind NNW casualties NIL	BSN
"	25th	"	As yesterday. Enemy bombarded our trenches W about 6-30 pm on 25th Wt with artillery T.M's, trench to Weather wet wind S.W. casualties nil	BSN
"	26th	"	As yesterday. Enemy quiet. 12 O.R. joined Battalion from Base. Relieved by 8th R. West Kent Regt on night 26th inst and Battalion marched into Divisional Reserve in Billets GRENAY. Weather wet wind SSW. Casualties 1 O.R. wounded	BSN

Army Form C. 2118.

WAR DIARY
or
INTELLIGENCE SUMMARY.
(Erase heading not required.)

Instructions regarding War Diaries and Intelligence Summaries are contained in F. S. Regs., Part II. and the Staff Manual respectively. Title pages will be prepared in manuscript.

Place	Date	Hour	Summary of Events and Information	Remarks and references to Appendices
BULLY GRENAY	27th	13 noon	Battalion in Divisional Reserve in Billets weather, Snowed Wind N.W. Casualties nil	ASN
"	28th	"	as yesterday, men bathing. ½ of the Battalion fire this Gas chamber as Gas Box Respirators	ASN
			A Coy inspected by Brig General W.F. Sweeney D.S.O. (B.G.C. 72 Inf. Bde.) weather fine wind S.W. as yesterday many working parties wind S.W. weather fine Casualties nil	ASN
"	29th	"	As yesterday many working parties Wind S.W. fine Casualties nil	ASN
"	30th	"	As yesterday Wind S.W. weather nice Casualties nil	ASN
"	31st	"	As yesterday. One platoon from B Coy sent to Divisional Training School at ALLOUAGNE for training. Wind S.W. weather nice. Casualties nil.	ASN

A.S. Johns Captain/Captain
for Lt Colonel Commdg
15th NL Staffs Regt
31/3/17

1st BATTN. N. STAFF. REGIMENT

72nd INFANTRY BRIGADE

24th DIVISION

APRIL 1917

1st Battn North Staffordshire Regt. "Vol 26"

War diary for month of April 1917.

Army Form C. 2118.

Instructions regarding War Diaries and Intelligence
Summaries are contained in F.S. Regs., Part II.
and the Staff Manual respectively. Title pages
will be prepared in manuscript.

WAR DIARY
or
INTELLIGENCE SUMMARY.
(Erase heading not required.)

Place	Date	Hour	Summary of Events and Information	Remarks and references to Appendices
	1917			
BULLY GRENAY	April 1	12 noon	Relieved 8th West Kent Regt. in Column left Sub section Trenches on right war. 3 O.R., James Battiston from Rue. 92, 17 L/cupt P. ONT.W. granted Military Medal for gallantry on the field. Wind NW. Weather Snowed. Casualties 2 O.R. wounded	ASH
MAROC	" 2	12 noon	Occupied Column left Subsection front line trenches, A, C, & D coys in line, B coy in Support communication quiet. Wind NW. N & NE weather Snowed. Casualties Nil	ASH
"	" 3	12 noon	As yesterday. Wind N.W. Weather fine. Casualties 1 O.R. wounded	ASH
"	" 4	12 noon	As yesterday. enemy artillery active. Capt. Q.O. WAY goes to England to attend Senior Officers Course elsewhere. Wind S.W. weather fine. Casualties 1 O.R. wounded	ASH
"	" 5	12 noon	As yesterday. Lt. A.H. ALLEN rejoined from F. Amb. Wind W. weather war Casualties Nil	ASH
"	" 6	12 noon	As yesterday. enemy artillery active. Wind S.S.W. weather fine. Casualties Nil	ASH
MAROC	" 7	12 noon	As yesterday. relieved by 8th R.W. Kent Regt. in Calonne Sub section. Battalion moved into Brigade Support in Calonne in MAROC D coy remained in MAROC. Wind S.W. weather fine. Cas. Nil	ASH
CALONNE	" 8	12 noon	Battalion in Brigade Support. Wind W. weather fine. Casualties 1 O.R. wounded	ASH
"	" 9	12 noon	As yesterday. Lt. G.T. BUTCHER rejoined from F. Amb. 2/Lt. R.F. HAYWOOD joined Battalion from training. Wind S.W. weather fine. Casualties 2 O.R. wounded. then snowed	ASH

Army Form C. 2118.

WAR DIARY
or
INTELLIGENCE SUMMARY.
(Erase heading not required.)

Instructions regarding War Diaries and Intelligence Summaries are contained in F.S. Regs., Part II. and the Staff Manual respectively. Title pages will be prepared in manuscript.

Place	Date 1917 APRIL	Hour	Summary of Events and Information	Remarks and references to Appendices
CALONNE	10th	12 noon	In Brigade Support CALONNE. Found enemy munitioning positions. 2/Lt C.A. HORE joined Battalion from RFC. Wind N.W. Snowed. Casualties 1 OR wounded.	PSN
"	11th	"	As yesterday. Wind W. Snowed. Casualties 1 OR wounded. Enemy shelled CALONNE fairly heavily ex intervals.	PSN
"	12th	"	As yesterday. Enemy's artillery very active on Brigade front, and CALONNE and back areas. Wind Weak. Casualties 2 OR wounded.	PSN
"	13th	"	As yesterday. Enemy retired towards LENS. 9th East Surreys and 8th R.W.Kent Regt. sent our strong patrols into enemy's trenches. Regiment moved into 9th East Surreys former line trenches in front of CALONNE, enemy artillery fairly active. Wind N.E. Remained. Casualties 2 OR, killed 3 OR wounded.	PSN
"	14th	"	Enemy continued to retire towards LENS, East Surreys and 8th Queens (who relieves 8 (Kents) pushed forward. Battalion remained as yesterday. Enemy shelling light. Whilst in above mentioned Regt's CALONNE trenches fire which Nr. 2/Lt R. BURRENS accidentally wounded Lt H.W.L.ANTHONY severely wounded very slightly (the latter shot the former in the leg and self in hand with German pistol) Lt BURRENS sent to F.A. Lt ANTHONY remained in duty. Casualties 2 OR wounded. D Company returned from MARIC and joined Battalion in CALONNE	PSN

2353 Wt. W2544/1454 700,000 5/15 D.D.& L. A.D.S.S./Forms/C.2118.

WAR DIARY
or
INTELLIGENCE SUMMARY.
(Erase heading not required.)

Army Form C. 2118.

Place	Date 1917	Hour	Summary of Events and Information	Remarks and references to Appendices
CALONNE	April 15th	12 noon	Relieved 8th Queens Regt in Cité St Pierre in front and to the WEST of LENS. A Coy (Capt THOMSON) Left front, C Coy (Lt HAPPLEBECK) right front. B Coy Right Support, D Coy Left Support, enemy's MGs returning to front. Our artillery fire increased in intensity. A Coy engaged an intermittent machine gun round S.W. Casualties 2 O.R. wounded.	BZN
Cité St PIERRE	16th	p.m.	A & C Coys pushed forward patrols and Rept Contact with enemy, but entrances blocked up missing. 46th Division on left of A Coy. Number of entrances, enemy artillery active, enemy MGs enemy's dugouts and cellars has been blown in by them, and they had also left various traps in others. Wind W. weather wet. S.O.R. James Burnham from Bone Casualties 3 O.R. wounded.	BZN
"	17th	"	Line held much same as yesterday viz. German trenches in front of Cité St PIERRE about 1½ miles N.W. of LENS. Unable to make further progress owing to night Rm of 6th Division (on our left) being unable to take a German strong point in junction of our left Coy and Division on right. Burnham ordered its component to piece of 6th Division. Casualties 2 O.R. wounded. Weather fine	BZN

Army Form C. 2118.

WAR DIARY
or
INTELLIGENCE SUMMARY.
(Erase heading not required.)

Instructions regarding War Diaries and Intelligence Summaries are contained in F. S. Regs., Part II. and the Staff Manual respectively. Title pages will be prepared in manuscript.

Place	Date	Hour	Summary of Events and Information	Remarks and references to Appendices
	1917 April			
Gre. St PIERRE	18th	12 noon	Position as yesterday. Commenced consolidation of line, enemy shelling severe at times. 1st Division made unsuccessful attack on the Strong point. Weather wet. Wind S.W. Casualties	BSN
"	19th	12 noon	As yesterday. Weather fine. Wind S.W. enemy shelling. 1 OR wounded. Chilly air moderate. Wind S.W. weather fine. Casualties 2 OR killed 4 OR wounded	BSN
"	20th	12 noon	Division relieved by 46th Division. Brigade by 136th Bde and Battalion relieved by 4th LEICESTERSHIRE Regt. in night of 19th inst and marched to PETIT SAINS. Wind S.W. weather fine	BSN
ALLOUAGNE	21st	"	Battalion marched to ALLOUAGNE on 20th inst and billeted for night. weather fine. wind. NW Casualties nil	BSN
"	22		Battalion marched from Allouagne to WESTREHEM on 21st inst and went into billets 8 other ranks joined from Base. weather cold	BSN
WESTREHEM	23	"	Battalion resting in billets in WESTREHEM. 2/Lt R. MANSELL joined the Battalion as yesterday. Bn. transferred from I Corps to II Corps (1st Division)	BSN
"	24th	"	Battalion marched from WESTREHEM to RECLINGHEM and went into billets. weather fine	BSN
"	25th	"	Battalion in this place to carry out training	BSN
RECLINGHEM	26th		Battalion Training commenced as per programme. 2OR joined Battalion. weather fine	BSN

Army Form C. 2118.

WAR DIARY
or
INTELLIGENCE SUMMARY.
(Erase heading not required.)

Place	Date	Hour	Summary of Events and Information	Remarks and references to Appendices
Reeling Hem	27th	12 noon	Battalion in Billets and carried out training programme as per programme.	BSA
"	28"	"	As yesterday. Weather fine and cool.	BSA
"	29"	"	As yesterday — weather warm.	BSA
"	30"	"	As yesterday — weather warmer.	BSA

B.D. Johnson Captain/Adjutant
1st N. Staffordshire Regt
30/4/17

1st Bn North Staffordshire Regt.

War Diary for May 1917.

WAR DIARY
or
INTELLIGENCE SUMMARY.

(Erase heading not required.)

Army Form C. 2118.

Place	Date	Hour	Summary of Events and Information	Remarks and references to Appendices
ROELINGHEM	1.5.17	12 noon	Battalion training for open warfare as programme. The weather was	BSM
"	2.5.17	"	As yesterday. C Coy inspected by Lt Genl Sir Claude JACOB KCB, Corps Commander II Corps Commander interviewed by him during afternoon re "STRAgglers" from France. weather fine & warm.	BSM
"	3.5.17	"	As yesterday. fine & warm	BSM
"	4.5.17	"	As yesterday. fine & warm	BSM
"	5.5.17	"	As yesterday. fine & warm	BSM
"	6.5.17	"	As yesterday. fine & warm	BSM
"	7.5.17	"	As yesterday. Capt. B.N. FLETCHER and 2/Lt R.W. SHARP joined from England. fine & warm	BSM
"	8.5.17	"	As yesterday. fine & warm	BSM
LIGNY-LEZ-AIRE	9.5.17	"	Battalion marched to LIGNY-LEZ-AIRE and billeted for the night. weather warm	BSM
BOESEGHEM	10.5.17	"	Battalion marched from the last named place to BOESEGHEM on 10th inst " "	BSM
"	11.5.17	"	Battalion inspected by Major Genl. J.E. CAPPER " "	BSM
nr ABEELE	12.5.17	"	Battalion marched from BOESEGHEM to near ABEELE a distance of 20 miles on 12th inst & 11th Joined Brigade Base	BSM
"	13.5.17	"	Battalion marched from last named place to BRAND HOEK on 13th inst " "	BSM
	11.5.17		5485 Sgt TAMS T.B. and 8029 Corpl RUTTER J. awarded military medal.	

Army Form C. 2118.

WAR DIARY
or
INTELLIGENCE SUMMARY.
(Erase heading not required.)

Place	Date 1917 May	Hour	Summary of Events and Information	Remarks and references to Appendices
BRANDHOEK	14th	11am	Battalion relieved 11th Sherwood Foresters in Brigade Support in ZILLEBEKE Sector trenches by train from BRANDHOEK to YPRES. Relief 24th Division now in IX Corps II Army. Casualties nil	BSN
ZILLEBEKE SECTOR	15th	"	Battalion in Support in trenches. Area Quentin HALFWAY HOUSE. Enemy ?quiet? in morning shelling our mmwerfers right subsector. Weather fine. Casualties nil	BSN
"	15th	"	left subsector.	
"	16th	"	On yesterday. Casualties nil	BSN
"	17th	"	As yesterday. 10 OR. joined from Base. Casualties nil	BSN
"	18th	"	As yesterday. Enemy attempted to raid 8th Gunners on right subsector. Casualties nil	BSN
"	19th	"	As yesterday. Casualties nil	BSN
"	20th	"	As yesterday. Enemy Survey Flyer machine left subsector in night 20/21st inst. B&D Coys in front A&C Coys in support. Casualties nil. Weather fine	BSN
"	21st	"	Relieved from line left subsector. Enemy very quiet - a little shelling. Standard weight 4.5" 5.9" and 77mm. 15 OR. joined from Base also Lieut E.A. COCHRANE from Base. Weather wet. Casualties nil	BSN
"	22	"	As yesterday. Weather fine. One OR wounded.	BSN

Army Form C. 2118.

WAR DIARY
or
INTELLIGENCE SUMMARY.
(Erase heading not required.)

Place	Date	Hour	Summary of Events and Information	Remarks and references to Appendices
ZILLEBEKE SECTOR	23	10 a.m.	Holding line as yesterday, enemy artillery active; enemy attempted to rush 2" R.W. Kent Regt in right subsection after violent bombardment. Weather fine. Casualties with one O.R. wounded	PSN
"	24th	"	As yesterday. Intercompany relief. D Coy relieved A Coy in front line. C Coy relieved B Coy in front line. B & A Coys go into support. One O.R. killed. Weather fine.	PSN
"	25th	"	As yesterday. Captain Y.G. THOMSON awarded Military Cross. Weather fine. Casualties One O.R. wounded	PSN
"	26th	"	As yesterday. Weather still hot. Enemy's artillery very active especially on track across our ridge.	PSN
"	27th	"	As yesterday. Weather war. One O.R. wounded	PSN
"	28th	"	As yesterday. Weather fine. 2/Lieut F.S.W. SHUTE and L.H. JULL joined Battalion Casualties nil	PSN
"	29th	"	As yesterday. Brigade relieved by 80th Brigade in this sector. Battalion by 19th Kings Liverpool Regt in night 29/30th inst. Battalion proceeded by train from YPRES to HOPOUTRE and marched into camp at the latter place. Weather fine. Casualties One O.R. killed	PSN

Army Form C. 2118.

WAR DIARY
or
INTELLIGENCE SUMMARY.

(Erase heading not required.)

Place	Date	Hour	Summary of Events and Information	Remarks and references to Appendices
HOPOUTRE (S.W. POPERINGHE)	May 1917 30th	12 noon	In camp. weather fine. Captain F.T.W. WINTER joined Battalion 2 O.R. joined Battalion. Casualties nil	BSA
"	31st		Battalion marched to cork wood into billets near ABEELE weather fine. Casualties nil	BSA

Total Casualties during May 1917 2 O.R. Killed 5 O.R. wounded

B.S. Jopling Captain & Adjutant
1st N. Staffordshire Regt.

1st Bn. North Stafford Shire Regt.
Programme of Training:

DATE	7.0am - 7.45am	9.0am - 10.0am	10.15am - 11.0am	11.30am - 12.30pm	2.0pm - 3.30pm	5.0pm - 5.30pm
MONDAY 30th	All Coys. Physical Training including "Swedish" running drill.	"A" Coy. Route March, not less than 10 miles practicing drilling formations as opportunity occurs. "B" Coy. Bayonet Fighting & Bombing practice & Lewis Gun. "B" Rifle range and Musketry Exercises		"C" Coy. Rifle Range & Musketry Exercises. "B" Bayonet Fighting & Bombing practice & Lewis Gun. "D" Bombing practice & Lewis Gun	"A" Coy. Bayonet fighting and as above. B, C, & D Coys. Training for open warfare. ※	5.0pm - 5.30pm Lecture by R.S.M. to senior NCO's of B & D Coys.
TUESDAY May 1st	All Coys as Yesterday.	"B" Coy. Route March as above. "A" " Bombing practice & Lewis Gun. "C" " Bayonet Fighting & Bombing drill. "D" " Rifle range as above		"A" Coy. Rifle Range as above. "C" " Bombing & Lewis Gun. "D" " Bayonet fighting as above.	"B" Coy. Bayonet fighting as above. A, C, & D Coys. Training for open warfare.	5.0pm - 5.45pm Lecture by M.O. to senior N.C.O's "B" & "D" Coys.
WEDNESDAY May 2nd	All Coys as Yesterday	"C" Coy. Route march as above. "A" " Bombing & Lewis Gun. "B" " Bayonet Fighting & Bombing drill. "D" " Rifle Range as above		"A" Coy. Bayonet Fighting as above. "B" " Bombing & Lewis Gun. "D" " Bombing & Lewis Gun	Half day holiday	
THURSDAY May 3rd	All Coys as Yesterday.	"D" Coy. Route March as above. "A" " Bayonet Fighting as above. "C" " Bombing & Lewis Gun. "B" " Rifle Range as above.		"A" Coy. Rifle range as above "C" " Bayonet Fighting as above. "B" " Bombing & Lewis Gun.	"D" Coy. Bayonet Fighting as above. A, B & C Coys. Training for open warfare.	5.0pm - 5.30pm Lecture by R.S.M. to senior NCO's A & C Coys. 5.30pm - 6.30pm Lecture by 2nd in Command to all junior officers.

Programme of Training (continued)

DATE	9.0 am – 9.45 am	9.0 am – 10.0 am	10.15 am – 11.0 am	11.30 am – 12.30 pm	2.0 pm – 3.30 pm	5.0 pm – 5.30 pm
FRIDAY May 4th	All Coys.	"A" & "C" Coys. Bayonet Fighting as above	"B" & "D" Coys. Bayonet Fighting. "B" Coy. Rifle Range. "A" Coy. Rifle Range. "D" Bombing & Lewis Gun. "C" Bombing & Lewis Gun.	All Coys. Platoon Drill	All Coys. training for open warfare.	Lecture by R.S.M. to senior NCOs B & D Coys. 5.30 pm – 6.30 pm. Lecture by M.O. to senior N.C.Os A & C Coys.
SATURDAY May 5th	All Coys. as yesterday	"A" Coy. Rifle Range. "C" Bombing & Lewis Gun. "B" & "D" Coys. Bayonet Fighting	"A" & "C" Coys. Bayonet Fighting. "B" Coy. Bombing & Lewis Gun. "D" Rifle Range.	All Coys. Platoon Drill.	Half day Holiday.	
SUNDAY May 6th	9.0 am – 10.0 am Batt. on Parade	10.0 am Divine Service				

One Corporal Per Coy to report to Sgt Tams each day for range taking from 2.0 pm – 3.30 pm. Junior NCOs (except specialists) from all Coys to report to R.S.M. between 10.15 am – 11.0 am daily. Those from Company doing systematic march will report to R.S.M. at 9.0 am.

Bn. Bombing Officers will arrange with O.C. Coys direct as to the number of men to throw live bombs for grenade during the Coys allotted time.

The Lewis Gun Officer will also arrange direct with O. Coys as to which teams are required for firing during the Coys Lewis Gun drill time. Lewis Gun drill fire at the same time as their Coys.

The following Lewis Gun Bomb Lectures will be under the Batt. Bomb. & Lewis Gun Officer on the afternoon between 2.0 & 3.30 pm. The May Coys do their route march.

✗ Practising Parade working ground taping touch with each other. Attacking troops during back information reports. Attacks by platoons on reviewing strong points, woods, houses, villages &c. Outflanking actions. H.Q.'s &c. Using Lewis Guns, rifle grenades &c. Artillery formation.

[signatures]
7/5/17

1st Bn North Staffordshire Regiment
Programme of Training

DATE	7.0 – 7.15 a.m.	9.0 – 10.0 a.m.	10.15 – 11.0 a.m.	11.30 a.m. – 12.30 p.m.	2.0 – 3.30 p.m.	5.0 – 5.30 p.m.
MONDAY May 7th	All Coys. Physical Training including ½ hour running drill	A Coy. Route march not less than 10 miles, practising Artillery formations, combats, patrols and advance guards etc. B " Platoon & Company drill C " Lewis Gun & Bombing D " Rifle Range & musketry exercises		B Coy. Bayonet fighting as above drill C " Platoon & Company drill D " Lewis Gun & Bombing	A Coy. Lewis Gun & Bombing B, C & D Coys. Training for open warfare ※	Lecture by R.S.M. to senior N.C.Os A & C Coys. 5.30 – 6.30 p.m. Lecture by M.O. to junior N.C.Os B & D Coys.
TUESDAY May 8th	All Coys. As yesterday	A Coy. Drill as above B " Bayonet fighting as above C " Rifle Range as above D " Lewis Gun & Bombing	A Coy. Bayonet fighting as above B " Rifle Range as above C " Lewis Gun & Bombing D " Drill as above	A Coy. Rifle Range as above B " Lewis Gun & Bombing C " Bayonet fighting as above D " Rifle Range as above	All Coys. Battalion Scheme in Training for open warfare	Lecture by R.S.M. to senior N.C.Os B & D Coys. 5.30 – 6.30 p.m. Lecture by M.O. to junior N.C.Os A & C Coys.
WEDNESDAY May 9th	All Coys. As yesterday	B Coy. Route march as above A " Bayonet fighting as above C " Lewis Gun & Bombing D " Rifle Range as above	→	A Coy. Lewis Gun & Bombing C " Rifle Range as above D " Bayonet fighting as above	Half day Holiday	
THURSDAY May 10th	All Coys. As yesterday	C Coy. Route march as above A " Rifle Range as above B " Bayonet fighting as above D " Lewis Gun & Bombing	→	A Coy. Bayonet fighting as above B " Lewis Gun & Bombing D " Rifle Range as above	C Coy. Lewis Gun & Bombing A, B & D Coys. Training for open warfare	Lecture by R.S.M. to senior N.C.Os A Coy. 5.30 – 6.30 p.m. Lecture by 2nd in Command to all junior Officers

Programme of Training (continued)

DATE	9.0 - 7.15 a.m.	9.0 - 10.0 a.m.	10.15 - 11.0 a.m.	11.30 a.m. - 12.30 p.m.	2.0 - 3.30 p.m.	5.0 - 5.30 p.m.
FRIDAY May 11th	All Coys. as yesterday	D Coy. Route march A " Bayonet fighting as about B " Lewis Gun & Bombing C " Rifle range as about ⊙	as above	A Coy. Lewis Gun & Bombing B " Rifle range as about C " Bayonet fighting as above	D Coy. Lewis Gun Bombing A, B, C Coy. Training for open warfare	Lecture by R.S.M. to junior NCOs B & D Coys
SATURDAY May 12th	All Coys as yesterday	All Coys drill as above.	All Coys drill as above.	A & C Coys. Lewis Gun & Bombing. B Coy. Rifle Range as about D " Bayonet fighting as above.	B & D Coy. Lewis Gun & Bombing. A Coy. Rifle Range as about C " Bayonet fighting as above.	Half day holiday
SUNDAY May 13th		All Coys drill as above	Divine Service			

✽ · Practising attacks on villages, woods, isolated strong points &c. Winning ground, open warfare, formation & extended order &c. Pushing forward patrols, sending back reports, keeping in touch with other troops, trying to be carried out in Bn. Respects?

⊙ A proportion of Lewis Gunners to report to Lieut. Wood for further shooting at 10.0 a.m. daily. One range shooting Corporal per Company to report to Sgt. Lane at 2.0 p.m. daily for range taking. Junior NCOs (except specialists) to report to R.S.M. between 10.15 - 11.0 a.m. daily. Three from Company on route march to report at 9.0 a.m.

Battalion Bombing Officer & Lewis Gun Officer to arrange with O.C. Coy. as before as to number of men to them for bombing & fire hours juno during Coys. allotted time.

Lecture will be under Battalion Officer that Lewis Gun Officer from 2.0 - 3.30 p.m. or daylight, dependent mean

Vol 28
"Confidential"

1st Batln North Staffordshire Regt.

War Diary month of June 1917.

Army Form C. 2118.

WAR DIARY
or
INTELLIGENCE SUMMARY.
(Erase heading not required.)

Instructions regarding War Diaries and Intelligence Summaries are contained in F. S. Regs., Part II. and the Staff Manual respectively. Title pages will be prepared in manuscript.

Place	Date JUNE 1917	Hour	Summary of Events and Information	Remarks and references to Appendices
Wy ABEELE	1st	10 am	Battalion in Billets training. 2/Lieut E. BALDRY, C.N. SILK, E.T. TOELS joined Battalion. Weather fine	ASH
"	2	"	As yesterday. Weather fine. 5 O.R. joined from France	ASH
"	3	"	As yesterday. Lieut J.M. Grenadi E.T. LANGRIDGE left Battalion to join R.F.C.	ASH
HOPOUTRE	4th	"	Marched into Camp at HOPOUTRE. Weather fine. Battalion (less Transport) now concentrated in X Corps Reserve.	ASH
"	5th	"	Marched by night to DOMINION Camp near BOSSEBOOM	ASH
DOMINION Camp	6	"	Battalion routines to spread sand loose down, &c. No great war up in trenches, 200 rds S.A.A. 6 bombs, 2 sandbags per man, qualities of rope generator, timber 10 hurdles, operating, permitting, tape laying, moved by night to MIC MAC Camp opposite the Scots — sent one ahead to reconnoitre the Country ahead. Casualties nil. Weather clear.	ASH
MicMac Camp	7th	"	Zero day on WYTSCHAETE - MESSINES Ridge Battle Divisional troops Assembly trenches thrown up. Enemy shown knocks up ridge on Short notice, received from Brigade new mac camp to G.H.Q. 2nd line (extending from YPRES Southwards) during afternoon. Battalion 1 sent to 23 Division for carrying parties, moved from GHQ 2nd line to "Rasslway" detached Dugouts (near YPRES) on MENIN RAILWAY) en route, writing casualties from enemy shelling and	ASH

Army Form C. 2118.

WAR DIARY
or
INTELLIGENCE SUMMARY.
(Erase heading not required.)

Instructions regarding War Diaries and Intelligence Summaries are contained in F. S. Regs., Part II. and the Staff Manual respectively. Title pages will be prepared in manuscript.

Place	Date	Hour	Summary of Events and Information	Remarks and references to Appendices
Railway Dugouts nr Mount Sorrel near Ypres	1917 June 8th	12 noon	Battalion attaches to 23rd Division under 69th Infy Bde doing work for 69th & 76th Infy Bde relieved the line from BATTLE WOOD northwards to MOUNT SORREL - OBSERVATORY RIDGE inclusive on the left flank of the above mentioned Battle. Casualties 9 OR wounded	A.S/1
"	9th	"	As yesterday. Attached Brigade moved up and relieved 70th Infty Bde on the MOUNT-SORREL - OBSERVATORY RIDGE sector. Battalion relieved 8th YORKS and 9th YORKS Regt's in the captured german trenches in front of MOUNT SORREL on nights of 9th/10th. Much needier than Casualties Capt 1 OR killed 9 OR. wounded	A.S/1
MOUNT SORREL Trenches	10th	"	Battalion holding occupied german trenches (and consolidating) in front of Mount Sorrel. enemy's Artillery fire very heavy at times intense. 2/Lieut G.T. BUTCHER killed Capt V.V. POPE (with Brigade) wounded 3. O.R. Killed 130.R. wounded. Trenches very much worked about after are lost and enemys present bombardment	A.S/1
"	11th	"	As yesterday enemys artillery fire violent at times, mostly from North & North East Lt. Col W.F.B.R. DUGMORE and Capt G.H. ROBINSON Killed Lieut (by some shell) 19 OR wounded Major A.S. CONWAY Killed own command of Battalion 3 OR Killed. weather to conditions, very low.	A.S/1
"	12th	"	As yesterday 2/Lt C.C. HARRIS and A/Lt A.E. HODGE Killed 6 OR. Killed 21 OR. wounded Bombardment continues to be as before	A.S/1

WAR DIARY or INTELLIGENCE SUMMARY

Army Form C. 2118.

Place	Date	Hour	Summary of Events and Information	Remarks and references to Appendices
Dicke Busch H	1917 June 13th	8.30 pm	As yesterday. Battalion relieved by 9th East Surrey Regt on night of 12/13th and moved back to Brigade Reserve unicamp nr Dicke Busch. Enemy's fire during casualties 2 OR wounded.	BN
"	14th	"	Battalion Resting. Lt W.D. RENWICK killed by shell when returning from ypres. 2 OR wounded.	BN
"	15th	"	As yesterday — weather hot.	BN
"	16th	"	As yesterday — weather hot. 2/Lt Pearson E.F. joined	BN
"	17th	"	As yesterday. Battalion relieved 9th East Surrey Regt in trenches on night of 17/18th. MAJOR A.S. CONWAY killed. 2/Lt COCHRANE wounded. Lt V.T.C. BENT R.A.M.C. wounded. All by same shell, from enemy's artillery. 3 OR wounded. Major Hicks 8th Queen's Regt took on temporary command.	BN
Mount Sorrel Trenches	18th	"	Battalion relieving front line. D Coy C Coy in front line. A Coy in support. B in reserve. Enemy shelling any active. Winches Bros casualties 4 OR/killed 16 OR/wounded in O.A TUNNICLIFFE tunnel. Capt Pelly came [illegible]	BN
"	19th	"	Battalion relieving day 3 RIFLE BRIGADE and moved into Divisional Reserve in MICMAC camp. casualties 4 OR killed 13 OR wounded	BN
McMac camp	20th	"	Battalion in Divisional Reserve resting. Capt V.V. PUPE took on temporary command of the Battalion. Casualties nil.	BN

2353 Wt. W.2544/1454 700,000 5/15 D. D. & L. A.D.S.S./Forms/C. 2118.

Army Form C. 2118.

WAR DIARY
or
INTELLIGENCE SUMMARY.
(Erase heading not required.)

Instructions regarding War Diaries and Intelligence
Summaries are contained in F. S. Regs., Part II.
and the Staff Manual respectively. Title pages
will be prepared in manuscript.

Place	Date 1917	Hour	Summary of Events and Information	Remarks and references to Appendices
MICMAC CAMP	June 21	11am	Battalion in Divisional Reserve resting and refitting. Weather uncertain	BSM
"	22	"	" " " " " " Wet	BSM
"	23	"	" " " Battalion Relieves the 7th Northamptons Regt in Brigade Support in BATTLE WOOD trenches. Major Lewis europhene's murdere - gassed from which was attacking one of our balloons. Two men wounded. Lt E.B.G. WOOD wounded. 6 O.R. wounded. Enemy opened a barrage of gas shells near Battalion on approaching trenches during relief. weather warm	BSM
BATTLE WOOD SUPPORT	24	"	Battalion in Brigade Support in the above trenches, enemy artillery very active Bn H.Q. in LARCH WOOD tunnels near HILL 60 which was constantly bombarded. Casualties 3 O.R. wounded	BSM
"	25th	"	as yesterday 1 O.R. wounded	BSM
"	26/6	"	Battalion relieved "9th East Surrey Regt" in front line BATTLE WOOD trenches on night of 26/27 A+B Coys in front line C+D Coys in support. enemy artillery very active. weather warm	BSM
"	27th	"	As yesterday —	BSM
"	28th	"	As yesterday — weather heavily overcast.	BSM

Army Form C. 2118

WAR DIARY
or
INTELLIGENCE SUMMARY
(Erase heading not required.)

Instructions regarding War Diaries and Intelligence Summaries are contained in F.S. Regs., Part II. and the Staff Manual respectively. Title Pages will be prepared in manuscript.

Place	Date 1917 June	Hour	Summary of Events and Information	Remarks and references to Appendices
Buttle Wood Trenches	29th	12 noon	As yesterday Battalion relieved by 11th West York's Regt on front line Buttle Wood trenches on night 29th/30th and marched to MICMAC CAMP. Weather fine 50 OR. joined from Base.	1 BN
Micmac Camp	30th	12 noon	Battalion marched from MICMAC Camp on morning of 30th to RENINGHELST SIDING and entrained; proceeded by train from here moved place to LUMBRES (near St OMER) and marched from LUMBRES to SENINGHEM & there moved into Billets and proceeded to train for Battle.	1 BN

Total Casualties during month of June

Officers
W. O/R   O. Ranks
K. W   K. W. M
7. 3.   29. 134. 1.
1 - 0

[signature] Captain & Adjutant
1st W. Riding S.nier Regt

[signature]

Secret

72/24 Vol 29

War Diary
of
1st Bn North Staffordshire Regt.
from 1/7/17 — 31/7/17
(Volume)

Army Form C. 2118.

WAR DIARY
or
INTELLIGENCE SUMMARY.
(Erase heading not required.)

Instructions regarding War Diaries and Intelligence Summaries are contained in F. S. Regs., Part II. and the Staff Manual respectively. Title pages will be prepared in manuscript.

Place	Date	Hour	Summary of Events and Information	Remarks and references to Appendices
Sevington	1-7-17		Battalion in Rest Billets. Church Parade. Weather warm.	
"	2-7-17		Battalion training. 119 Other Ranks joined. Weather fine.	
"	3-7-17		Battalion training. 2/Lt B.J. SOELS reported sick at Field Ambulance. One C.S.M. and 34 Other Ranks joined. Weather fine.	
"	4-7-17		Battalion training. Lt. S. A. AITSON reported sick at Field Ambulance. Capt. C.O. WAY rejoined from England. Weather fine.	
"	5-7-17		Battalion training. Weather warm.	
"	6-7-17		Battalion training. Six Other Ranks joined from B.E.F. Learne to all officers by G.O.C. 72nd Bde. Weather warm.	
"	7-7-17		Battalion training. Twenty-nine Other Ranks joined from England. The Battalion was field firing in Bullets strict. Second firing in water cart, released firing in officers changes at Home School. Led in the Transport lines of 8th C.S. The Queens. Weather warm	
"	8-7-17		Church Parade. Lieut. R.S.M. MURRAY joined from England. Weather warm.	
"	9-7-17		Battalion training. Inspection of Coys by C.O. Parties warm.	
"	10-7-17		Battalion training. Lewis March. Party for O.R's only on 13 and 14. weather warm	
"	11-7-17		Training of batt. Helmets by Company Comdrs. C.O's Parade. Conferences. Weather warm	

Army Form C. 2118

WAR DIARY
or
INTELLIGENCE SUMMARY
(Erase heading not required.)

Instructions regarding War Diaries and Intelligence Summaries are contained in F. S. Regs., Part II. and the Staff Manual respectively. Title Pages will be prepared in manuscript.

Place	Date	Hour	Summary of Events and Information	Remarks and references to Appendices
Sandgham	12.7.17		Battalion training. Lectures by Major Parts on Bayonet Fighting. Weather warm.	
	13.7.17		Battalion training. Lt S.D.S. OXLEY joined. Weather warm.	
	14.7.17		Battalion training. Practised attack in connection with 8th Queens under orders of 72nd Infantry Brigade. 2/Lt JOLL 4 rejoined. Instruction from X Corps School. Weather wet.	
	15.7.17		Church Parade. "D" coy formed "C" coy 7th Yorkshire at Foulness, the remainder being Northumbrian 9 als Staffords 3 Lectures by Colonel Hay, 24th Div, on the attack. 2/Lt E.S.GORE to Sea Ambulance. 2/Lt S.SHUTE to Sea Ambulance. Visit 8th Queens came on Saturday (the 14th inst.)	
	16.7.17		Battalion training. Practised attack. 2/Lt E.H.W HIGGINBOTHAM joined.	
	17.7.17		Battalion training. Practised attack. Gas arrangements & Infantry stragglers. Lecture to Coys by C.O.	
	18.7.17		2/Lt BALDAY E.S. to Sea Ambulance. Capt PELLY.L.R.A.M.C (and 2nd North Staffs) to Sea Ambulance. Lieut MITCHELL. R.A.M.C. reported for duty. Lecture to Coys by C.O.	
RENESCURE	19.7.17		The Bn moved from SENINGHEM ——— Entrained at RENESCURE the Bn marched 2 am to arrived at RENESCURE about 10 am (a distance of about 16 miles)	
CAESTRE	20.7.17		The Bn moved from RENESCURE —— Bivouacked on near CAESTRE, a distance of about 10 miles. Lieut S.E. STEELEY joined the Bn.	

1875 Wt. W593/826 1,000,000 4/15 J.B.C. & A. A.D.S.S./Forms/C. 2118.

Army Form C. 2118.

WAR DIARY
or
INTELLIGENCE SUMMARY.
(Erase heading not required.)

Instructions regarding War Diaries and Intelligence Summaries are contained in F. S. Regs., Part II. and the Staff Manual respectively. Title pages will be prepared in manuscript.

Place	Date	Hour	Summary of Events and Information	Remarks and references to Appendices
EECKE.	21/1/17		The Bn moved from the CAËSTRE Area - Billets in the EECKE Area. 13 O.R's were, 1 C.S.M. and 7 O.R's joined.	
STEENVOORDE	22/1/17		The Bn moved from the EECKE Area - STEENVOORDE Area. Weather warm. Capt. M°tr. FLETCHER rejoined Bn.	
"	23/1/17		An address by the Archbishop of York to the 7th Infantry Bde. to which the Bn. is attached temporarily. Weather warm.	
Micmac Camp	24/1/17		The Bn moved from the STEENVOORDE Area - Micmac Camp. Weather wet.	
" "	25/1/17		Battalion training. Major D.M.DAWES (Middx. yeomanry) joined Bn. (attached) also C.N. LOMAX reported sick at Field Ambulance. 2/Lt. C.A. HORE rejoined Bn. from hospital. Weather warm.	
" "	26/1/17		Battalion training. 14 O.R's. joined.	
" "	27/1/17		Battalion training. 2/Lt. E.R. BYAS wounded in action. Weather warm.	
" "	28/1/17		Battalion training. 2/Lt. R.W. SHARP reported sick at Field Ambulance. Weather warm. Six O.R's joined. Bn. moved into Reserve Trenches, prior to taking up Battle position. Weather wet. Col. G. MADLEBEEK and 5 O.R's wounded in action. Lt. A.W.L. ANTHONY evacuated sick at Field ambulance. Lt. C.N. LOMAX rejoined	

WAR DIARY
or
INTELLIGENCE SUMMARY.
(Erase heading not required.)

Army Form C. 2118.

Instructions regarding War Diaries and Intelligence Summaries are contained in F. S. Regs., Part II. and the Staff Manual respectively. Title pages will be prepared in manuscript.

Place	Date	Hour	Summary of Events and Information	Remarks and references to Appendices
Bois Grenier	30/4/17		Capt G.D. MAPPLEBECK died of wounds received in action.	
"	3/5/17		The Bn. attacked in the early morning about 4 am, and suffered the following casualties. About 11 officers and 280 O.R's reported casualties. 2/Lt BIRD rejoined Coy.	

D.G. Tunnicliffe Lieut 10/5/17.
a/adjt. North Staffs Regt.

"Account of

"Action of 1st North Staffordshire Regt in THIRD Battle of YPRES
Commencing 31st July 1917

On night of 29th July
The Battalion which had marched up from SENINGHEM where it had been practicing the attack for the past three weeks moved up from MICMAC Camp to trenches just South of MENIN-YPRES. Railway and remained there all day 30th inst. A coy who was to be Company in Support took over front line trenches from 9th East SURREY Regt in front of MOUNT SORREL

On night of 30th/31st July
B. C. & D coys moved across the front and took up their assembly positions in the MOUNT SORREL System. C Company on right in IMMAGE CRESENT. D coy on left on tape line in continuation of C Coy. B Coy in close support to the two former & A Coy back in reserve.

ORDER OF BATTLE.

The 72nd Infty Bdge. attacked on a two Battalion front. 8th Queens Regt on right and N. Staffs on left. 8th R.W. KENTS in Support and 9th EAST SURREYS in reserve.

The two attacking Battalions attacked each on a two company front. N. Staffs with C coy (Lieut. ALLENAH Commdg) on right. D Coy (Capt M.L.B. SHAW commdg) on left. B Coy (2nd Lt. J. SWALLOW commdg) in Support & A Coy (Capt G.G. THOMSON Commdg) in reserve.

On the right of 8th Queens was 41st DIVISION (20th D.L.I.)
On " left of N. Staffs " 7th NORTHANTS Regt. (73rd Infy Bdge. 24th DIVISION)

OBJECTIVES (See Map attached)

The objectives of 72nd I.B. were JEHOVAH TRENCH. GREENBUG FM. JORDAN TRENCH and if possible to push forward patrols to WEST edge of BULGAR WOOD &c. thus conforming to movements to be carried out by a big attack northwards and form part of a defensive flank to that attack.

Battle

Zero hour was fixed for 3.50AM on 31st inst. and from midnight until that time the enemy kept up a fairly active bombardment on our trench system and back areas with guns of all calibres, as had been his custom for some weeks past. This bombardment was erratic and caused the Battalion few casualties.

At Zero. our barrage descended and the attacking troops (D. C & B coys) went forward close under it in a few minutes the enemy dropped a barrage with 77 mm guns on our front line and a barrage of 5.9 & 4.2" on our Support and reserve lines.

The attacking line got clear of the enemy's barrage with

few casualties and met with little opposition until they reached JEHOVAH TR. here the enemy made resistance but was either killed, taken prisoner or driven out and the trench quickly occupied by our men. But owing to a Company of Northants on our left loosing direction and the remainder of that Regt being unable to keep up with our Barrage owing to the ground and tell stumps in SHEWSBURY FOREST, a gap was caused in the attacking line, and the enemy opened a heavy infilading machine gun fire from SHEWSBURY FOREST on our left and also opened with machine guns from BULGARS WOOD to our front. thus causing a great many casualties to this Battalion, especially among the officers, who were all either killed or wounded by 6.30am except two Lieut Allen & 2/Lieut PIERSON. The men however advanced beyond JEHOVAH TR and commenced to dig themselves in. 2/Lt PIERSON and a few men reached JORDAN TRENCH but afterwards came back.

6455 A/CSM AVERILL. D Coy. acted with great gallentry, as when all the officers of his Company became casualties, he led the men on to their objective.

10918 Sgt AUSTIN & 8179 Pte WALKLATE. with a Lewis gun engaged, put out of action and captured an enemy machine gun & crew, which was causing casualties to our men from JEHOVAH TR.

At about 6am BGC commanding 72 I.B. gave orders that the attack would not continue owing to the situation on our left and right flanks; the line gained was therefore consolidated forthwith. At about 7am Capt G.G. THOMSON went up and took command of the front line which consisted of men of B.C. & D coys and some men of Queens & Northcants all very much mixed up together.

During the night of 31st inst. it rained heavily and continued to rain throughout the following day, the line taken and our old trenches and surrounding country was quickly turned into a mass of mud and water which severly handicapped all movement.

The enemy's artillery machine guns and snipers were at all times during the attack and consolidation very active. his artillery increasing in intensity at different periods on our old front and support lines and the ground between these and the newly captured position.

The Battalion was relieved by 9th EAST SURREY Regt on night of August 1st/2nd and moved back to MICMAC Camp to rest and reorganize.

Attached is Summary is report of Lt. A.H. ALLEN.

The following officers took part in the action.

Lt. Colonel V.V. POPE. D.S.O. M.C. — Commanding ⎫
Captn P.D. HARRIS — Adjutant ⎬ Battalion HQ
2/Lt. A.N WESTLAKE — INTELL. OFFICER ⎭

Captn G.G. THOMSON. M.C. — Commanding ⎫
Lt. K.F.M. MURRAY ⎪
" S.E. STEELEY — Wd ⎬ A Coy
2/" W.R. LAWTON ⎭

Wd = Wounded
Kd = Killed.

Lt. L.J. SWALLOW ⱽ — Wd — Commdg ⎫   ⱽ Wounded missing believed Killed
" R.A. HOPE — Kd ⎪
" F BOURNE — Kd ⎬ B Coy
2/" C.H SILK — Wd ⎭

Lt. A.H. ALLEN ⊕ — Commdg ⎫   ⊕ Captn G.W. MAPPLEBECK, who
2/Lt. L.H. JULL — Wd ⎬ C Coy   should have commanded, was
" E.T. PIERSON ⎭   mortally wounded on night
                            of 29th/30th whilst marching
                            up and died on 31st July.

Captn M.I.B. SHAW — Wd — Commdg ⎫
2/Lt. B.D. MARTIN — Wd ⎪
" N.M TOFT — Wd ⎬ D Coy
" D.J. CRUICKSHANK — Wd ⎭

Total casualties for this action were —

Officers
K or D of W | Wounded | missing
3 | 87 | nil
                        wounded+missing
                        1

Other Ranks
K or D of W | Wounded | missing
36/42 | 239 | 21

none of the missing are believed to have been taken prisoner, but are probably Killed.

The Battalion captured between 40 & 50 German prisoners also one german machine gun.

The Battalion was congratulated by the B.G. Comdg and Major General commanding on the part they took in the action.

P.D. Jeffris Captain & Adjutant
4/8/17   1st N Staffs Regt

REPORT ON THE OPERATIONS OF 31ST JULY, 1917.
.o.o.o.o.o.o.o.o.o.o.o.o.o.o.o.o.o.o.o.o.o.o

Ref. HILL 60& SHREWSBURY FOREST.
....

At 3-0 a.m. on the morning of 'Z' day I got my Company out of the Assembly Trench and lined up in waves running parallel to IMAGE CRESCENT, the last platoon just resting on the trench, and the first line some 50 or 60 yards ahead. I was in touch with "D" Company on my LEFT and "D" Company of the 8th QUEENS on my RIGHT.

At ZERO 3-50 a.m. the Company moved close up to the Barrage and on the Barrage moving forward the attacking lines moved forward close up to it. The enemy sent up various coloured Rockets and his Heavy Artillery opened on IMAGE CRESCENT and some 100 yards in front of it, but not at all heavily. At the same time he opened Rifle and Machine Gun fire principally from the direction of SHREWSBURY FOREST about I.31.a.8.8. and JEHOVAH TRENCH about I.31.a.5.7. This latter point he had a Machine Gun which was firing in oblique direction across our front and causing a certain amount of damage. About mid-way across 'No man's land' enemy posts were encountered and these put up some little resistance until our men were close upon them and then they tried to surrender. They were either cleared by the Rifle or Bayonet.

The assault on JEHOVAH TRENCH was carried out very successfully little opposition being put up except in one isolated case of the Machine Gun about I.31.a.5.7. which kept in action until our men got into the trench and then its crew ran into two concrete shelters close to their gun and from this they threw several bombs. No. 10918, Sergt. Austin E.A. of "B" Coy. who was working along the trench sent Bombers on the flanks of these Shelters and then got a Lewis Gun to fire into the entrance of the Shelter where six of the crew were and thereupon the entire crew of fourteen men surrendered. He captured the gun and its crew complete No. 8479, Pte. Walklate was the Lewis Gunner who brought the Lewis Gun into action firing it as he advanced along the trench from the Hip and this man acted with commendable coolness and presence of mind and compelled the surrender of the gun crew.

On arriving at JEHOVAH TRENCH I found that direction had been lost by the 7th NORTHAMPTONS who should have been in touch with "D" company on my LEFT by the 8th QUEENS who should have been on my RIGHT, and by a party of the 20th DURHAM LIGHT INFANTRY belonging to the 41st DIVISION on our RIGHT the whole parties being mixed up very badly, I ascertained the direction of GREEN BUG FARM, got the men going in this direction, and pushed forward the whole of the men with me in that direction. I then came under heavy Machine Gun and Rifle Fire from my LEFT flank SHREWSBURY FOREST, and saw that this Wood was still held by a large number of the enemy with several Machine Guns in concrete emplacements, and that none of our troops were in the wood at all. The NORTHAMPTONS should have been in this Wood and their not being there left my left flank in the air and a gap of some three hundred yards existed.

(Sheet No. 2).

I formed a defensive flank to protect my Left by pushing out posts of Riflemen and Lewis Guns and engaged the enemy Machine Guns with Lewis Guns and Rifle Fire. At the same time the remainder of my men were pushed forward towards GREEN BUG FARM and reaching the edge of that place dug themselves in near the edge of the MOAT, as far forward as possible having regard to the great quantity of water and marshy ground there found. I decided that to push forward whilst I had the gap on my Left consisting of a wood held in some strength by the enemy would be both futile and dangerous. In addition the ground in front constituted some difficulty on account of the Moat and Marshy ground in which it was quite impossible to dig. A portion of my leading platoon under 2/Lieut. Peirson did as a matter of fact push on over JORDAN TRENCH and close to the edge of BULGARS WOOD but owing to the situation on the flank they were compelled to retire on to the line we were now consolidating. This Officer went forward with great coolness under enemy Machine Gun fire from an enfilade position and in this and the earliest portion of the attack did excellent work getting his platoon forward. Part of the enemy were seen running from the EASTERN Edge of SHREWSBURY FOREST through GREEN BUG FARM and over what was apparently JORDAN TRENCH back into BULGARS WOOD. These were fired upon and casualties caused. Two enemy were seen moving back towards the GUN EMPLACEMENTS at the edge of BULGARS WOOD carrying a Machine Gun which they tried to get into action on the rising ground near the GUN EMPLACEMENTS. These men were dealt with by Rifle Fire. I found that the ground around GREEN BUG FARM for a considerable distance was a quagmire and impassable except on making a wide detour to a flank. No enemy were in GREEN BUG FARM or JORDAN TRENCH but a Machine Gun and enemy Snipers caused some trouble from houses in rear of the farm about 25.d.2.1. These buildings were on the rising ground and in fair condition as regards cover for enemy troops. About this time a party of troops were seen coming through SHREWSBURY FOREST from a Northerly direction but were held up by Machine Gun firing from the GUN EMPLACEMENTS. This gun was fired upon and ceased firing, whether it was hit I am unable to say. The Support Companies of the NORTHAMPTONS were then seen moving in file up to SHREWSBURY FOREST from the direction of our old line and thereupon the enemy in the wood came out of his dug-outs without firing a shot at them and surrendered. Enemy aircraft were now active, one aeroplane coming low over our positions at the same time as our own contact machine and this enemy machine bore the same distinguishing contact marks. Shortly afterwards the enemy heavily shelled around our new positions, and we had to push forward in some cases. He was using 8 inch shells but did not inflict much damage. I was in touch with the QUEENS on my RIGHT and with a portion of the NORTHAMPTONS on my LEFT but they in turn were not in touch with their other Companies until some little time afterwards.

Sheet No. 3.

when they moved down to the correct positions. As this Regiment did not move forward I did not think it advisable to move forward until they had gone through SHREWSBURY FOREST but this they did not do and I accordingly proceeded to consolidate the line where I was, and this I carried out without much loss from shelling, but rather numerous casualties from Machine Gun Fire and Sniping from the direction of BULGARS WOOD. Digging was extremely difficult on account of the great number of shell-holes nearly all of which were half full of water.

With regard to the loss of direction, I think it was due (a) to the darkness prevailing at ZERO and (b) To the nature of the ground over which we had to advance. Men were inclined to make for the thinner portion of the wood instead of going straight ahead to their objectives. In addition the gully leading to GREEN BUG FARM may have had something to do with it. These points do not apply to this Regiment as our portion of front was not very thick with trees.

With regard to casualties I think a great many of these were caused by Machine Gun Fire going across 'No man's land' and I think the captured Machine Gun was responsible for most of these. A good many were also caused during our advance whilst SHREWSBURY FOREST was held by the enemy, and during the consolidating. Shelling casualties were, I believe, light. I do not think that any of the Officer casualties were caused by their not wearing G. S. tunics. The morning was too dark to pick out individuals and also most Officers wore their Stars on the Shoulder Straps.

The Artillery Barrage was exceedingly good and no difficulty was experienced in keeping close to it. I do not think we had any Casualties from this. The Machine Gun Barrage too was very good.

The men behaved with the utmost coolness and bravery and there was not the slightest hesitation amongst them in moving close up to the Barrage.

                (Signed) Arthur H. Allen, Lieut.
                "C" Company.

4/8/1917.   1st Battn. North Staffordshire Regt.

Vol 30

WAR DIARY.

OF

1st. BATTALION   NORTH STAFFORDSHIRE REGIMENT.

From 1st. to 31st. August 1917.

Army Form C. 2118.

WAR DIARY
or
INTELLIGENCE SUMMARY.
(Erase heading not required.)

Instructions regarding War Diaries and Intelligence Summaries are contained in F.S. Regs., Part II. and the Staff Manual respectively. Title pages will be prepared in manuscript.

Place	Date	Hour	Summary of Events and Information	Remarks and references to Appendices
	August 1917			
MOR	1st	12 noon	Description of the Battalion action in 3 Battle of YPRES commencing 31-7-17 attached hereto.	
Mount SORREL				
			Battalion holding newly captured trenches, enemy's artillery very active in times relieve enemy positions particularly in support Company and around Battalion Hqr. Previous evening Battalion relieved by 9th EAST SURREY Regt and returned to MICMAC camp in rear and arriving in camp at 4½ a.m.	BN
MICMAC CAMP	2		Battalion resting and reorganizing, weather very wet.	BN
"	3rd	"	as yesterday	BN
"	4th	"	as yesterday	BN
"	5th	"	as yesterday (one) J Company went up to LARCHWOOD in Brigade Support. Lt K.G. MARRIN and 2/Lt A.N. WESTLAKE transferred to RFC	BN
"	6th	"	as yesterday Lt I.K.G. MARRIN and 2/Lt SHUTE F.S.W. returned from F.A.	BN
"	7th	"	as yesterday weather finer A Coy returned from Brigade Support at LARCH WOOD.	BN
"	8th	"	as yesterday weather finer	BN
"	9th	"	as yesterday Lt G.B. STARTIN joined and 2/Lt W.J.A. CRESSWELL joined and Lt D.M. SMYTHE returned from F.A.	BN
"	10th	"	as yesterday 2/Lt. J.G. COOK joined Battalion. weather finer.	BN
"	11th	"	Brigade moved from Divisional Reserve to Divisional Support in DICKEBUSCH Battalion relieves	

Army Form C. 2118.

WAR DIARY
or
INTELLIGENCE SUMMARY.
(Erase heading not required.)

Instructions regarding War Diaries and Intelligence Summaries are contained in F. S. Regs., Part II. and the Staff Manual respectively. Title pages will be prepared in manuscript.

Place	Date	Hour	Summary of Events and Information	Remarks and references to Appendices
	August 1917			
MICMAC	11th	12pm	Relieved 9th Royal Sussex Regt in Dickebusch wester [Brigade] and Battalion in Divisional Reserve. Showery cool weather	PSA
DICKEBUSCH	12th	12	Lieut T.S. MOORE joined from 72" T.M. Battery	PSA
"	13	12	As yesterday. 2/Lieut R. MANSELL transferred to 72" T.M. Battery. Lieut R. MOORE must Captn B.M. FLETCHER to Divisional appointment as COMMANDANT. LOCKWOOD & Mc SORLEY Tunnels	PSA
"	14th	12 noon	As yesterday. Reconnoitring parties went up to front line	PSA
"	15th	"	Relieve 9th R. Sussex Regt in left Subsector OBSERVATORY RIDGE trenches on night of 15/16". D.C & B Coys in front line. A Coy in close support Bn Hq HEDGE St Tunnels. Enemy line as above. Enemy artillery very active by Bellewaarde & Inverness Copse to which did no succeed. 18035 A/Cpl GIBSON was awarded bar to military medal and the following awarded the military medal A/15 L/Cpl JONES T. 8372 Tilbury B. D. 16903 Pte SLEAMAN R.C. 8047 Pte BRENNAN T.C. and 15261 Pte BURNYEAT M.C. all for devotion to duty and gallantry in the Ypres sector fire. 9 Lieut W. T. A. CRESSWELL wounded.	PSA
line	16	"		PSA
"	17th	"	Holding line as above. Enemy very active and artillery message exorcised active. Especially in brown wood and environs. Showery weather	PSA

2383 Wt W2541/1454 700,000 5/15 D.D.&L. A.D.S.S./Forms/C. 2118.

WAR DIARY
or
INTELLIGENCE SUMMARY
(Erase heading not required.)

Army Form C. 2118.

(3) Summary of Events and Information

Place	Date	Hour	Summary of Events and Information	Remarks and references to Appendices
Line	August 18th 1917		Holding line as above. Continued hostile artillery fire on our front Battalion Boys.	ASN
"	19	noon	Brigade relieved by 17th Infy Boys and Battalion on orders moved back to MICMAC Camp in DIVISIONAL RESERVE. Shell on back areas throughout night. Enemy very active with gas	ASN
MICMAC Camp	20th		Battalion in Divisional Reserve. Battalion thoroughly inspected.	ASN
"	21st		As yesterday. Weather warm. Inter platoon rifle match won by Lce/Corp Drummonds team.	ASN
"	22		As yesterday. Weather warm. Played 9th Bn N.Staffs at football. 2/Lieut G. B. BROWN joined Battalion	{2/Lieut A.H. ALLEN 6th A ASN
"	23		Bayonets returned 73 IB in Divisional Support. Battalion relieved 9th R. Sussex Regt. in camp at DICKEBUSCH	ASN
DICKEBUSCH	24		Inspection attacked by enemy 7th Brigade moved up to reserve. Battalion moved in CHATEAU SEGARD area. 2nd Lieut A PEACOCK joined Battalion at DICKEBUSCH	ASN
"	25		Bayonets moved back into Divisional Support. 2/Lieut A.H. ALLEN and 2/Lieut A.N. WESTLAKE awarded "Military Cross" 64855 A/CSM AVERIL T & 109/18 Sgt AUSTIN A awarded D.C.M. and 203 62 Pte SALT T awarded "Military Medal" all for "gallantry and distinguished conduct in the field" (see 38th ullen)	ASN

Army Form C. 2118.

WAR DIARY
or
INTELLIGENCE SUMMARY.
(Erase heading not required.)

Instructions regarding War Diaries and Intelligence Summaries are contained in F.S. Regs., Part II. and the Staff Manual respectively. Title pages will be prepared in manuscript.

Place	Date 1917	Hour	Summary of Events and Information	Remarks and references to Appendices
DickeBusch	August 26th	12 noon	Battalion in Divisional Reserve in camp	PSN
"	27th	"	72 I.B. relieves 73 I.B. — 9th R. Sussex Rgr in Brigade support. Observatory Ridge sector — enemy line British line. 2/Lt E.T. BALDRY & 2/Lt R.W. SHARP rejoined from leave.	PSN
Tournai	28th	"	Battalion in Brigade support. LARCHWOOD & HEDGE ST. Tunnels re: enemy party quiet. Captn A.M. FLETCHER rejoined from Divisional employment. 30 O.R. rejoined from leave. Battalion from leave.	PSN
"	29th	"	At yesterday's enemy working party 3 Pr. R.F. to meanwhile new as yesterday 2nd Division transferred to X corps. II army 28th inst.	PSN BSN
"	30th	"	At yesterday Reveille relieved by 17 I.B. Battalion by 1st R. Fusiliers. Battalion returned to Divisional Reserve in camp at MICMAC. 25 O.R. rejoined from leave.	BSN
"	31st	"	7658 L/Cpl SMITH.E wounded D.C.M. for Devotion to Duty & gallantry in the field. (31st wling) (Recommended by 2.O. PVC)	PSN

Total Casualties for Month of August 1917

Officers			Other Ranks		
K. (& Dow)	W.	M.	K. (& Dow)	W.	M.
—	—	—	—	3	—
				15 (& Dow)	
				24	

[signatures]

Confidential

Vol 31

War Diary
1st Battn. North Staffordshire Regt.
September

(Volume)

WAR DIARY
INTELLIGENCE SUMMARY

Army Form C. 2118.

Place	Date 1917 September	Hour	Summary of Events and Information	Remarks and references to Appendices
MICMAC CAMP	1st	12 nn	Battalion relieved from Bde Supt on 31st midnight. 7th Infy Bde in Divisional Reserve in Micmac Camp. Training & reorganizing.	PSN
"	2nd	"	Yesterday 15 CIR rejoined from BdeR	PSN
"	3rd	"	Brigade relieved 73 IB in Divisional Support DICKEBUSCH. Battalion relieved 13 MIDDLESEX REGT in Camp K. 2/Lt W.R. LAWTON to Field Ambulance	PSN
DICKEBUSCH	4th	"	Battalion in Divisional Support 2/Lts E.C. KEBLE and F.T. SHUTT joined from Base. 15 CIR rejoined from Base. Enemy aircraft very active bombing back areas at nights. Weather fine	PSN
"	5th	"	2/Lt E STEEL, REDFERN, E RAMSDEN and B. BROOKS joined from Base. Capt. L.D. ADAMS went at Brigade HQ to 17 I.B. Capt Croucher joined	PSN
"	6th	"	O.C. yesterday. B. MORLEY-FLETCHER to Base, Permanent Board. Weather Fine. The Battalion relieved the 7th B. Northants in Brigade Support in the Hoaw's sector. Weather fine. Capt GALBRAITH, C.F, RAMC to take place Rev'd Capt W.R. CATHCART RAMC joined.	
France	7th	"	In the trenches. Major O.M. DAWES returned from Hospital. Our trenches were bombed and one died of wounds (?) Weather Fine	
"	8th	"	In the trenches. One casualty (wounded). Weather Fine	

WAR DIARY or INTELLIGENCE SUMMARY

Army Form C. 2118.

Place	Date	Hour	Summary of Events and Information	Remarks and references to Appendices
Renescure	10th		Weather Fine	
"	11th		The Battalion was reviewed by Lt Col Morris Preston. Came back into Divisional Reserve at MICMAC CAMP. Weather Fine.	
			Battalion training. Weather Fine	
MICMAC CAMP	12th		Battalion training. 2/Lieuts RATHBONE G.P. and CLARK L. joined Bn. from base march. Entrance of 1/North Staffords + 1/North Staffords, the Bn. East (see entry 2.-1.) Weather Fine.	
"	13th		The Battalion moved from MICMAC CAMP to MORRIS Area by motor buses. Lorries taken on Pte EVERITT wounded carrier out. Weather Fine.	
STAPLE	14th		Battalion training. Weather Fine	
"	15th		The Battalion was visited by Major General Daly (G.O.C. 24th Div.) + Lieuts COOLTON, W.L. and LATIMER, A.J. joined the Bn. and eight O.Rs. rejoined from R.E.E. Col. MORLEY-FLETCHER	
"	16th		Battalion training. Weather Fine	
"	17th		Inspection of Battalion by G.O.C 24th Division (Major General DALY). Weather Fine.	
"	18th		Battalion training. Weather Fine	
"	19th		In morning Battalion training. Weather fine. In the evening Battalion entrained at CAESTRE	
"	20th		en route for the SOMME.	

2353 Wt. W2544/1454 700,000 5/15 D. D. & L. A.D.S.S./Forms/C. 2118.

WAR DIARY
or
INTELLIGENCE SUMMARY.

(Erase heading not required.)

Army Form C. 2118.

Place	Date	Hour	Summary of Events and Information	Remarks and references to Appendices
LE TRANSLOY.	21st		In the early morning Bn. detrained at MIRAUMONT and marched, via BARAUME, to a camp near LE TRANSLOY. Weather fine. 2/Lt. J. CRUICKSHANK and 5 O.R. rejoined from France.	
"	22nd		Battalion training. Weather fine.	
"	23rd		Church parade, attended en route to Infantry Bde. Weather fine. 20 entry min O.R. joined from France.	
"	24th		Coy. training. Weather fine. A Coy. to provide party of officers and men who fell in DEVILLE WOOD (Capt. W.G.) checked in DEVILLE WOOD	
HAUT ALLAINES	25th		Bn. marched from LE TRANSLOY — HAUT ALLAINES CAMP. Weather fine.	
"	26th		Coy. training. Weather fine.	
BERNES.	27th		Battalion moved by motor buses from HAUT ALLAINES CAMP — BERNES arriving 14.00. Coy. into Bde. in reserve. Weather fine. Lieut. R.D.W. SISSONS M.A. and 2/Lieut. D. CUNNINGHAM and 20 o.r. joined 2/Lt. S. BARDAY rejoined Bn. from training Bn. from Base.	
TRENCHES	28th		Bn. relieved 2 Bn. Bn. Northumberland Fusiliers in right sub. Sector right of sub 28/29. in line from Base. Weather fine.	
"	29th		Weather fine. Thirteen new O.R.'s joined Bn.	

A. Sommerville Coy of off
Bn. North Staff. Regt.

Vol 32

Secret.

War Diary
1st Battn North Staffordshire Regiment
October 1917.

Army Form G. 2118.

WAR DIARY
or
INTELLIGENCE SUMMARY.

(Erase heading not required.)

Instructions regarding War Diaries and Intelligence Summaries are contained in F. S. Regs., Part II. and the Staff Manual respectively. Title pages will be prepared in manuscript.

Place	Date	Hour	Summary of Events and Information	Remarks and references to Appendices
In the Trenches	1-10-17		Weather fine.	
"	2-10-17		Weather fine.	
"	3-10-17		Weather fine.	
"	4-10-17		Bn. relieved on night 4th/5th by 8th Bn. The Queen's Regt. Bn. moved into Support line. Weather wet.	
Support Line	5-10-17		Eight O.R's joined Bn.	
"	6-10-17		Weather wet.	
"	7-10-17		Weather wet.	
"	8-10-17		Weather wet.	
"	9-10-17		Eight O.R's joined Bn. Weather wet.	
"	10-10-17		Weather wet.	
"	11-10-17		Bn. relieved 8th Bn. The Queen's Regt in right sub-section on night 10th/11th. Weather wet.	
In the Trenches	11-10-17		Weather fine.	
"	12-10-17		Weather wet.	
"	13-10-17		Weather fine. 2/Lt. P. Cunningham evacuated to base wounded.	
"	14-10-17		Weather fine.	
"	15-10-17		Weather fine.	

Army Form C. 2118.

WAR DIARY
or
INTELLIGENCE SUMMARY.
(Erase heading not required.)

Instructions regarding War Diaries and Intelligence Summaries are contained in F. S. Regs., Part II. and the Staff Manual respectively. Title pages will be prepared in manuscript.

Place	Date	Hour	Summary of Events and Information	Remarks and references to Appendices
VOGELLES				
SUPPORT LINE	16.10.17		Bt. relieved by 2nd Bt. The Queens Regt. Came into Cable Support, relieving 2nd R.W. Kents	
"	17.10.17		Weather fine	
"	18.10.17		Weather fine	
"	19.10.17		Weather fine	
"	20.10.17		Weather fine	
"	21.10.17		Ready - Seven O.R's joined Bt. from Base. officer S. SEALY joined Bt. Weather fine	
"	22.10.17		Weather fine	
TRENCHES	23.10.17		Bt. relieves 8th Bt. The Queens Regt. in right sub-sector. Weather fine	
"	24.10.17		Weather wet	
"	24.10.17		Weather fine	
"	25.10.17		A successful raid was carried out by Queens Trenches. Operation Orders attached. Weather wet.	
"	26.10.17		Bt. relieved by 8th Bt. The Queens Regt. Bt. moved to VENDELLES, remainder into Divl. Reserve. Weather wet.	
VENDELLES			Bt. training. Weather fine.	

Army Form C. 2118.

WAR DIARY
or
INTELLIGENCE SUMMARY.
(Erase heading not required.)

Instructions regarding War Diaries and Intelligence Summaries are contained in F. S. Regs., Part II. and the Staff Manual respectively. Title pages will be prepared in manuscript.

Place	Date	Hour	Summary of Events and Information	Remarks and references to Appendices
VENDELLES	28.10.17		Bn. training. Weather fine.	
"	29.10.17		Bn. training. Weather fine. One hundred and twenty eight OR's joined Bn. from Base.	
"	30.10.17		Bn. training. Weather fine.	
"	31.10.17		Bn. training. Weather fine.	

Commanding Col. 17 West [?]
1st West Staffs.

Secret

War Diary
of
1st Battn: North Staffordshire Regt
1st - 30th November 1914.

Army Form C. 2118.

WAR DIARY
or
INTELLIGENCE SUMMARY.
(Erase heading not required.)

Instructions regarding War Diaries and Intelligence Summaries are contained in F. S. Regs., Part II. and the Staff Manual respectively. Title pages will be prepared in manuscript.

Place	Date	Hour	Summary of Events and Information	Remarks and references to Appendices
Front line	1/11/17		Batt relieved 8th Batt, the Queens Regt in the front trenches. Weather fine.	
"	2/"		Weather fine. 1 O.R. wounded.	
"	3/"		Weather fine. Capt Thorpe proceeded to England for a month and 2lt Murray taking over H.Q. from him	
"	4/"		Weather fine.	
"	5/"		Weather fine. Shells Capt Tunncliffe proceeded on leave and handed over duties of Adjt to 2lt Students	
"	6/"		Weather wet. 1 O.R. wounded. Captain Egerton to hospital. 1 O.R. wounded. Lieut J.S. Hunt wounded M.E. 70148 Sgt Austin & Hunt and D.R. Batt relieved by 8th Batt. the Queens R. and moved into Batt. Dugouts. Weather wet.	
Suffolk lines	7/"		Weather wet. 2 Lt Browne J. R. to Special Coy by R.E.	
"	8/"		Weather wet.	
"	9/"		Weather wet.	
"	10/"		Weather fine.	
"	11/"		Weather fine.	
"	12/"			
Front line	13/"		Batt relieved 8th Batt. The Queens R. in Front line trenches. Weather fine.	
"	14/"		Weather fine.	
"	15/"		Weather fine.	
"	16/"		Weather fine.	

WAR DIARY or INTELLIGENCE SUMMARY

Army Form C. 2118

(Erase heading not required.)

Instructions regarding War Diaries and Intelligence Summaries are contained in F. S. Regs., Part II and the Staff Manual respectively. Title Pages will be prepared in manuscript.

Place	Date	Hour	Summary of Events and Information	Remarks and references to Appendices
Festubert	17/11/17		Weather fine. 1 O.R. wounded	
St Hilaire	18/"		Batt. relieved by 2/4th Queens R. in right sub-sector and moved in Bde 2 support in relief work fatigues.	
"	19/"		Weather wet. Battalion finding working parties.	
VENDELLES	20/"		Batt. relieved by 4/5 East Surrey Regt. in Bde. Support. Batt. moved to Vendelles and came into Divisional Reserve. Weather wet. Lt. Eely returned from hospital & Lt. Saunders	
"			returned from Base. 2 Lts. Coe, Wilson, MacHardy, McSweeney Gray, Irvine 3rd Border Regiment join Batt.	
"	21/		Weather wet.	
"	22/		Weather fine. Capt. Tunnicliff returned from leave and resumed duties of Adjutant	
"	23/		Bn. training. Weather fine.	
"	24		Ch. training. Weather fine.	

Army Form C. 2118

WAR DIARY
or
INTELLIGENCE SUMMARY
(Erase heading not required.)

Instructions regarding War Diaries and Intelligence Summaries are contained in F.S. Regs., Part II. and the Staff Manual respectively. Title Pages will be prepared in manuscript.

Place	Date	Hour	Summary of Events and Information	Remarks and references to Appendices
TRENCHES	24/5		Bn. relieved 1st Bn. "The Queens Regt" in right sub sector. Weather fine	
" "	25/5		Lieut. D.C. BUTTERWORTH and Lieut C. SPREY SMITH joined Bn.	
" "	26/5		Weather wet.	
" "	27/5		Weather wet.	
" "	28/5		Weather fine.	
" "	29/5		Weather fine.	
" "	30/5		Weather fine.	

E Grunicliffe Capt. & Adjt.
1st North Staffords.
30-11-1.

Secret.

Vol 34

War Diary

1st Bn. North Staffordshire Regt.

1st – 31st December 1914

(Volume)

WAR DIARY
or
INTELLIGENCE SUMMARY
(Erase heading not required.)

Army Form C. 2118

Place	Date	Hour	Summary of Events and Information	Remarks and references to Appendices
TRENCHES	1st		Weather fine. Bn. relieved from in front line & we went into Support.	
"	2nd		Weather fine.	
"	3rd		Gas projectors were fired on Enemy front line with satisfactory results. Weather fine.	
VENDELLES	4th		Bn. relieved in 8th Bn. The Queens Regt. in night relief order. Weather fine. Bn. proceeded to billets at VENDELLES and came into Divisional Reserve.	
"	5th		Bn. training. Weather fine. The Bn. worked through Gas Chamber at foot basse, named Work Shoppers 6.9am. East Surreys 1 Ent. Conference on Bn. tos attack on G.O.C. R.Q.G.	
"	6th		Bn. Training. Bn. 16 raid hidden hump Trench. Raid did not take place owing to Artillery opening before Zero hour. Weather fine. Captain W. Stevens took at assistance from Capt. O.A. Tunnicliffe M.C.	
"	7th		Bn. training as per attached programme. Poly from the Bn. to raid enemy Trenches on the Same Scheme as yesterday. No results as Bangalores Torpedos failed to explode.	
COTE WOOD	8th		15th relieved the 8th Bn. mounted Cavalry and "B" Coy 9th Bn. E. Surrey Regiment in Support. "B" Coy remained at VENDELLES. Weather Stormy.	
TRENCHES	9th		Bn. relieved the 8th Bn. the Queens R to S Regiment in the night Subsection. Major G.O. Gray D.S.O in Command of the 15th. Lt.Col V.V. Pope D.S.O. Mc tenured at Jehal G.H.Q.	
"	10th		Weather fine. Hostile balloons were up in abundance. Our Artillery and T.M.'s carried out a shoot on the enemy's front line system & back areas during the early morning. Capt. P.D. Hornis reported Bn.	
"	11th		Weather fine - off enemy artillery activity abnormal. Enemy fired for shells into our front and support line. Lt. Col. V.V. Pope D.S.O., M.C. travelled on a months leave to U.K.	
"	12th		Our artillery & T.M.'s carried out a shoot on enemy's front line system a trench every three rifles - two raids & several bombs were left on our wire by enemy day enemy patrol.	

Army Form C. 2118

WAR DIARY
or
INTELLIGENCE SUMMARY
(Erase heading not required.)

Instructions regarding War Diaries and Intelligence Summaries are contained in F. S. Regs., Part II. and the Staff Manual respectively. Title Pages will be prepared in manuscript.

Place	Date	Hour	Summary of Events and Information	Remarks and references to Appendices
TRENCHES	13th		Weather fine but misty. Enemy fired about 200 gas shells from T.M's into our front and support line. A dud dog was found - this is believed to belong to the enemy.	
"	14th		Bn was relieved in the right Sub-Section by the 8th Bn the Queens R.W.S. Regt. Bn proceeded to Subport line in COTE WOOD. Operation Orders No 201 attached.	
COTE WOOD	15th		Weather fine. There was considerable aerial activity on either side. One hostile aeroplane was brought down near COTE WOOD and about three bombs.	
"	16th		Weather moderate, wind light. The Colonel of the 13th relieving us - came up to reconnoitre. It commenced to snow during the afternoon.	
"	17th		The weather was fine - It had snowed hard during the previous night - leaving about 4" of snow on the ground in the morning.	
"	18th		The weather was fine but a little misty - a few aeroplanes of both sides were seen - Capt P.D. Harris & 2/Lieut R. Byan proceeded on leave to U.K.	
"	19th		Weather fine. Thick fog.	
"	20th		Weather fine. Thick fog.	
"	21st		Bn was by "B" Bn Dismounted Cavalry. 5th Cavalry Bde, in Support. Bn proceeded to billets in the VRAIGNES AREA. Operation Order No 204 attached.	
VRAIGNES	22nd		Bn worked as per attached Programme. Weather fine. Capt K.J.M. Murray returned from leave from U.K.	

WAR DIARY
or
INTELLIGENCE SUMMARY.
(Erase heading not required.)

Army Form C. 2118.

Instructions regarding War Diaries and Intelligence Summaries are contained in F. S. Regs., Part II. and the Staff Manual respectively. Title pages will be prepared in manuscript.

Place	Date	Hour	Summary of Events and Information	Remarks and references to Appendices
VRAIGNES	23rd		Weather fine. Bn worked as per attached programme. Bn played D.A.C. at football – result D.A.C. 3 – N.S.H.rs 0.	Bn played
"	24th		Weather moderate. Sleet fell at intervals during the day – it commenced to thaw during the evening. Bn. Training as per attached programme. Lieut W.R. Lawton went on leave to U.K.	
"	25th	–	Weather fine – Church Parade by Rev. Poole at 12·15 p.m. Stopford Hawtn	
"	26th	–	Weather fine. Holiday – all Officers attended a lecture by The B.G.C. at VRAIGNES – Drew lottery money handed in – Officers 485 frs O.R's 1340 frs.	A & B Boys had Their Xmas dinner in 3rd Army Hut. C & D Boys had Their Xmas dinner at VRAIGNES – BOUVINCOURT Rd. On arrival D Coy came in 1st. Lt R.W. Sharp
"	27th	–	Weather fine. Bn worked as per attached programme.	
"	28th	–	Weather fine. Range Practices carried out as per attached programme. Fatigue parties cleared snow from VRAIGNES – BOUVINCOURT Rd.	
"	29th	–	Bn worked as per attached programme. Inter-Coy Cross Country Race. Distance 2½ miles. A Boys Team of 15 won. Provided on a course to V Army School. Weather fine.	

Army Form C. 2118.

WAR DIARY
or
INTELLIGENCE SUMMARY.
(Erase heading not required.)

Instructions regarding War Diaries and Intelligence Summaries are contained in F. S. Regs., Part II. and the Staff Manual respectively. Title pages will be prepared in manuscript.

Place	Date	Hour	Summary of Events and Information	Remarks and references to Appendices
VRAIGNES	30th	—	Weather fine slight thaw. Church Parade at 11.30 B.G.C. present. B.G.C. inspected the Bn at 12.30. He appeared to be satisfied with the appearance of the men. 2nd Lt. G.A Hoare M.C. proceeded to HESDINS to rejoin the R.F.C.	
"	31st	—	Weather fine. Brigade Boxing Contest in Recreation Hut at HANCOURT. No.7243 Pte B. Sweatman & No.17677 Pte S. Turner both of the 1st North Staffordshire Regt. fought 3 Exhibition rounds in the Bridleweight B. No.8129 Pte J. Davies & No.7893 Pte R. Layton won the Finals. The C.B.J. Brigade Concert Party performed at VRAIGNE'S at 5.30 P.M. 100 seats were allotted to the Bn.	

2353 Wt. W2544/1454 700,000 5/15 D. D. & L.   A.D.S.S./Forms/C. 2118.

t.t. War Diary

Reference the attached Training Programme.

1. The first two days will be spent in cleaning all mud from Clothing Great-coats, etc.
   Equipment including entrenching tool handles to be thoroughly scrubbed, Bayonet Scabbards to be greased or oiled. Inspections to be carried out.

2. On arrival in VRAIGNES Area Company Commanders will make themselves acquainted with the location of the Range, P.T. and B.F. Course and the Bombing Ground as soon as possible.

3. Buttons will be polished daily during the rest.

4. I want all Companies to do a grouping practice at 200 yards and an application practice at 200 yards during time Range is allotted to them. If time permits ½ a minute's rapid fire should also be practised.

20/12/1917.   ....Major,

Commdg. 1st Battalion North Staffordshire Regiment.

1st Batt. North Staffordshire Regiment
Programme of Training for week ending Dec 29/15

PLACE	DATE	LOCATION	TIME	NATURE OF TRAINING	REMARKS
	22-12-15 23-12-15	Coy. Billets	All Day	Inspections. Cleaning up. Work on Camps	Fitting Clothing by arrangement between O.C. Coy's & Q.M. Stor.
	24-12-15	Coy Parade Grounds	Inspection by O.C. Regt by C.O. "A" Coy 9.30 a.m. "B" Coy 10.30 a.m. "C" Coy 11.30 a.m. "D" Coy 12.30 p.m.		
	25-12-15		CHURCH PARADE		
	26-12-15	Range Coy. Parade Ground	9.30 a.m. — 12.30 p.m. 2.0 p.m. — 4.0 p.m. 9.30 a.m. — 12.0 a.m. 10.0 a.m. — 10.30 a.m. 10.40 a.m. — 11.30 a.m. 11.40 a.m. — 12.30 p.m.	Musketry to "A" Coy "B" Squad Drill. Rifle Exercises. P.T. & R.F. Saluting Drill & Gas Helmet Practice	Men not actually at firing point must be Practising in judging distance & musketry. Bar'k & Trench Range Finders to be taken. Bombing Ins: will be at disposal of "C" Coy 9.30 a.m. — 11.0 a.m. D' Coy 11.0 a.m. — 12.30 p.m. "B" Coy to cease work in time to have dinners & be at Range at 1.0 p.m.

PLACE	DATE	LOCATION	TIME	NATURE OF TRAINING	REMARKS
KRIGNES	24-12-17	Coy Parade Grounds	9.30 a.m — 10.0 a.m 10.0 " — 10.30 " 10.30 " — 11.0 " 11.0 " — 11.30 " 11.40 " — 12.30 p.m	Squad Drill. Recreational Training Rifle Exercises. P.F. & B.F. Extended Order Drill.	
	28-12-17	Range Coy Parade Grounds	9.30 a.m — 12.30 p.m 1.0 p.m — 4.0 p.m 9.30 a.m — 10.0 a.m 10.0 " — 10.30 " 10.40 " — 11.30 " 11.40 " — 12.30 p.m	Rifles to "C" Coy D" " "L" Squad Drill Rifle Exercises P.F. & B.F. Saluting Drill, Gas Helmet Drill	Men not actually at firing point must be practiced at Judging distance, & Musketry. Ranges & Butts. Range Parties to be taken. Bombing Pit will be at disposal of:- "A" Coy 9.30 a.m to 11.0 a.m "B" Coy 11.0 " to 12.30 p.m "D" Coy to cease work in time to have dinner & reach Range 1.0 p.m
	29-12-17	Coy Parade Grounds	9.30 a.m — 10.30 a.m 10.30 a.m — 11.30 " 11.30 " — 12.30 p.m	Coy Drill. P.F. & B.F. Guards Drill	P.T. B.F. course allowed to:- A Coy 9.30 a.m — 11 a.m B Coy 11.0 a.m — 12.30 p.m Class 1", N.C.O.'s per platoon under C.S.M. Thompson commencing 9.30 a.m on 27's B.S. course

Thursday Dec 6th

Training Programme

Hours	7.15 to 7.30	9.15 to 10 am	10.15 to 11.15 am	11.15 to 12 noon	12.15 to 12.45	2.0 pm to 2.45	Remarks
Att A. Coy	Short march	Close order Drill & Rifle Exercises	Bayonet fighting & P.T.	Musketry	Saluting drill.	Wiring	Lewis Gunners under B.M. L.G.O. all day.
B. Coy	"	Musketry	Bayonet fighting & P.T.	Close order Drill & Rifle Exercises	Signalling & Scouting	Wire cutting with Cutters on Rifles.	Lewis Gunners under B.M. L.G.O. all day.
C. Coy	"	Close order Drill & Rifle Exercises	Bayonet fighting & P.T.	Semaphore Wiring	Saluting Drill.	Musketry	Lewis Gunners under C.L.G.O. all day.
D. Coy	"	Musketry	B.F. & P.T.	Close order Drill & Rifle Exercises	Wire cutting with Cutters on Rifles.	Saluting Drill.	Lewis Gunners under Coy. L.G.O. all day.

Friday Dec 7th.

	7.15 to 7.30	9.15 to 10 am	10.15 to 11 am	11.15 to 12 noon	12.15 to 12.45	2 pm to 2.45 pm	
"A" Coy	parade	Musketry with to connect with sights	B. F & P.T.	S.os Helmet Drill	Extended order Drill	Wire cutting with cutters on Rifles.	Lewis Gunners under L.G.O. all day
"B" Coy	"	"	B. F & P T	"	Extended order Drill	Wiring.	Lewis Gunners under L.G.O. all day.
"C" Coy	"	"	B. F & P T	"	Wire cutting with cutters on Rifles.	Extended order Drill	Lewis Gunners under L.G.O. all day
"D" Coy	"	"	B. F & P.T.	Wiring	S.os Helmet Drill	Extended order Drill	Lewis Gunners under L.G.O. all day.

SECRET.   OPERATION ORDER NO. 201,
                      1st Battalion North Staffordshire Regiment.
                      :-:

Map Reference Sheet NAUROY edition 2B, 1/20,000

1. The Battalion less "B" Coy. will relieve the 8th Bn. DISMOUNTED CAVALRY, and "B" Coy. 9th EAST SURREYS in SUPPORT on 8th December. Relief to be complete by 2-0 p.m.

2. "B" Coy. will remain in present billets in VENDELLES.

3. Relief will be as follows :-
    "D" Coy. N.STAFFS. Regt. relieves "B" Coy. 9th E.SURREYS, in trenches roughly from L.10.A.1.1. to L.10.D.4.9.
    "A" Coy. N.Staffs Regt. relieves CAVALRY in trenches from L.10.D.1.1. to L.16.C.3.7.
    "C" Coy. N.STAFFS. Regt. relieves CAVALRY in trenches from L.22.C.8.9. to L.22.C.6.1.

4. Coys. will march by platoons at five minutes interval :-
    "A" Coy. will leave VENDELLES at 11-0 a.m.
    "C" Coy.   "   "   "   11-30 a.m.
    "D" Coy.   "   "   "   12-0 noon.

5. Advance parties consisting of one Officer per Coy. and one N.C.O. per platoon will go on at 9-30 a.m. to take over trenches.

6. ~~xxxxxxxxxxxx~~   O.C. Coys. will detail one man per Coy. to remain with Officers Trench Kits, Cooking Utensils, Lewis Gun Magazines, etc. until picked up by Transport at 4-0 p.m.

7. 50% Lewis Gun Magazines will be left with Trench Kit to be collected by Transport at 4-0 p.m.

8. Officers Valises, Surplus Kit, and Blankets, will be ready for collecting outside Coy. H.Q. at 12-0 noon.

9. Coy. Cooks, and Cooking Utensils, rations etc., for cooking dinners will be ready to be collected at Coy. H.Q. at 9-45 a.m.
   Five men per Coy. and two men Battn. Head Qrs. to accompany this Transport as carrying party.

10. O.C. Coys. will report to Battn. Hd.Qrs. in SUPPORT when relief is complete by using the code word "F I N"

11. Maltese Cart to report at Dressing Station VENDELLES at 4-0 p.m.

12. Lewis Guns will be carried.

8/12/1917.   ....Captain & A/Adjutant
                                1st Battalion North Staffordshire Regiment.

Copy No. 1. War Diary.
   "   2. "A" Company.
   "   3. "B"   "
   "   4. "C"   "
   "   5. "D"   "
   "   6. 9th East Surreys.
   "   7. 8th Dismounted Cavalry Battn.
   "   8. Transport Officer & Quartermaster.

War Diary.

SECRET.   OPERATION ORDER NO. 202.
                  1st BATTALION NORTH STAFFORDSHIRE REGIMENT.
                  :-:

1.   The Battalion will relieve the 8th Bn. THE QUEENS' (R.W.S.Regt.)
   in the RIGHT SUB-SECTION on the night 9/10th December.

2.   The order of relief will be as follows :-
   "B" Coy. N.STAFFS. relieves "A" Coy. QUEENS. in FARM TRENCH.
   "A" "   "   "   "C" "   "   in RAILWAY TRENCH.
   "D" "   "   "   "D" "   "   in THOMSON'S REST.
   "C" "   "   "   "B" "   "   RIGHT COMPANY SECTOR.

3.   "A" Coy. will leave SUPPORT LINE at 2-30 p.m.
       "B" "   "   " VENDELLES   at 2-0 p.m.
       "C" "   "   " SUPPORT LINE at 3-0 p.m.
       "D" "   "   " SUPPORT LINE at 3-30 p.m.

4.   "A", "C" & "D" Coys. will move by Sections with 50 yards distance
   between Sections.

5.   O.C. Coys. will send an advance party, consisting of one Officer
   per Coy. and one N.C.O. per platoon to take over Stores, etc.,
   from the Company they are relieving.

6.   O.C. Coys. will render certificates of Stores taken over to
   Orderly Room by 9-0 a.m. 10th December.

7.   Valises and Surplus Kit of "B" Coy. to be stacked outside
   Coy. Hd.Qrs. at 1-0 p.m. when Transport will collect it.

8.   "B" COMPANY: 50% Lewis Gun Magazines, Officers Trench Kits,
   Cooking utensils, etc., to be stacked outside Coy. Hd.Qrs. by
   3-30 p.m. Transport will call for this at 4-0 p.m.

9.   Battn. Hd.Qrs., "A", "C" & "D" Coys. Officers Trench Kits,
   Cooking utensils, etc., will be collected from Coy. Ration Dumps
   at 5-0 p.m. One man per Coy. to remain with Kits until they are xxx
   collected.

10.   Maltese Cart to be at Dressing Station in SUPPORT LINE at
   5-0 p.m.

11.   O.C. Coys. will report to Battalion Head Qrs. at the EGG when
   relief is complete by using code word "F L U F F"

                                           [signature]

   8/12/1917.   ....Captain & A/Adjt.
                          1st Battalion North Staffordshire Regiment.

   Copy No. 1.   War Diary.
        "   2.   "A" Company.
        "   3.   "B" "
        "   4.   "C" "
        "   5.   "D" "
        "   6.   Transport Officer & Quartermaster.
        "   7.   O.C. 8th QUEENS.

                          (War Diary)

SECRET.   OPERATION ORDER NO. 203.   Copy No. 1

1ST BATTALION NORTH STAFFORDSHIRE REGIMENT.

1. The Battalion will be relieved by the 8th Bn. THE QUEENS (R.W.S.) Regt. in the RIGHT SUBSECTION on the night 14/15th December.

2. On relief the Battalion will move into BRIGADE SUPPORT taking over accommodation occupied at present by 8th Bn. THE QUEENS Regt.

3. "C" Coy. QUEENS. will relieve "A" Coy. N.STAFFORDS. about 3.30 p.m.
   "D" "   "   "B" "   "
   "B" "   "   "C" "   "
   "A" "   "   "D" "   "

4. Accommodation in SUPPORT is allotted as follows :-
   "A" Coy. N.STAFFORDS. will relieve "B" Coy. 8th QUEENS in FERVAQUE TRENCH.
   "B" "   "   "   "C"   "   "   in COTE TRENCH.
   "C" "   "   "   "D"   "   "   in LE VERGUIR QUARRY at L.28.a.50.95. (approx).
   "D" "   "   "   "A"   "   "   in dug-outs at L.10.a.2.5

5. O.C. Coys. will send an advance party of one Officer per Company and one N.C.O. per Platoon to take over Stores etc.
   These parties will leave at 10-0 a.m.

6. All Trench Stores, Work in hand, etc., will be carefully handed over to relieving Unit.

7. O.C. Coys. will render a return of all Stores taken over from 8th QUEENS to Orderly Room by 12-0 noon 15th inst.

8. Lewis Guns and Magazines will be carried.

9. Officers Trench Kit, Petrol Tins, Cooking utensils, etc., to be at Company Ration Dumps ready for removal by 5-30 p.m.
   O.C. Coys. will leave a N.C.O. and two men as a guard until these kits have been removed.

10. O.C. Coys. will be responsible that all Petrol Tins (at least 10 per Coy.) are collected and dumped with above kit.

11. Transport Officer will arrange to bring up Officers Valises, Blankets, Rations, Water, etc., to Company Dumps in Support by 5-0 p.m.

12. Advance parties will be responsible for taking over this Kit etc., from the Transport.

13. "D" Coy. dump in Support will be the same as that used by "A" Coy. QUEENS.

14. O.C. Coys. will send on orderlies to act as guides to the Coy. on relief.

15. Completion of relief in the front line will be notified to Battalion Head Quarters by wire or runner using the code word "NUFSED"

16. O.C. Coys. will report the arrival in Support Line by using the code word "HERE"

13/12/1917.   ....Captain & A/Adjt.
                                1st Battalion North Staffordshire Regiment.

Copy No. 1. War Diary.   Copy No. 6. "D" Coy.
"   "   2. C.O.   "   "   7. T.O. & Q.M.
"   "   3. "A" Coy.   "   "   8. O.C. 8th QUEENS.
"   "   4. "B" "   "   "   9. R.S.M.
"   "   5. "C" "

SECRET.　　　　　　　　OPERATION ORDER NO. 204.　　　Copy No...
　　　　　　　　1ST BATTALION NORTH STAFFORDSHIRE REGIMENT.
　　　　　　:-

Map Reference Sheet 36c. 1/40,000.

1. The Battalion will be relieved by "B" Battn. DISMOUNTED CAVALRY 5TH CAVALRY BRIGADE in SUPPORT on 21st December.

2. On relief the Battalion will move to Camp "B" at VRAIGNES.

3. "C" Coy. N.STAFFORDS. in LE VERGUIR QUARRY will not be relieved but will move to VRAIGNES on receipt of the message "MOVE"

4. "A", "B" & "D" Coys. will send one guide per platoon to A.D.S. JEANCOURT by 9-0 a.m. 21st December.

5. Advance parties of one Officer per Coy. and one N.C.O. per platoon will leave for VRAIGNES at 6-30 a.m. 21st December, to take over the Camp.

6. "A", "B" & "D" Coys. and Bn. H.Q.　Transport will call for Officers Kits, men's blankets, cooking utensils, etc., at 6-0 a.m. 21st December.

7. A G.S. wagon will be at A.D.S. JEANCOURT at 10-30 a.m. to collect all Coy. Lewis Guns, Magazines, etc.

8. Transport Officer will arrange to collect all "C" Coys. Kit at 9-30 a.m. on 21st December.

9. All Trench Stores, Aeroplane Photographs, Defence Schemes, Trench Maps and Sketches, will be handed over and receipts obtained.

10. Coys. will move by Sections at 500 yards distance to JEANCOURT where Coys. will be reformed, and remainder of march will be completed by Coys.

11. All men must be dressed in the same manner.. Overcoats can be carried or worn as Coy. Commander wishes.

12. Any man who falls out will be brought before the M.O. on arrival at VRAIGNES, and before the Commanding Officer at Orderly Room on 22nd December.

13. Completion of relief will be notified to Battalion Head Qrs. by wire or runner using the code word "REST"

14. Coy. Commanders will notify Battn. H.Q. when Coys. arrive at VRAIGNES.

15. ACKNOWLEDGE.

19/12/1917.
　　　　　　　　　　　　　　　　　　　　　　Captain & Adjutant.
　　　　　　　　　　　　　　　　　　1st Battalion North Staffordshire Regiment.

Copy No. 1.　War Diary.
　　"　　2.　"A" Company.
　　"　　3.　"B"　"
　　"　　4.　"C"　"
　　"　　5.　"D"　"
　　"　　6.　Commanding Officer.
　　"　　7.　R.S.M.
　　"　　8.　O.C. "B" Battn. Cavalry.
　　"　　9.　Transport Officer.
　　"　　10.　Quartermaster.

SECRET.   OPERATION ORDER NO. 204.   Copy No....
                    1ST BATTALION NORTH STAFFORDSHIRE REGIMENT.
                    :-

Map Reference Sheet 8cc. 1/40,000.

1. The Battalion will be relieved by "B" Battn. DISMOUNTED CAVALRY 5TH CAVALRY BRIGADE in SUPPORT on 21st December.

2. On relief the Battalion will move to Camp "B" at VRAIGNES.

3. "C" Coy. N.STAFFORDS. in LE VERGUIR QUARRY will not be relieved but will move to VRAIGNES on receipt of the message "MOVE"

4. "A", "B" & "D" Coys. will send one guide per platoon to A.D.S. JEANCOURT by 9-0 a.m. 21st December.

5. Advance parties of one Officer per Coy. and one N.C.O. per platoon will leave for VRAIGNES at 6-30 a.m. 21st December, to take over the Camp.

6. "A", "B" & "D" Coys. and Bn. H.Q. Transport will call for Officers Kits, men's blankets, cooking utensils, etc., at 6-0 a.m. 21st December.

7. A G.S. wagon will be at A.D.S. JEANCOURT at 10-30 a.m. to collect all Coy. Lewis Guns, Magazines, etc.

8. Transport Officer will arrange to collect all "C" Coys. Kit at 9-30 a.m. on 21st December.

9. All Trench Stores, Aeroplane Photographs, Defence Schemes, Trench Maps and Sketches, will be handed over and receipts obtained.

10. Coys. will move by Sections at 500 yards distance to JEANCOURT where Coys. will be reformed, and remainder of march will be completed by Coys.

11. All men must be dressed in the same manner. Overcoats can be carried or worn as Coy. Commander wishes.

12. Any man who falls out will be brought before the M.O. on arrival at VRAIGNES, and before the Commanding Officer at Orderly Room on 22nd December.

13. Completion of relief will be notified to Battalion Head Qrs. by wire or runner using the code word "REST"

14. Coy. Commanders will notify Battn. H.Q. when Coys. arrive at VRAIGNES.

15. ACKNOWLEDGE.

19/12/1917.   ....Captain & Adjutant.
                                    1st Battalion North Staffordshire Regiment.

Copy No. 1.   War Diary.
    "   2.   "A" Company.
    "   3.   "B"   "
    "   4.   "C"   "
    "   5.   "D"   "
    "   6.   Commanding Officer.
    "   7.   R.S.M.
    "   8.   O.C. "B" Battn. Cavalry.
    "   9.   Transport Officer.
    "   10.   Quartermaster.

SECRET.   ADDENDUM TO OPERATION ORDER No. 204.   Copy No. 1
                    1ST BATTALION NORTH STAFFORDSHIRE REGIMENT.
                :-:

1.   O.C. Coys. will detail an Officer to be in charge of guides at JEANCOURT at 9-0 a.m. 21st December.

2.   O.C. Coys. will report exact location of Coy. Parade Grounds and alarm posts as soon as possible after arrival in VRAIGNES Area.

3.   "A" Coy. N.STAFFS. will be relieved by OXFORD HUSSARS Coy.
     "B" "   "   "   "   "   "   3rd HUSSARS Coy.
     "D" "   "   "   "   "   "   6th DRAGOON GUARD Coy.

4.   O.C. Coys. will order their own Chargers.

5.   ACKNOWLEDGE.   *W.D. Stamer*
     20/12/1917.   ....Captain & Adjutant,
                            1st Battn. North Staffordshire Regiment.

     Copy No. 1. War Diary.
         "   2. "A" Coy.
         "   3. "B" "
         "   4. "C" "
         "   5. "D" "
         "   6. Commanding Officer.
         "   7. R.S.M.

*To J.O.
for War Diary
WJS.*

ADDRESS TO:

1. My Company / Platoon has reached .... Mark position on map and give map reference

2. I am at .... and { Am consolidating, Have consolidated, Am ready to advance to

3. We are held up by { Wire / Machine Gun / Rifle Fire } at ....

4. I have sent patrols forward to ....

5. I need:– S.A.A.
   Bombs.
   Rifle Grenades.
   Water.
   Very Lights, S.O.S, Signals, Rockets.
   Stokes Shells.
   Stakes, Wire.
   Spare Lewis Gun Drums.
   Stretcher Bearers.

6. Enemy Troops Strength estimated at .... { Assembling at / Advancing from / Retiring from.

7. I am in touch with .... on Right / Left at ....

8. I am not in touch on Right / Left

9. Am being shelled from .... Nature of shell ....

10. I estimate my present strength at .... rifles

11. Hostile { Battery / Machine Gun / Trench Mortar } Active at .... and is shooting at ....

12. I intend to

Time.............. am. (p.m.)   Name...... ....
Date.........   Platoon...... Company......
                                     Battalion.

NB:– The R.F. of map overleaf is 1:10,000.

War Diary. (Confidential.)

1st Battn: North Staffordshire Regt:

Month of January 1918.

Army Form C. 2118.

WAR DIARY
or
INTELLIGENCE SUMMARY.
(Erase heading not required.)

Place	Date	Hour	Summary of Events and Information	Remarks and references to Appendices
VRAIGNES	1/1/18	—	Weather fine, slight thaw. Considerable aerial activity. Brigade Runs in the afternoon. A Coy repeated bath & finished 3rd Training carried out as per attached programme. Lt Col L.T. WYATT D.S.O. returned from ENGLAND. 2nd Lts G.P. RATHBONE, C. SPREY-SMITH, B. BROOKES & E. STEEL returned from courses.	ENS
MONTIGNY	2nd		Weather fine thaw continued. Bath relieved the 8th Batt the BUFFS in MONTIGNY as per OO 205 attached	ENS
"	3rd		Weather fine, frosty. The CO & Coy Commrs reconnoitred line held by the 9th ROYAL SUSSEX Regt. Coy inspections carried out.	ENS
"	4th		CAPT P.D. HARRIS & 2nd Lt E.R. BYAS rejoined from leave. Capt HARRIS took over duties of Transport Officer. 2nd Lt E.R BYAS took over duties of Intelligence Officer vice 2nd Lt. KEEBLE who went on a course of PT at 3rd Army School. Batt relieved 9th Bn ROYAL SUSSEX in front line A.B, & D Coys front line C Coy support as per O.O. 206 attached	ENS
LINE	5th		Weather fine. fall of snow during day. Situation quiet.	ENS
"	6th		Weather dull. Situation quiet. HARGICOURT & TEMPLEUX e Guerin with 5.9s + 4.2s. 2nd Lt. PEACOCK went on leave	ENS

WAR DIARY or INTELLIGENCE SUMMARY

Army Form C. 2118.

(Erase heading not required.)

Place	Date	Hour	Summary of Events and Information	Remarks and references to Appendices
LINE	7/4/18	—	Thaw set in. Situation quiet	Nil
"	8th	"	Batt relieved by 8th Bn the QUEENS (RWK) in Centre Sector front line as per O.O. 207 attacked & came into Brigade support. Batt HQ & A & D Coys to TEMPLEUX QUARRIES. B Coy L/3 a central C Coy Quarry at L5b 30 35 in close support to 8th A QUEENS. Heavy fall of snow during day	Nil
			Casualties during tour — Nil	Nil
SUPPORT	9th		Thaw set in. Situation quiet	Nil
"	10th		Snow continued. Increased shelling of back areas TEMPLEUX & battery positions behind QUARRIES. 2 5"gd.howitzers + 1 4·2 battery firing continuously all day	Nil
"	11th		Bn Major V.P.POPE DSO MC rejoined from 1 month's leave. Remained as transport until Batt relieved.	Nil
"	12th		Batt relieved by 12·4 Bn ROYAL FUSILIERS & moved to VENDELLES as per O.O. 208 attached. Lt WR LAWTON rejoined from leave	Nil
VENDELLES	13th		Coys bathed & carried out kit inspections	Nil
"	14th		Scale of working parties Required every day. 200 men required nightly	

Army Form C. 2118.

WAR DIARY
or
INTELLIGENCE SUMMARY.
(Erase heading not required.)

Instructions regarding War Diaries and Intelligence Summaries are contained in F. S. Regs., Part II. and the Staff Manual respectively. Title pages will be prepared in manuscript.

Place	Date	Hour	Summary of Events and Information	Remarks and references to Appendices
VENDELLES	14th	—	for work on defences near TEMPLEUX. Capt. C.B. STARTIN went on leave. Lt. W.R. LAWTON took over command of "B" Coy.	ENDS
"	15th	—	Battalion mess begun. All officers including Batt. HQs. 2nd Lt. L. REDFERN went on leave	ENDS
"	16th	—	Weather mild, snow all gone. Batt. Scouts made up to 16 Comer of instruction under Intelligence Officer. RSM started class for young NCOs	ENDS
"	17th	—	2nd Lt. TATTERSAL (4th Batt.) joined Batt. from England	ENDS
"	18th	—	Weather dull + misty. Working parties as usual.	ENDS
"	19th	—	Guest night at Officers mess. Batt. HQ + some members of Brigade staff guests	ENDS
"	20th – 24th	—	Weather fine. Working parties as per programme Walls built round huts as protection from bombs etc. Training as per programme. CO's inspection of Coys — one per day. Capt. R.D. HARRIS left to be Zone Commandant in TEMPLEUX area	ENDS
"	25th	—	A Coy moved to VERMAND for work as per OO 209 attached. 2nd Lt WHITING	ENDS

WAR DIARY
or
INTELLIGENCE SUMMARY.

(Erase heading not required.)

Army Form C. 2118.

Place	Date	Hour	Summary of Events and Information	Remarks and references to Appendices
VENDELLES	26/1/18	–	Reported from duty with Tunnelling Coy	
"	27th	–	Weather fine. Work & training as per programme.	
"	28th	–	Quiet night. 9 O.C. + adj.-in-camp. B. 9 C. + staff + B HQs guests	enn
			2nd Lt. PEACOCK rejoined from leave. Considerable aerial activity during	
			day. Bombs dropped on MONTIGNY. A.Coy & B. Coy rejoined from VERMAND.	enn
"	29th	–	A.M. relieved 7th Bn NORTHAMPTON REGT in support at TEMPLEUX	
			QUARRIES as per OO 210. attached. Batt HQ + HQ Coys in QUARRIES. B Coy	
			at LION central & D Coy at Quarry in support. C Coy & 8" QUEENS in line	enn
			Capt 90 WAY DSO took over duties of Transport Officer	
SUPPORT	30th		Weather mild. Situation quiet. Work carried out in granaries.	enn
"	31st		Weather misty. Situation quiet. Sgt HILL signaller awarded	
			D.C.M. in NEW YEARS HONOURS LIST	
			2nd Lt. SHUTT went on leave	enn
			* Major - Lieut Col Mc Daly CMG, Major Mac Lennon MC, A-Cos. Pickthorn DSO	
			A-Lt. Riddell DSO, Burgon Mc Morgan DSO, Capt Hanby (act A.M.)	
			Tunnicliffe MC, Wownds MC, O'Connor MC, Riddell, Capt. Gordon Mc, Truscombe Officer	
			Lt. Thomas Mc, Mackenzie	
			(signed) W.N. Lt.Col	

SECRET.　　　　　　　OPERATION ORDER NO. 205.　　　　　COPY No. 1

1ST BATTALION NORTH STAFFORDSHIRE REGIMENT.

1. The Battalion will relieve the 8th Battalion The BUFFS. in SUPPORT at MONTIGNY on January 2nd, 1918.

2. The following distances will be maintained between Platoons 200 yards, and between each six Transport Vehicles 200 yards.

3. The Quarter-master will allot billets to advanced parties on arrival.

4. O's. C. Coy's. will send in advance one Officer per Coy. and one N.C.O. per platoon, to take over billets, these parties to leave billets at 11.0 a.m.

5. Order of march will be :-

        H. Q.　　　1.15 p.m.
        "A" Coy.　1.30　"
        "B"　"　　1.45　"
        "C"　"　　2.0　"
        "D"　"　　2.15　"

6. Officer's Valises, spare kit, men's blankets, cooking utensils, etc. to be stacked outside Coy. billets at 1.0 p.m. when they will be called for by Transport.

7. 8th Batt. The BUFFS. will not commence moving until Batt. H.Q. and 1 Coy. of this Battalion have arrived at MONTIGNY.

8. A G.S. Wagon will be outside Orderly Room at 1.0 p.m. to collect Lewis Guns and Magazines.

9. O's. C. Coy's. will notify Batt. H.Q. on arrival at MONTIGNY.

10. Exact location of Coy. alarm posts should be sent to Batt. H.Q. as soon after arrival in MONTIGNY as possible.

11. Acknowledge.

                                                      ....Capt. & Adjt.

30/12/17.　　　　　　　　　1st Battalion North Staffordshire Regt.

Copy. No. 1. War Diary.
        2. C.O.
        3. "A" Coy.
        4. "B"　"
        5. "C"　"
        6. "D"　"
        7. O.C. 8th Buffs.
        8. R.S.M.
        9. T.O.
       10. Qr.Mr.

SECRET.   OPERATION ORDER NO. 206.   Copy No. 2

                    1ST BATTALION NORTH STAFFORDSHIRE REGIMENT.

            Map Reference Sheet 62C.
            ----

1.   The Battalion will relieve the 9th Batt. ROYAL SUSSEX. Regt.
        in the front line during the Evening of 4th January, 1918.

2.   Order of relief will be :-
        "A" Coy. 1st N. Staffordshire Regt. relieves "B" Coy. R. Sussex Regt.
        "B"   "   "   "   "D"   "   "   "
        "D"   "   "   "   "C"   "   "   "
        "C"   "   "   "   "A"   "   "   "

3.   "D" Coy. will leave MONTIGNY at 4.30 p.m.
            "B"   "   "   "   " 4.45 "
            "A"   "   "   "   " 5.0   "
            "C"   "   "   "   " 5.15 "

4.   1 guide per platoon and 1 guide per Coy. H.Q. will be at
        L.4.c.95,45. at 5.30 p.m. also 1 guide for Batt. H.Q.

5.   All movement EAST of NIRVILLY will be by platoons at 200
        yards interval.

6.   All men's blankets, Officer's spare kit etc. to be stacked
        outside Coy. H.Q. by 4.30 p.m. when Transport will collect them.

7.   All Officer's Trench Kits, cooking utensils etc. to be
        stacked outside Coy. H.Q. by 4.30 p.m. One Servant per Coy. to
        remain with these kits until collected by Transport at 6.0 p.m.

8.   O's. C. Coy's. will render a certificate of Stores taken over
        by 9.0 a.m. January 5th.

9.   One Runner per Coy. and four Batt. H.Q. Runners, all Scouts,
        and three linesmen to parade at Orderly Room under 2/Lieut.
        E.C. Keble at 11.0 a.m. to proceed to Trenches.

10.   All requisitions for Gum Boots to be sent to Batt. H.Q. 200
        pairs are available for the Battalion.

11.   Coy. Pack Cobs to be at Coy. H.Q. half an hour before Coy.
        is due to move from MONTIGNY for the purpose of carrying
        Lewis Guns and Magazines.

12.   Twenty Petrol Tins of Water to be sent up nightly to "A" Coy.
        and 8 tins nightly to "B" "C" and "D" Coy's. A water Cart will be
        brought up and left at Regimental Aid Post nightly.

13.   O's. C. Coy's. will notify completion of relief to Batt. H.Q.
        by using the code word POST.
14.   Acknowledge.   W.D. Sta......
        3/1/18.   ....Capt. & Adjt.
                                        1st Battalion North Staffordshire Regt.

        Copy No. 1. Commanding Officer.   Copy No. 7. Transport Officer.
                2. War Diary.   8. Quartermaster.
                3. "A" Coy.   9. R.S.M.
                4. "B" "   11. H.Q. Mess.
                5. "C" "   12. 9th R. Sussex Regt.
                6. "D" "

                                J.O.

SECRET.   OPERATION A
                     OPERATION ORDER NO. 224.   Copy No. 1.
              1ST BATTALION NORTH STAFFORDSHIRE REGIMENT.

Reference HARGICOURT Special Sheet 1/10,000

1.   The Battalion will be relieved by the 8th Batt. The QUEENS (R.W.S.)
     Regt. in the WINTER SECTOR front line during the afternoon of
     January 6th, 1918.

2.   On relief the Battalion will move into SUPPORT.

3.   "D" Coy. N. Staffords. Regt. will be relieved by "C" Coy. Queens.
     "B" "   "   "   "   "   "   "   "   "A" "   "
     "A" "   "   "   "   "   "   "   "   "B" "   "
     "C" "   "   "   "   "   "   "   "   "D" "   "

4.   Coy's. will provide Guides as follows :-
     "D" Coy. 1 guide per two sections and 1 for Coy. H.Q. at 1.30 p.m.
     "B" "   "   "   "   "   "   " "   "   "   " 2.30 "
     "A" "   "   "   "   "   "   " "   "   "   " 3.30 "
     "C" "   "   "   "   "   "   " "   "   "   " 4.30 "
     Rendezvous for guides at Batt. H.Q.

5.   On relief "D" Coy. will move into accommodation in QUARRY at
     L.5.d.10.35 relieving "C" Coy. Queens.
     "B" Coy. will come under command of O.C. 8th Batt. The Queens.
     "C" Coy. will move into accommodation at L.10.a. Central (old
     73rd. Bde. H.Q.) relieving "D" Coy. Queens.
     "A" Coy. will move into TEMPLEUX QUARRIES relieving "B" Coy. QUEENS.
     "B" Coy. will move into TEMPLEUX QUARRIES   "   "A" "   "

6.   O's.C. Coy's. will hand on an advanced party consisting of
     1 Officer per Coy. and 1 N.C.O. per platoon at 10.30 a.m. to take
     over Trenches and accommodation, Trench Stores, etc.

7.   H.Qrs. and "A" "B" and "D" Coy's. to have all Officer's Trench
     Kits, petrol tins, scoring utensils, etc., stacked at Coy. Dumps
     by 5.0 p.m. when Transport will call for them. 1 N.C.O. and 2 men
     per Coy. to be left as Guard over these Kits.

8.   Transport Officer will arrange to bring up Officer's Valises,
     one blanket per man, rations and water etc., to Coy. Dumps in
     SUPPORT area and hand them over to advanced parties by 5.30 p.m.

9.   All Trench Stores, work in hand, etc., will be carefully handed
     over to relieving Unit.

10. Lewis Guns and Magazines will be carried.

11. O's.C. Coy's. will send Orderlies with advanced parties if
     necessary, to act as guides to Coy's. on relief.

12. O's.C. Coy's. will report arrival in correct area by using code
     word "JUMP".

13. Transport Officer will arrange to bring up the following number
     of petrol tins nightly while the Battalion is in SUPPORT.
     "D" Coy. 8 Tins.
     "B" "   12 "
     A water cart will be kept permanently at Batt. H.Q. for the use
     of Batt. H.Q. and "A" and "B" Coy's. This will be replaced by a

                                                  Full one/..........

full one at 12.0 Noon and 5.0 p.m. daily.

14. The Regimental Aid Post in SUPPORT will be at L.10.a. Central, where the M.O. will live.

15. Officer i/c of "B" Coy's. advanced party will take over all secret Documents, etc., at Batt. H.Q. in SUPPORT.

16. O's.C. Coy's. will inform Batt. H.Qrs. of completion of relief in the front line by using the code word "SHOY".

17. "A" "B" and "D" Coy's. will hand in their Gum Boots to the store in HARGICOURT and obtain receipts. "C" Coy. will retain theirs and hand them in for exchange when necessary.

18. Acknowledge.

W. J. Skinner

7/1/18. ....Capt. & Adjt.
1st Battalion North Staffordshire Regt.

Copy No:1. War Diary.
2. Commanding Officer.
3. H.Q. Mess.
4. "A" Coy.
5. "B" "
6. "C" "
7. "D" "
8. Transport Officer.
9. Quartermaster.
10. R.S.M.
11. O.C. 6th Batt. The Queens (R.W.S.) Regt.
12. War Diary.

SECRET.   OPERATION ORDER NO. 208.   Copy No. 2

1ST BATTALION NORTH STAFFORDSHIRE REGIMENT.

1. The Battalion will be relieved by the 12th Batt. Royal Fusiliers in Support on January 12th.

2. On relief the Battalion will move into huts at VENDELLES.

3. "A" Coy. N.Staffords. Regt. will be relieved by No. 1. Coy. R. Fus.
   "D" "   "   "   "   "   "   "   3. "   "
   "B" "   "   "   "   "   "   "   4. "   "
   "C" "   "   "   "   "   "   "   2. "   "

4. Coy's. of 12th Royal Fusiliers are leaving BERNES at 12.30 p.m.

5. O's.C. Coy's. will send on an advanced party of 1 Officer per Coy. and 1 N.C.O. per Platoon to take over Billets. The Quartermaster will allot Billets. Advanced parties will leave Trenches at 11.0 a.m.

6. All special maps, aeroplane photographs, etc., and HARGICOURT special sheet 1.A. will be handed over and receipts obtained.

7. H.Qrs. and "A" "B" and "D" Coy. All Officer's Trench Kits, men's blankets, cooking utensils, petrol cans, etc., to be stacked at Coy. Dumps by 2.0 p.m. when Transport will call for it.

8. O.C. "C" Coy. will leave a Guard of 1 N.C.O. and 2 men with Officer's Trench Kits, cooking utensils, etc., until collected by Transport at 5.0 p.m.

9. Transport Officer will arrange to hand over Officer's Valises, men's blankets, etc., to advanced parties at VENDELLES by 1.0 p.m.

10. All men doing duty at Brigade Gum Boot Store, bomb store, HARGICOURT and Traffic Control HARGICOURT will be relieved by 1.0 p.m. and will rejoin their Coy's.

11. The party at Brigade H.Q. Bomb Store will rejoin their Coy. in VENDELLES.

12. O.C. "C" Coy. will return any Gum Boots to Gum Boot Store in HARGICOURT.

13. All movement will be by Platoons at 200 yards distance.

14. Pack Cobs will be at Coy's. Dumps to carry Lewis Guns and magazines at 2.0 p.m. all Coy's.

15. O's.C. Coy's. will notify Batt. H.Q. on completion of relief by using the code word "BON"

16. O's.C. Coy's. will inform Batt. H.Qrs. on arrival in
    VENDELLES.

17. Coy. Commanders will order their own Chargers.

18. Acknowledge.

                                    W.J. Starnes
11/1/18.   ....Capt. & Adjt.
                                1st Battalion North Staffordshire Regt.

Copy No. 1. Commanding Officer.
         2. War Diary.
         3.   "
         4. H.Qrs. Mess.
         5. O.C. "A" Coy.
         6. O.C. "B" "
         7. O.C. "C" "
         8. O.C. "D" "
         9. R.S.M.
        10. O.C. 12th Royal Fusiliers.
        11. Transport Officer.
        12. Quartermaster.

OPERATION ORDER No. 209   Copy No.
1st Battn. North Staffordshire Regiment.

1. "A" Company less Company Head Qrs. and classes will move to VERMAND on January 25th.

2. Officer in charge should report to a representative of 288th Tunnelling Company with his party at VERMAND CHURCH at 9.0 a.m.

3. Company will leave VENDELLES at 8.0 a.m.

4. Transport Officer will arrange for sufficient transport for Blankets, Officers Kit, Petrol Tins, rations, men's packs, etc., to be at "A" Coys. Billet at 7-30 a.m.

5. Company Cooker will go with the Company.

6. Rations for this Company will be sent from MONTIGNY daily.

7. Company will be employed in making Huts.

8. They will be accommodated in these Huts.

9. Company will rejoin Battalion after work on January 28th.

24/1/1918.   ....Captain & Adjutant,
                  1st Battalion North Staffordshire Regiment.

Copy No. 1. War Diary.
     "   2.   do.
     "   3. Commanding Officer.
     "   4. O.C. "A" Company.
     "   5. Quartermaster.
     "   6. R. S. M.

J O for War Diary
WDS

SECRET.   OPERATION ORDER NO. 210.   Copy No. ...

1ST BATTALION NORTH STAFFORDSHIRE REGIMENT.

1. The Battalion will relieve the 7th Bn. NORTHAMPTON Regt. in SUPPORT on January 29th.

2. "D" Coy. N.STAFFS. will relieve "D" Coy. NORTHANTS. in Reserve to Battn in the Line.
   "B" "   "   "   "   "A" "   "   at L.10.a.
   "A" "   "   "   "   "B" "   "   at Templeux Quarries
   "C" "   "   "   "   "C" "   "   "

3. O.C. Coys. will send advance parties of one Officer per Coy. and one N.C.O. per platoon. Officer in charge of "C" Coys. advance party will take over for Battalion Head Quarters.

4. The Regimental Aid Post will be in Templeux Quarries, not at L.10.a.

5. Companies will leave VENDELLES at the following hours :-
   Head Qrs.   1-10 p.m.
   "A" Company.   1-0 p.m.
   "C"   "   1-15 p.m.
   "B"   "   1-30 p.m.
   "D"   "   4-0 p.m.

6. "A", "B", "C" Coys. and Head Qrs. All Officers Trench Kit, Cooking utensils, and one blanket per man to be stacked outside Company Billets by 1-0 p.m. and transport will collect them.

7. All Officers Spare Kit, men's Blankets, etc., to be stacked outside Company Billets by 12-0 noon.

8. The following intervals will be kept up on the march :-
200 yards between platoons.   200 yards between each six transport vehicles.

9. Transport officer will arrange to bring up the following number of Petrol Tins nightly while the Battalion is in Support :
   "D" Company   6 Tins.   "B" Company.   12 tins.

   A water cart will be kept permanently at Battalion Head Qrs, for the use of Battalion Head Qrs. and "C" and "A" Coys. This will be refilled at 12-0 noon and 5-0 p.m. daily.

10. Company Pack Cobs to be at Coy. Hd.Qrs. half an hour before the Company moves off to carry Lewis Guns and Magazines.

11. O.C. Companies will notify completion of relief to Battalion Hd.Qrs. by wire using the code word "MUD"

12. Transport Officer will arrange to collect "D" Coys. kit at 4-0 p.m.

13. O.C. "D" Coy. will report in person to O.C. 8th QUEENS when his relief is completed, and wire Battalion Head Quarters.

14. ACKNOWLEDGE.

28/1/1918.   ....Captain & Adjutant,
                            1st Battalion North Staffordshire Regiment.

Copy No. 1.   War Diary.
      " 2.   War Diary.
      " 3.   Commanding Officer.
      " 4.   "A" Company.
      " 5.   "B"   "
      " 6.   "C"   "
      " 7.   "D"   "
      " 8.   O.C. 7th Northants.
      " 9.   Quartermaster.
      " 10.   R.S.M.

Vol 36

Secret

War Diary

1st Battn. North Staffordshire Regiment

Period - February 1918

Volume

WAR DIARY
INTELLIGENCE SUMMARY. February 1918.

Army Form C. 2118.

Place	Date	Hour	Summary of Events and Information	Remarks and references to Appendices
SUPPORT TEMPLEUX QUARRIES	1/2/18		Weather misty. Situation quiet. Capt. STARTIN and 2/Lt REDFERN back from leave. Capt. MURRAY left to be instructor on gymnastic staff. Lt LAWTON took over command of A Coy. Lt BUTTERWORTH arrived back from Lewis Gun course.	SNR
"	2/2/18		Weather fine. Great amount of aerial activity. Our artillery active. 2/Bn relieved the 6th Bn The QUEENS in the centre sector. (00 21.0 attached) (our of relief postponed owing to fog.) (Addendum to 00 21.0 attached)	SNR
FRONT LINE	3/2/18		Weather fine. Considerable trench mortar activity during day. 2 ORs wounded. Lt SHARP arrived back from infantry course. 2/Lt COE returned from Field Ambulance.	SNR
"	4/2/18		Weather bright. Situation quiet during day. Considerable amount of artillery activity at night. Particularly from 10.15 p.m. to 11.15 p.m. and again at 4.30 a.m. to 6 a.m. 3 ORs wounded. Lt Col WYATT D.S.O. left to take temporary command of 72nd Inf. Bde. Major POPE D.S.O. M.C. took temporary command of Batt.	SNR

Army Form C. 2118.

WAR DIARY
~~INTELLIGENCE SUMMARY.~~

(Erase heading not required.)

Instructions regarding War Diaries and Intelligence Summaries are contained in F. S. Regs., Part II. and the Staff Manual respectively. Title pages will be prepared in manuscript.

Place	Date	Hour	Summary of Events and Information	Remarks and references to Appendices
LINE	4/2/18 (contd)		2nd Lt HAYWARD rejoined from Hospital	OMB
"	5/2/18		Weather fine. Situation quiet. Readjustment made in line the Coy ("C" Coy) relieved by a Coy of 8th ROYAL WEST KENTS & proceeded to MONTIGNY & Billets in trenches (OO 21.1. 50 (Sickles) "D" Coy to MONTIGNY. Bath relieved by 3rd Bn RIFLE BRIGADE & moved to VRAIGNES & became Brigade reserve. "C" & "D" Coys rejoined Batt. Batt. accommodated in B camp (OO 21.2 stankes)	OMB
"	6/2/18		Weather dull. Situation quiet.	OMB
VRAIGNES	7/2/18		Weather dull. Coys bathed. Reinforcement of 3 ones.	OMB
"	8/2/18		Weather dull. Bn. Coys to went for 4 hours per day on FREBY LINE. Run during morning. Lt Col WYATT DSO. rejoined Batt from Brigade. 2/Lt. COULTON to Field Ambulance. 2nd Lt Mac HARDIE Left for Infantry course at 5th ARMY School. 2nd Lt MANSELL & Lieut. off strength & taken on strength of Yeut TRENCH MORTAR BATTERY	
"	9/2/18		Weather dull. Work as above Capt SYMTHE & 2nd Lt STEEL went on leave	OMB
"	10/2/18		Weather fine. CSM HAND + SGT BARNARD to England for 6 months tour of duty	OMB

Army Form C. 2118.

WAR DIARY
or
INTELLIGENCE SUMMARY.
(Erase heading not required.)

Instructions regarding War Diaries and Intelligence Summaries are contained in F. S. Regs., Part II. and the Staff Manual respectively. Title pages will be prepared in manuscript.

Place	Date	Hour	Summary of Events and Information	Remarks and references to Appendices
VRAIGNES	11/2/18		Weather fine. Work as above. LT + QM ELSEGOOD + 2nd LT RAMSDEN proceeded on leave	ENDS
"	12/2/18		Weather fine. Coy Commanders reconnoitred new line. This Bn will take over.	ENDS
"	13/2/18		Weather dull + rainy. Work as above.	ENDS
"	14/2/18		Weather fine + frosty. 2nd LT KEEBLE reported from hospital. Bath redeemed. HtHOW the mounted Pole at front line (60 213 attached)	ENDS
FRONT LINE	15/2/18		Weather fine + frosty. Situation quiet.	ENDS
"	16/2/18		Weather fine + frosty. Situation quiet. 2nd LT. O.E. attached to 103 Coy R.E.	ENDS
"	17/2/18		Weather fine. LT SEALY proceeded to ENGLAND for duty at Machine Gun Training Centre + struck off strength	ENDS
"	18/2/18		Weather dull. Bn relieved by the 8th Bn R.W. KENTS (09214s/12th) 3 Coys to MONTIGNY "A" Coy to U 22 central in support 6 R W KENTS. 6 bombs dropped on MONTIGNY. 8pm No damage done.	ENDS
MONTIGNY	19/2/18		Weather fine + frosty. Coy inspections carried out by Coy Officers.	

Army Form C. 2118.

WAR DIARY
INTELLIGENCE SUMMARY.
(Erase heading not required.)

Place	Date	Hour	Summary of Events and Information	Remarks and references to Appendices
MONTIGNY	20/2/18		Weather fine. Paraded during morning. D Coy relieved A Coy in support to R W KENTS. A & C Coy entered D Coy. Proceeded to MONTIGNY (OO 21.5 attached) 2nd LT BROOKES went on leave. 2nd LT PEIRSON rejoined from 3rd Corps School.	ENS 2N3.
"	21/2/18		Weather fine. Paraded during morning.	
"	22/2/18		Batt (less D Coy) relieved 9th/EAST SURREY REGT in support (OO 216 attached) Weather dull & rainy. LT LAWTON proceeded to ENGLAND for 6 months tour of duty. LT TATTERSAL took over command of "B" Coy. LT BUTTERWORTH took over Adjutants. Capt STAMER to Field Ambulance	ENS.
SUPPORT	23/2/18		Weather fine. Work on trenches & wiring of battle position carried out. 2nd LT HAYWARD proceeded on a course to 5th Army School	ENS
"	24/2/18		Weather fine. Capt SMYTHE & 2nd LT STEEL returned from leave. LT SHUTE MC rejoined from hospital & joined C Coy	ENS.
"	25/2/18		Weather fine. Officers & relieving batt arrived to look over line. Major V.V. POPE DSO/MC left to carry out inspection of Army Schools	ENS.

Army Form C. 2118.

WAR DIARY
INTELLIGENCE SUMMARY.
(Erase heading not required.)

Place	Date	Hour	Summary of Events and Information	Remarks and references to Appendices
SUPPORT	25/2/18 - 26/2/18	(contd)	2nd LT. KEEBLE proceeded on leave. Reinforcement of 85 ors joined Batt. Divisional relief by 66th Division. Batt. relieved by 2/4 MANCHESTERS 199 Bde + marched to BERMES by train from TEMPLEUX. (NO 214 attacked) LT & QM EISEGOOD + 2nd LT RAMSDEN reported from leave. Capt. STAMER reported from Field Ambulance	4/43, CRB
BERMES	27/2/18		Bn entrained ROISEL at 5pm. arrived at VILLERS-BRETONNEUX at 6.30pm. Marched to CORBIE + billetted in houses in CORBIE. Reinforcement of 19 ors joined Batt.	" ens. CRB
CORBIE	28/2/18		Weather fine. Coys at disposal of Coy commanders.	CRB

A.R. Rops. 10
Lt. Col.
1st North Staffords Regt

SECRET.   OPERATION ORDER No. 210   Copy No. 1.
                  1ST BATTALION NORTH STAFFORDSHIRE REGIMENT.

Map Reference.- HARGICOURT Special Sheet.

1. The Battalion will relieve the 6th Bn. The QUEENS (R.W.S.) Regt. in the Centre Section on February 2nd.

2. "A" Coy. N.STAFFS. will relieve "B" Coy. QUEENS (LEFT Coy).
   "B" "   "   "   "   "A" "   "   (CENTRE Coy.)
   "C" "   "   "   "   "D" "   "   (RIGHT Coy.)
   "D" "   "   "   "   "C" "   "   (SUPPORT Coy.)

3. Coys. will leave the present positions at the following times -
        "D" Company.   1-45 p.m.   "A" Company   2-45 p.m.
        "B"   "   3-45 p.m.   "C"   "   4-45 p.m.

4. No guides are being provided. Advanced parties will be used as guides if necessary.

5. Gum Boots will be drawn as follows :-
        "C" Coy.   One pair per man.   "A" Coy.   20 pairs.
        "B" "   20 pairs.   "D" Coy.   20 pairs.
   These will be drawn from the Brigade Gum Boot Store in HARGICOURT by Companies direct. Indents for additional pairs should be sent to Battalion Head Quarters.

6. All Officers spare kit, men's blankets, etc. to be stacked on Company Dump before moving off. A guard will be left with this kit until collected by Transport about 6-0 p.m.

7. All Officers Trench Kit, cooking utensils, etc., to be stacked on Company Dump before 4-0 p.m. when Transport will collect them.

8. Transport Officer will arrange to bring up Petrol Tins nightly as follows while the Battalion is in the forward area.
        "A" Coy.   26 tins.   "C" Coy.   6 tins.
        "B" "   6 tins.   "D" "   6 tins.
   A water tank will come up nightly to fill tank at Battalion Hd.Qrs.

9. Coys. will do their own ration, etc. carrying parties as before.

10. O.C. Coys. will send advanced parties of one Officer per Coy. and one N.C.O. per platoon.

11. Reserve Rations to be carefully taken over. A list of all stores taken over to reach Battn. Hd.Qrs. by 12-0 noon Feb. 3rd.

12. Lewis Guns and Magazines will be carried.

13. All men employed on Guard at Brigade Gum Boot Store etc., will rejoin their Coys. to-morrow on relief.

14. O.C. Coys. will notify Battalion Head Qrs. on completion of relief by using the code word "R U M"

15. ACKNOWLEDGE.

                                    W.J. Staemer
1/2/18.   ....Captain & Adjutant,
                                    1st Battalion North Staffordshire Regiment.

Copy No. 1.   War Diary.
     "   2.   War Diary.
     "   3.   Commanding Officer.
     "   4.   O.C. "A" Coy.
     "   5.   O.C. "B" "
     "   6.   O.C. "C" "
     "   7.   O.C. "D" "
     "   8.   O.C. 8th Queens.
     "   9.   Quartermaster.
     " 10.   Transport Officer.
     " 11.   R.S.M.
     " 12.   File.

SECRET.   ADDENDUM TO OPERATION ORDER No. 210.

Operation Order No. 210, para. 3. is cancelled and the following will be substituted :-

| "D" Coy. | 4-30 p.m. | "A" Coy. | 4-0 p.m. |
| "B" " | 4-45 p.m. | "C" " | 5-15 p.m. |

ACKNOWLEDGE.

W.D. Stawer

2/2/16.   ....Captain & Adjutant,
                          1st Battalion North Staffordshire Regiment.

Copies to all recipients of Operation Order No. 210.

SECRET.　　　　　　　　OPERATION ORDER No. 211.　　　Copy No. 1.
　　　　　　　　1ST BATTALION NORTH STAFFORDSHIRE REGIMENT.

1. The following reliefs and readjustment of the line will take place to-night February 5th.

2. "C" Coy. will be relieved by " " Coy. 8th R.W.KENTS. One guide per platoon to be at Battn. Hd.Qrs. at 6-0 p.m.

3. On relief "C" Coy. will move to MONTIGNY and report to the Quartermaster for accommodation.

4. "B" Coy's post in FERRET LEFT will be relieved by 8th R.W. KENTS. A guide will be at Battn. Hd.Qrs. at 6-0 p.m.

5. On relief, platoon from FERRET LEFT will relieve "D" Coy. in COLOGNE LEFT.

6. "D" Coy. will be relieved in COLOGNE RIGHT by 8th R.W. KENTS.

7. On relief "D" Coy. will move to MONTIGNY and report to the Quartermaster for accommodation.

8. "A" Coy. will relieve 9th Bn. E.SURREY Regt. in VALLEY POSTS with one platoon. This relief to be complete by 6-0 p.m.

9. O.C. "C" and "D" Coys. will arrange to have all Officers Trench Kit, Petrol Cans, Cooking Utensils, etc. stacked on Coy. Dumps by 7-0 p.m. when Transport will collect them.

10. O.C. Coys. will notify Battn. Hd.Qrs. on completion of relief by using the code word "B U M P".

11. The boundary between CENTRE and RIGHT Battns. will be EAST end of RUBY LANE (exclusive to Centre Battn.) - (FERRET LEFT also exclusive to CENTRE Battn.) - Cross Roads L.5.c.2.3. - point where HARGICOURT TRENCH cuts HARGICOURT - TEMPLEUX ROAD (inclusive to Centre Battn.)

12. Boundary between CENTRE and LEFT Battns. - CARBINE TRENCH (inclusive to Centre Battn.) F.29.d.3.3. (VALLEY POSTS inclusive to Centre Battn.) - Cross Roads F.28.d.1.2. (Pimple locality exclusive to Centre Battn.) - F.27.d.0.0.

13. O.C. "C" and "D" Coys. will arrange to return all Gum Boots to Brigade Gum Boot Store in HARGICOURT.

14. ACKNOWLEDGE.

5/2/1918.

　　　　　　　　　　　　　　　　　　　　C. D. Stamer.
　　　　　　　　　　　　　　　　...................Captain & Adjutant,
　　　　　　　　　　　　　　　　1st Battalion North Staffordshire Regiment.

Copy No. 1. War Diary.
    "   2. War Diary.
    "   3. Commanding Officer.
    "   4. "A" Company.
    "   5. "B"   "
    "   6. "C"   "
    "   7. "D"   "
    "   8. File.
    "   9. R.S.M.
    "   10. Quartermaster.
    "   11. Transport Officer.
    "   12. O.C. 8th R.W. Kent Regt.
    "   13. O.C. 9th Bn. E. Surrey Regt.

SECRET.   OPERATION ORDER No. 212.   Copy No. 1.
                  1ST BATTALION NORTH STAFFORDSHIRE REGIMENT.

1.   The Battalion (less "C" & "D" Coys.) will be relieved by the
      3rd Bn. RIFLE BRIGADE in the Centre Section on the night Feb. 6/7th.

2.   On relief "A" & "B" Coys. will move to VRAIGNES, Camp "B", by
      trains from TEMPLEUX.

3.   Train arrangements as follows :-
      7-30 p.m. "A" Coy. and Battn. Hd.Qrs. from C.Y.211 to VRAIGNES.
      8-30 p.m. "B" Coy. from C.Y.211 to VRAIGNES.

4.   "A" & "B" Coys. All Officers Trench Kit, Petrol Tins, Cooking
      utensils, etc. to be stacked on Company Dumps by 6-0 p.m. when
      Transport will collect them.

5.   Transport Officer will arrange to take all Officers valises,
      men's blankets, etc. to VRAIGNES to-morrow.

6.   "C" & "D" Coys. will move from MONTIGNY to VRAIGNES on Feb. 6th,
      leaving MONTIGNY at 1-0 p.m. The Drums will accompany this half
      Battalion on the march.

7.   Quartermaster will allot Billets in Camp "B" at VRAIGNES.

8.   O.C. "A" & "B" Coys. will arrange to return all Gum Boots to
      the Brigade Gum Boot Store on relief.

9.   All Trench Stores, work in hand and proposed, Defence Schemes,
      Aeroplane Photographs, Reserve Rations, etc. will be handed over
      on relief and receipts obtained.

10.   O.C. Coys. will report completion of relief to Battn. Hd.Qrs.
      by using the code word "R O C K".

11.   No guides will be required.

12.   ACKNOWLEDGE.

                                        C. J. Stamer.
5/2/1918.   ....Captain & Adjutant,
                                   1st Battalion North Staffordshire Regiment.

      Copy No. 1.   War Diary.
        "   2.   War Diary.
        "   3.   Commanding Officer.
        "   4.   File.
        "   5.   "A" Company.
        "   6.   "B"   "
        "   7.   "C"   "
        "   8.   "D"   "
        "   9.   R. S. M.
        "   10.   Quartermaster.
        "   11.   Transport Officer.
        "   12.   O.C. 3rd Rifle Brigade.
        "   13.   Signalling Sergeant.

SECRET. OPERATION ORDER No. 213. Copy No......

1ST BATTALION NORTH STAFFORDSHIRE REGIMENT.

1. The Battalion will relieve MHOW DISMOUNTED BDE. arranged in depth, and one Dismounted Regiment distributed – 2 platoons HETTY, and Posts 6 and 7 on the night 14/15th February. Relief to be complete by midnight.

2. "A" Company will be LEFT Company.
   "D"   "   " LEFT CENTRE Company.
   "B"   "   " RIGHT CENTRE Company.
   "C"   "   " RIGHT Company.

3. Advanced Parties as under will parade outside Orderly Room at 9-0 a.m. to-morrow :-
   One officer per Coy. One N.C.O. per platoon. Three Battn. Runners, Four Battn. Signallers. Provost Sergeant. Intelligence Officer and two Scouts. A lorry will take this party to JEANCOURT. They will report to Hd.Qrs. MHOW Dismounted Cavalry Bde. at the EGG.

4. Coys. will parade at 12-30 p.m. and entrain at D.Z. 215 at 1-0 p.m. Trucks will go as far as JEANCOURT.

5. Lewis Guns and Magazines will be taken on the train.

6. Transport Officer will arrange for Pack Cobs to meet Coys. at JEANCOURT to carry Lewis Guns and Magazines.

7. All Trench Kit, Cooking utensils, etc. to be stacked outside Coy. Billets by 12-30 p.m. when Transport will collect it.

8. All spare kit, men's blankets, etc. to be stacked in 3rd Army Hut at present occupied by Drummers before marching off.

9. R.S.M. will arrange for a guard to be found from The Battalion Drummers to guard this kit until collected by Transport on Feb. 15th.

10. Transport Officer will make following arrangements for supply of water in the forward area.
    "A" Coy.)
    "B" "   ) 10 petrol cans nightly.
    "D" "   )

    "C" "   6 petrol cans nightly.
    A water cart to come up nightly and fill Battn. H.Q. water tank.

11. All Trench Stores, returns of work, special maps, aeroplane photographs, reserve rations, will be carefully taken over, and receipts forwarded to Orderly Room by 12-0 noon February 15th.

12. No guides will be provided. Advanced Parties will be used as guides if necessary.

13. The following distance will be kept on the march EAST of JEANCOURT. 200 yards betwwen Platoons. Order of march will be "C","A","D","B".

14. O.C. Coys. will draw what Gum Boots they require from the Store at the EGG.

15. Coys. will do their own ration carrying.

16. O.C. Coys. will report as soon as possible after relief position and number of S.O.S. Rockets and Reserve Rations taken over.

17. O.C. Coys. will notify Battn. Hd.Qrs. on completion of relief by using the code word "B E A N".

18. ACKNOWLEDGE.

13/2/1918.

..................Captain & Adjt.
1st Battn. North Staffordshire Regiment.

P. T. O.

Copy No. 1. War Diary.
"   2. War Diary.
"   3. Commanding Officer.
"   4. "A" Company.
"   5. "B"   "
"   6. "C"   "
"   7. "D"   "
"   8. Transport Officer.
"   9. Quartermaster.
"   10. R. S. M.
"   11. MHOW Dismounted Bde.
"   12. File.
"   13. Signalling Sergeant.

SECRET.   OPERATION ORDER No. 214.   Copy No. 3.
1st BATTALION NORTH STAFFORDSHIRE REGIMENT.

Map Ref. HARGICOURT - Special Sheet.

1. The Battalion will be relieved by the 8th Bn. R.W. KENT Regt. on Feb. 18th.

2. On relief Hd.Qrs. and "B", "C" & "D" Coys. will move to MONTIGNY. "A" Coy. will occupy accommodation at L.22. central.

3. "A" Coy. will send an advanced party of one Officer, and one N.C.O. per platoon.

4. Coys. of 8th R.W. KENT Regt. will leave the intermediate line at 4-0 p.m.

5. All Trench Kit, Petrol Tins, Cooking utensils, etc. will be stacked on Coy. Dumps by 6-0 p.m. when Transport will collect it.

6. Transport Officer will arrange for all Officers valises, men's blankets, etc. of Hd.Qrs. and "B", "C" & "D" Coys. to be taken to the Camp at MONTIGNY during the day. All Officers valises "A" Coy. and one blanket per man "A" Coy. to be taken to L.22 central.

7. Quartermaster will allot billets in MONTIGNY.

8. All Defence Schemes, Special Maps, Aeroplane Photographs, work in hand, etc. to be carefully handed over.

9. Coy. Pack Cobs. will be at Coy. Dumps at 6-0 p.m. to carry Lewis Guns and Magazines.

10. Guides will be as arranged between Company Commanders concerned.

11. O.C. Coys. will inform Battn. Hd.Qrs. on completion of relief by using the code word " O F F ".

12. Company Commanders will order their own horses.

13. ALLEC [illegible]

17/2/18.
.....................Captain & Adjutant,
1st Battalion North Staffordshire Regiment.

Copy No. 1. Commanding Officer.
 "   2. War Diary.
 "   3.   do.
 "   4. File.
 "   5. O.C. "A" Company.
 "   6. O.C. "B"   "
 "   7. O.C. "C"   "
 "   8. O.C. "D"   "
 "   9. O.C. 8th R.W. Kent Regt.
 "   10. R. S. M.
 "   11. Transport Officer.
 "   12. Quartermaster.
 "   13. Signalling Sergeant.

SECRET.   OPERATION ORDER No. 215   Copy No. 1

1ST BATTALION NORTH STAFFORDSHIRE REGIMENT.

1. "D" Coy. will relieve "A" Coy. at L.22 central on Feby. 20th.

2. On relief "A" Coy. will move into Billets at MONTIGNY.

3. Transport Officer will arrange for necessary Transport to be at "D" Coy's. billet at 3-30 p.m.

4. "D" Coy. will leave present Billets at 4-0 p.m.

5. "A" Coy's. Officers Trench kit, Cooking utensils, blankets, etc. to be stacked on Company Dump by 4-30 p.m.

6. Transport Officer will provide Pack Ponies to carry Lewis Guns and Magazines.

7. "D" Coy. will send an advanced party of one officer and one N.C.O. per platoon

8. 200 yards interval will be maintained between platoons on the march.

9. All Trench Stores, etc. will be carefully handed over.

10. "D" Coy. will report completion of relief by wiring the time.

11. "A" Coy. will report arrival in Billets.

12. ACKNOWLEDGE.

20/2/18.

..........................Captain & Adjt.

1st Battalion North Staffordshire Regiment.

Copy No. 1. War Diary.
"   2.   -do-
"   3. File.
"   4. "A" Company.
"   5. "D"   "
"   6. R. S. M.
"   7. Quartermaster.
"   8. Transport Officer.
"   9. Signalling Sergeant.

SECRET.   COPY NO. 1

OPERATION ORDER NO. 216.

1ST BATTALION NORTH STAFFORDSHIRE REGIMENT.

1. The Battalion (less "D" Coy.) will relieve the 9th Batt. East Surrey Regt. in BRIGADE SUPPORT on Febry 22nd.

2. "D" Coy. will remain in present position.

3. "B" Coy. N. Staff. Regt. will relieve "B" Coy. E. Surrey's. in FERVAQUE TRENCH.
   "C" "   "   "   "   " "A" "   " in COTE TRENCH.
   "A" "   "   "   "   " "D" "   " at L.10.a.

4. Coy's. will leave present Billets at the following times :-
   "A" Coy. 2.0 p.m.
   "B" "   2.15 p.m.
   "C" "   2.30 p.m.
   200 yards distance between Platoons will be kept on the March.

5. O.C. Coy's. will send advanced parties of 1 Officer per Coy. and 1 N.C.O. per Platoon, to leave present Billets at 11.0 a.m.

6. All Officers Trench Kit, one Blanket per man, Cooking Utensils etc. to be stacked outside Coy. Billets at 2.0 p.m. when Transport will collect them.

7. All Officers spare Kit, one Blanket per man, etc. to be taken down to the Qr Mr's. Stores during the Morning.

8. Transport Officer will arrange for Pack Ponies to carry Lewis Guns and Magazines.

9. Transport Officer will arrange to send up Water Carts nightly to fill Tanks at Batt. Hd. Qrs. and Right Coy. Hd. Qrs. Ten Petrol Tins will be sent up nightly to "A" "B" and "C" Coy's.

10. O.C. "B" Coy. will detail an N.C.O. and Six men for Machine Gun escort duty at BOCHE VIEW. O.C. "A" Coy. will detail Six men for Machine Gun escort duty at BOBBY QUARRY. O.C. "C" Coy. will detail a N.C.O. and 3 men for S.O.S. Guard at Batt. Hd. Qrs.
    All above parties will report to R.S.M. 9th Batt. East Surrey Regt. at 3.0 p.m. to-morrow at COTE WOOD Hd. Qrs.

11. Coy's. will work nightly on their Battle positions. Work in hand etc. should be carefully taken over.

12. Receipts for Trench Stores taken over, and a separate receipt for all Iron Rations and Reserve Water taken over to reach Batt. Hd. Qrs. by 12.0 Noon, Febry. 23rd.

13. The Batt. Intelligence Officer, a percentage of Batt. Runners and Signallers will go with advanced parties.

14. O.C. Coy's. will notify Batt. Hd. Qrs. on completion of relief by wiring the time.

15. ACKNOWLEDGE.

                                          W.D. Stamer
21/2/18.   ....Capt. & Adjt.
                                          1st Battalion North Staffordshire Regt.

Copy No. 1. War Diary.
        2.   "
        3. File.
        4. "A" Coy.
        5. "B" "
        6. "C" "
        7. "D" "
        8. Hd. Qr. Mess.
        9. Transport Officer.
        10. Quarter Master.
        11. R.S.M.
        12. Signalling Sergt.
        13. O.C. 9th East Surrey Regt.

SECRET.　　　　　　　OPERATION ORDER NO. 217　　Copy No....

1ST BATTALION NORTH STAFFORDSHIRE REGT.

1. The Battalion will be relieved by the 2/6 MANCHESTER Regt. in BRIGADE SUPPORT on 26/2/18.

2. Coys. will make their own arrangements with regards to inter-Company reliefs.

3. 2/6th MANCHESTER Regt. arrives Railhead at TEMPLEUX at 2-0 p.m. 26th inst., and will be met by one guide per platoon from Coys. and one guide from Battalion Head Qrs.

4. On relief Coys. less "D" Coy. will move to Railhead at TEMPLEUX. Platoons will be at 200 yards interval.

5. Battalion less "D" Coy. will entrain at TEMPLEUX for BERNES at 4-30 p.m. 26th inst.

6. Captain D.M. Smyth will meet all C.Q.M.Sgts. at 10-0 a.m. 26th inst., at DALY'S THEATRE, MONTIGNY, and with them he will take over and allot accommodation at BERNES.

7. All C.Q.M.Sgts. will meet Coys. on arrival at BERNES and guide them to Billets.

8. Blankets in 10's, men's cooking utensils, petrol tins, etc. will be stacked at Orderly Room by 2-30 p.m. 26th inst.

9. O.C. Coys. will detail 4 men per Coy. to remain at Orderly Room with Blankets, etc. These men will load above on to Transport arriving at 6-30 p.m. O.C. "D" Coy. will detail one Officer and one N.C.O. for duty with this party. The Officer marching the party to BERNES on completion of loading. This party will be provided with tea rations.

10. O.C. Coys. are held responsible for cleanliness and good order of their trenches and dug-outs on relief.

11. All maps, aeroplane photographs, defence schemes, work in hand, proposed work, etc. will be handed over.
Separate receipts will be obtained for reserve rations of water etc.

12. O.C. Coys. will inform Battn. Hd.Qrs. on completion of relief by wiring the time. "D" Coy. will report on arrival at BERNES.

13. ACKNOWLEDGE:

25/2/1918.　　　　　　　　　　..............Lieut.
　　　　　　　　　　　for Captain & Adjutant,
　　　　　　　　　　1st Battalion North Staffordshire Regiment.

Copy No. 1. War Diary.
　　"　　2. War Diary.
　　"　　3. Commanding Officer.
　　"　　4. "A" Company.
　　"　　5. "B"　"
　　"　　6. "C"　"
　　"　　7. "D"　"
　　"　　8. Transport Officer.
　　"　　9. Quartermaster.
　　"　　10. R.S.M.
　　"　　11. Signalling Sergeant.
　　"　　12. O.C. 2/6th Manchester Regt.
　　"　　13. File.

72nd Brigade.

24th Division.

1st BATTALION

NORTH STAFFORDSHIRE REGIMENT

MARCH 1918

Appendices :-

Account of Operations 21st March - 6th April.

Confidential.

WAR DIARY.

OF

1st. BATTN: NORTH STAFFORDSHIRE REGT.

1st. March 1918 to 30th April May 1918.

Volume V

Army Form C. 2118.

WAR DIARY
or
INTELLIGENCE SUMMARY.
(Erase heading not required.)

Instructions regarding War Diaries and Intelligence Summaries are contained in F. S. Regs., Part II. and the Staff Manual respectively. Title pages will be prepared in manuscript.

Place	Date	Hour	Summary of Events and Information	Remarks and references to Appendices
CORBIE	1.3.18		The Battalion left their rest Billets at CORBIE at 6.30 a.m. & marched to VILLIERS BRETTENEUX where Ry entrained for BRIE. From BRIE Ry Battalion marched to DEVISE & took over billets from Dismounted Cavalry	
DEVISE	2.3.18		Day spent in reorganisation. Cleaning of billets etc.	
do	3.3.18		Training began. Range practices carried out with rifle & Lewis Gun. Practice fired	
do	4.3.18		Training continued. Capt. P.D. HARRIS arranged Football & Rifle Competitions who were counting now	
do	5.3.18		Final heats played & run off.	
do	6.3.18		Weather having which was carried out in huts as far as possible. Recoiless practices fired. Training continued throughout Battalion – Major Pope returned from tour of S. of F.	
do	7.3.18		Day spent in training	
do	8.3.18		Battalion was exercised in ceremonial drill for Brigade Church Parade at DEVISE.	
do	9.3.18		Battalion took part in Brigade ceremonial service for Church Parade	
do	10.3.18		Battalion took part in Brigade General which consisted of inspection by Corps Commander XIX Corps Lt.Genl (Gene Gwrage) & Brigade Church Parade. Gen Crozby men were seen by 'A'Cof(Similan) shooting Competitions held. Also transport show judged by O.C. Divisional Train 20-21 Dismounted Cavalry Brigade Capt E.D.B. Oxley	
do	11.3.18		Battalion marched to VERMAND. Took over billets from Dismounted Cavalry Brigade. Proceeded on 14 days leave to England.	

WAR DIARY
or
INTELLIGENCE SUMMARY.

Army Form C. 2118.

Place	Date	Hour	Summary of Events and Information	Remarks and references to Appendices
VERMAND	11.3.18		Battalion in Support to 92nd Infy. Brigade. Bn. Officers mess formed under direction of Capt. HARRIS.	
	12.3.18		Training commenced but had to be abandoned as 2 Companies of the Battalion were detailed for working parties. Night considerable activity by our 60 pounder batteries during day & night.	
	13.3.18		Day was uneventful.	
	14.3.18		d/o	
	15.3.18		d/o. Owing to information received battle positions were manned by A Coy at MAISSEMY.	
	16.3.18		Brig. Genl. Morgan proceeded on leave. The command of 92nd Infy. Bde. devolved on Lieut. Col. Wyatt D.S.O. Command of the Battalion taken over by Maj. Pope.	

WAR DIARY or INTELLIGENCE SUMMARY

Army Form C. 2118.

(Erase heading not required.)

Hour, Date, Place	Summary of Events and Information	Remarks and references to Appendices
Night of 17/18 March 1918	1st N. Staffords relieved the 9th Bn East Surrey Regt in the front line, Sub sector of Brigade Front. B Coy commanded by Capt. S.B. STARTIN on the left night in SAMPSON TRENCH. Bn. Headquarters at MUQUET WOOD. "D" Coy were on left in PONTRUET commanded by Capt. D.M. SMYTH, "A" Coy were in ESSLING REDOUBT commanded by Lieut. H.V. TATTERSALL, "C" Coy were in outpost in MAISSEMY commanded by Lieut. F.S. SHUTE M.C. The Battalion was commanded by Maj. V.V. POPE DSO MC Lieut Col. T. WYATT DSO. being in Command of the 72nd Brigade. Battalion Headquarters was located in the Quilken Road about 500x South of MAISSEMY.	
18.3.18	The day was quiet & uneventful.	
19.3.18	The day was quiet & uneventful — Lieut J.G. COOK left the Battalion & proceeded for 6 months tour of duty in England.	
20.3.18	Quiet day — Information was received from Intelligence reports that Enemy offensive was to commence on morning of 21st. Enemy prisoners captured on the 20th confirmed his giving details. Action was taken as follows: — 2 platoons of "C" Coy under Lieut. REDFERN M/M. reinforced 'A' Coy in ESSLING REDOUBT. — One Company of the 9th Bn E. SURREY'S was brought from VERMAND to reinforce "C" Coy & hold the RED LINE, North	

WAR DIARY or INTELLIGENCE SUMMARY

Place	Date	Hour	Summary of Events and Information	Remarks and references to Appendices
Contd.	20.8.14		of the Bn ordered to be held by personnel of Battalion Headquarters. One Coy of Machine Gunners was brought up to hold the REDLINE immediately on the right of MAISSEMY. One Company of the 12th Pioneer Battalion SHERWOOD FORRESTERS was in reserve at VILLECHOLLES.	
	Night of 20 inst.		Uneventful Night.	
	21.8.14	4.30 am	At 4.30 am enemy barrage opened heavily on all trenches, all communications were cut by 4.45 am. There was a considerable amount of gas shelling & Bn Hqrs dugout soon became full of gas. In addition a dense fog was present which prevented any idea of junctions out enemy or our own movements by observation or otherwise.	
		8.00 am	Liaison with Battalion on our right was established they knew nothing more than we did of events which may have been occurring in forward positions	
		9.30 am	A runner from 7th - Bde Headquarters arrived with orders to man Batt positions - this also came immediately had already been given by Maj. POPE. Battalion Headquarters personnel having manned REDLINE in front of Headquarters	
		10.30 am	A creeping barrage passed over RED LINE but no signs of enemy were seen gas shelling by the enemy was now less constant.	
		11 am	Lieut. B. BROOKS arrived from "D" Coy with the information that enemy had broken through our front line battalions	

WAR DIARY
or
INTELLIGENCE SUMMARY.
(Erase heading not required.)

Army Form C. 2118.

Hour, Date, Place	Summary of Events and Information	Remarks and references to Appendices
	Major Pope took over command of Bn Hqrs personnel in RED LINE. Bn Hqrs dug out was abandoned the right of position was held by servant's orderlies & runners with 1 Lewis Gun & 1 Machine Gun. The left of the position was held by signallers runners with 1 Lewis Gun manned by Sgt. HARPER & one Machine gun by 3 men of the Machine Gun Corps.	
11.15 a.m.	Major Pope with Capt. BYAS attempted to establish communication with Battalion on our right. This was done & in 12 stores journey Major Pope was wounded. Fire was now opened by the enemy from the rear of Bn Hqrs position also from its left front. The enemy in force were now in the rear & dealt with by the Left Lewis Gun & rifles. The 3 men of the M.G.C were hit & the machine gun put out of action. The remaining Lewis gun developed a stoppage which could not be rectified. Enemy fire increased from our left rear & several casualties occurred. Capt. W.D. STAMER was hit.	
11.30 a.m.	Capt. Stamer ordered a rush to be made to the rear with the object of dislodging the enemy left & half of known left & half of this was carried out. On the enemy were to the left of the point rushed & we then came under enfilade fire & also M.G. fire from our original front. Capt. Stamer then gave the orders for a withdrawal in the direction of the VILLECHOLLES – VERMAND road which was carried out by short rushes & such there were

inflicted on the enemy during this withdrawal. The VILLECHOLLES-VERMAND road was reached but was found to be untenable owing to enfilade M.G. fire from the direction of MAISSEMY and a further withdrawal in the direction of VERMAND became necessary & was accomplished under the leadership of Capt Skinner who continued to command the party left until they joined the O.C. 2n E. Surrey Regt who had taken up a position on a ridge between VERMAND & MAISSEMY.

Army Form W.3091.

Cover for Documents.

Nature of Enclosures.

Details obtained from 2/Lt. A. PEACOCK 21.3.18-6.4.18.

Notes, or Letters written.

Army Form C. 2118.

WAR DIARY
or
INTELLIGENCE SUMMARY.
(Erase heading not required.)

Instructions regarding War Diaries and Intelligence Summaries are contained in F. S. Regs., Part II. and the Staff Manual respectively. Title pages will be prepared in manuscript.

Hour, Date, Place	Summary of Events and Information	Remarks and references to Appendices

The following details were obtained from 2nd Lt. A Cockburn 4th R. Scotts the only officer of the battalion who remained with the battalion from the 21st of March till it was relieved on April 8th:—

On the morning of March 21st 1918 "C" Coy (2/4 F.S.W.S.A. attd. 7/8 the date of the German attack on a 50 mile front) on ARRAS & LA FÈRE. "C" Coy (2/4 F.S.W. Shots) was less two platoons, which had been sent to reinforce 4th Coy in ESSIGNY Redoubt, were the Coy in Reserve and located in the inner Village of MAISSEMY situated some 2½ miles N.E. of VERMAND. During the early morning there was a thick mist which lasted till late at the day rendering it impossible to see more than 50 yards. The enemy opened a heavy bombardment at 4.30 a.m. with guns of all calibres, using amongst other arms a large number of gas shells, so that as Craofs were allowed to remain than four hornets formed and the sheltrs being up, the Coy became almost immediately inelgable often some 3 hours. It is unlikely to date a later to Company further communicated. Shortly fellowing forward movement was made, easy ... from wounded men and "C" Coy had no news of other Companies. Communication front the forward Coys was already fact, a "C" Coy act as not allowance Communication between what the enemy had a counter attacked, no attempt at them what was tapping on which the Coy had a counterattacked was the sound of rifle & M.G. fire coming from C.C.O. of all of them from C.O. of various Coys. It was learned later that a forward company which had been ordered up had become involved, they [illegible] them in afternoon W.am. the Coy then were informed...

up a defensive position in & around MAISSEMY; on eastern position stay forward & covered their flank & upon. This position was maintained till the garrison was practically surrounded when a withdrawal towards the Brown Line was ordered. The first move was to a point where the MAISSEMY–VILLECHOLE Rd crosses shortly to the S.W. here a position along the road was taken up & a L.G. placed in position in a farm hit.

In withdrawing to the position "C" Coys front experienced from Rifle & M.G. fire; a certain % of men were wounded & taken prisoners. Moreover the enemy did not have time to throw all the men away & heavy casualties were inflicted on them by our rifle & M.G. fire.

This position was held for about an hour when a further withdrawal west became necessary, a position across the VILLECHOLE – MAISEMY Road was taken up. This line was situated about 1000 yds N.E. of VILLECHOLE & extended about 600 yards. The left flank extended about 200 yds on the left of the road & rested on a wood, the right flank extended 400 yds on the right of the road & was in touch with the 9th East Surrey Regt. From this position also heavy casualties were inflicted on the enemy. The Cherwell Staffords were reinforced by a platoon of the 12th Sherwood Foresters, the strength of the Battalion having been reduced to 8 officers (2nd Lt Shute, R. J. Past Peacock) & 190 O.R.

At 2.am on 22.3.18. the N. Staffords were relieved & returned to B^{de} H.Q at VERMAND. The remainder of the night was spent.

At daylight the Staffords were ordered in the event of enemy attack, to take up a position man[n]ing the VERMAND Cemetery, situated a short distance S.W. of the town. This they did about 10. am remaining there till 1.P.M. when orders were received to withdraw to a front 300 yds E of the GREEN line which crossed the VERMAND – ESTRÉES-en-CHAUSSÉE Rd some 200 yds E of the village of POEUILLY.

At this point a line was manned by the Staffords. 103 Coy R.E. men of the T.M.B. & M.G. B^{n} together with a few stragglers from various other units. The green line in rear was at this time held by the 50 to division.

These troops were held while the remainder of the B^{de} passed through, then en route for MONCHY-LA-GACHE where the troops had orders to rendezvous.

Shortly after arriving here the B^{de} was ordered to take up a position on the high ground, to the E of the town. While the Staffords were too much reduced in strength to hold any front of the line was detailed to form a mobile reserve.

The night of 22/23 was quiet & at 7.am on 23rd orders were given for the B^{de} to withdraw to LICOURT crossing the SOMME by the bridges at St CHRIST. This was accomplished a rear-guard action being fought back as far as the river. The r. Gard was held by the 8th division. while the 72 B^{de}

(4)

Continued the march to LICOURT where the night was passed.

At this time the Stafford Coys made up of two of [?] (2/Lt Reeves & Ryus) were placed under the command of the O.C. 8th R. West Kent Regt (Stat H.J.Wenyon. D.S.O.).

At 7 am on 24.3.18 the 72nd Bn were ordered to proceed to CHAULNES.

Instead of further advance was ordered to proceed on a line E. of FONCHES across the CHIÉCOURT - LIANCOURT Rd. This plan tour of a reinforcement of 2 officers (2/Lt R.Hayward & A. Whiting) & some 60 men was received. These consisted of men returned from leave, reinforcements, officers & orderlies, as were had commenced at the transport lines for any available man to be sent up.

The night of 24/25 passed without incident.

On the 25th at 11 am orders were received to take up a line E. of FOUCAUCOURT. Here the 8th & ? came into contact with the enemy, & except the enemy Right & L.G. fire on the road there was practically no shelling. & nothing with. The position on [?] of [?] orderlies was [?] to be scaffold, there left front was in contact with the 7th Bn (NORTHANTS?) but on their right was a gap of 300 [?] between them & the 8th R.W. Kent Regt. The enemy were about 1000 yds away while holding the position 2/Lt E.R. Nyas was wounded.

5

26th March. Orders were received for the withdrawal to a line E of HALLU to a position in rear. Tanks were plenty of ammn. in front was taken up & held till 10 am. when an account of the units on the flanks having forced back orders were received to withdraw to a line E of ROUVROY.

On night 26/27th the 72nd Bn. was billeted in WARVILLERS & for the first time since the opening of the German offensive were the weary troops able to wash & to obtain a full nights rest. Inspite of all the troops had undergone during the previous six days, the distances they had marched, hardships & lack of sleep they had endured, the spirits & morale of all ranks was remarkable & worthy of the highest praise.

The midday on the 27th the 72nd Bn. took up a line between ROUVROY & WARVILLERS. The Bn afford. holding an advanced position about 300 yds E of the main line. Two two officers of 2nd Regiment & following were killed by snipers. This position was held till 5 P.M. when to avoid being surrounded & were withdrawn to the main line. became necessary. On the night of the 27th/28th. 2/Lieut Benson returned from leave & joined Capt. Peacock, then the only remaining officer.

At 2 am. on the 28.3.18 the withdrawal across the open plain to W of the town of WARVILLERS was ordered & at 10 am a further withdrawal across the open plain to W of the town as far as the CAIX – LE QUESNEL line of defences became necessary. During this much dreaded heavy casualties were inflicted on the enemy by our Rifles & L.G. fire, but also our gunners came into action & put open sten sights on the advancing enemy at a range ranging from 2000 – 800 yds.

(6)

The Cavé - a ravine, this was an excellent ambush, have been the scene of holding up the enemy after advance for a long time but owing to the flanks withdrawing, it became untenable & the 7 & 15 th were ordered to retire to VILLERS-aux-ERABLES via BEAUCOURTz MEZIÈRES. On this march the rearguard were engaged with troops of an absorption troops, artillery detachment, forming a fine target to the enemy, of which however he failed to take advantage any where on sections of battery units of element.

During the night 28/29th the Brigade marched to proceed to their respective Brandes lines which were then situated at the S. Bend of the BOIS de SENE at, Just N of the CASTEL – ROUVREL Rd, line Beymard over the AVRE at CASTEL. a short time. They were ordered to form the two troops covering the bridge over AVRE at CASTEL.

About 1. am + shirt comment of shirt. with arms at 12 noon.

During night period at 3.30 a.m. (29th.) + with their arms at 12 noon.

In the morning of the 29th the 18th marched to HAILLES + spent the night of 29/30 on a ridge s. of the river AVRE. In the afternoon the Battalion was reorganized. after the 8th west Kents, The losses then consisted of. - 2 brgs. Bn West Kents 1 Bn, gallant cover of 4 Bay. 1st North Staffords. All that time our strength was 2 officers, 70 O.R.'s + one platoon were formed, under 2/Lieut. Penson, C Coy. + Lgt Goodfellow, D Coy. Capt. A. Peacock commanded the Company.

The 30th was spent in digging position W of the town of DOMART + S. of the BOIS de GENTELLES.

From March 31st - April 3rd the Bn was in rserve + owing to our other manning there position Durring this afternoon of March 31st, a stand-To was ordered owing to heavy enemy attack on the town of THÉZY, HANGARD, MOREUIL front. A position was taken up + while NE of THEZY, +while/posh[?]/during the night of 31st March/1st April the Battalion was ordered to fill in THÉZY on the morning of the 1st.

On April 1st the Bn marched to the Bois de BLANGY + Bois l'ABBÉ in support positions when it remained till relieved by australian troops on the night 5/6 April.

The troops were taken by Motor Lorry to SALEUX where they night was spent entraining in the afternoon of 6th for St. VALERY, where the Stafford marched to St. BLIMONT, moving the following day (8th April) to NIBAS.

How the work of reorganising the battalion was begun.

Copy of letter from Capt. W.D.Stamer, M.C.

FIFTH ARMY CHAPTERS.

(24th - 31st March 1918.)

....

1/N.Staffs
72nd Bde.
24th Div.
XIX Corps.
Fifth Army.

Naval & Military Club,
94 Piccadilly. W.1.

23rd May 1930.

Director,
　　Historical Section.

I am so sorry I have not returned these documents before, they got mislaid in the/my heavy baggage from the Sudan.

I regret that I cannot add anything, but I was wounded so early in the day (21st March) that I saw very little.

The two attached accounts were written for me by two of my officers before demobilisation, as they only knew what happened to the Battalion. Would you mind returning them to me sometime. I only hope they may be of some use.

　　　　　　　　　Yours sincerely,

　　　　　　　　　　(sgd) W.D.Stamer. Capt.
　　　　　　　　　　N. Staffordshire Regiment.
　　　　　　　　　　　　Gibraltar.

....

Copies of accounts.

60 Picton Street,
Leek,
Staffordshire.

21st April 1919.

Dear Colonel.

　　　I received a latter from Purson this morning, and he tells me that you would like a written account of last years March show, so I will try to tell you as much as I know about it; I don't guarantee to spell the names of all the villages properly, but you will know them by pronunciation if by nothing else.

You are already aware of the Bn. dispositions and the kind of morning 21st March was, and as you know I was with Shute who was commanding C.Coy, with two platoons in Maisemey, and two platoons in Esselling Redoubt, with Redfern in command.

The bombardment opened out at 4.30 a.m. and went out to "stand to" and we got what ~~men we had got what~~ men we had in the trench just north of Headquarters, and the bombardment at (sic) gas continued till about 8.30 a.m. after that there was a lull, but at 9 a.m. the Boche started again with H.E. and kept it up till about 11.50 a.m. when the situation seemed to improve and get much quieter; up to this time we saw no-one come back, either had we heard of any rifle fire, but about 12 o'clock machine-gun bullets found us, coming from direction of Vadencourt Chateau; we took up a position in Maisemey and enemy infantry came in contract with us, and we hung on till 12.30 p.m. when they attacked us from the front in over-whelming numbers.

Just a few men were now falling back on us, R.F.A., one or two of our D. Coy., and A. Coy, and two men of B. Coy.

/ Villecholles

Major Graves of the R.F.A. came along and took command of the line and gave orders for everyone to retire to the brown line just in front of ~~Villecholles~~, which we did a few at a time.

When I got back there I met Byno and we counted the remaining men of the battalion up and collected them together, and there were 22 men, 3 officers; Shute, Byno, and Myself.

The Boche did not drive us back that day any further, and at 2 o'clock on the morning 22nd March we were relieved, by 16 men of the 11th Hussars, and we went back to Vermand, and placed under the command of Colonel Winyon.

We stayed in Vermand till 10 o'clock and then were sent to Puilly to fight a rear guard action whilst the 24th Division went through the 30th Div. and then we followed last; we had no casualties this day.

After we left the 30th Div. to hold the line we were marched to Monchy - Lagache and the whole of the 24th Division was mustered and promised a rest, but two hours later the whole division had to reinforce again as the Boche was breaking through, but he was checked, and an organised retirement was arranged for 9 o'clock on the morning of the 23rd, and at the said time we marched in parties and crossed the Somme river at Licourt, fighting rear guard actions all the way, five or six lines in depth.

We stayed at Licourt the night and on the morning of the 24th the 8th Division relieved us and we went back to Chaulnes and stayed about five hours and after we marched forward again to Fonches where we stayed the night; up to this time enemy artillery had been very heavy but at Fonches just one or two 8-inch were all he had forward.

On the morning of the 25th we had to take up a position in front of Fonches, a village I do not know the name of, and here about 20 more men were sent to us, returned from leave etc., also the drums.

Everything was quiet up to 3 o'clock and then enemy machine guns troubled us and about 4 o'clock Bynu got one in the leg, and Cryer(?), the Adjt. to the Kents, got hit in the hand.

This day Hayward and Whiting joined us and the position was a critical one, for we had very few men and no rations, but we stuck to the position as we had been ordered not to retire further at any cost, and we fired rapid and bluffed the Boche a bit, and stopped him for the time being, and here we had about 6 men killed and 5 wounded.

We hung on till 2 o'clock on the morning of the 26th and then had orders to retire to the Hallu line which was about 8 miles, and we reached our destination at about 5 o'clock; here we had a good position, a good trench, and plenty of barbed wire, and we held on till 10 a.m. and then both flanks went, and Colonel Winyon ordered a retirement but the Surrey's C.O. was at Brigade and they would not go, so Major Clarke went back but he was taken prisoner; Captain Diamond had started back but hearing of Major Clarke's fate, went back, but could do no good so was taken as well, and we went back to Warvillers and stayed there the night in billets, the first billet we had since the show started.

On the morning of the 27th March we had orders to take up a position in an advanced post between Warvillers and Rouvroy, which we did about 1 p.m.; it was very quiet then but about 3 o'clock we were fired on from Rouvroy and Whiting was killed, Sergt. Cooper mortally wounded, and several others wounded about the same time, then Hayward was sniped and as we had no-one on either flank and thought the wisest plan was to go back to the Kents, who were the main line of resistance 500 yards in rear, so this I did and we had about 12 men wounded in doing so, only one seriously; Whiting and Hayward were left unburied and no personal effects taken from them.

We stayed in the main line of resistance till 2 a.m. on the morning of the 27th March and then what few were left of us were taken to Warvillers and we rested till 10 a.m. in a dug-out, then the Boche had attacked again and was coming on very fast.

Purson had now joined us and we waited for the line to fall back and then we fought a rear guard action to the Quex/Quesnel Line which was about 5 miles away, and took up a commanding position there ~~until~~ about 2 p.m. the afternoon, but one hour later both flanks gave way and the remaining men of three divisions were nearly surrounded and we had orders to retire via Boucourt to Villers where we reached about 7 o'clock and rested in a barn until 9 p.m. and after that we marched to Castel and were commandeered by the Brigadier for piquet over the bridge, but Purson knows more about that than I do.

I think Purson has told you what happened after we reached Castel - I may add that I cannot say much of what happened after that till we entrained at Saleux for St. Valery; I certainly could not give in truth the movements of 29th, 30th, and 31st March, and the 1st, 2nd and 3rd April.

After landing at St. Valery we marched to St. Blimont where we stayed with the W. Kents for three(?) days and from there were allotted an area for reinforcements and reorganising at Nubas where, Colonel Hodson joined us along with officers who had been on leave, and after having 900 of a draft, we moved to Huclier.

The casualties on the first morning of the show we as near as possible as follows:-

```
Officers wounded.      4 (?)
    "    Prisoners.    6.
    "    Killed.       6.
```

and approximately 500 other ranks killed, wounded, and missing.

Hayward and Whiting were killed about 3 p.m. on the 27th.

Well I think I have given you as much information as I can now, you will have to /....(?) Parson's epistle where I've left off.

∧ (? join)

I may add that you will find a very good account of the Battn. movements about that time in the War Diary, for I helped Major Way to make it out after the show.

I hope this is the kind of report you wanted, it is not very elaborate, but if you re-write it I don't doubt you can make it look much better.

I trust you are still keeping well; personally I am A.1. and quite settled down to civilian life again. Give my kind regards to any officers with the battalion now, and same to yourself with the best of luck.

Yours etc.

(sgd) Arthur Peacocke.

....

THE RETIREMENT OF MARCH-APRIL 1918.

Events affecting the 1st Battn., North Staffordshire Regt. from 28th March - 7th April 1918.

....

28th March.

The Battn. (with 8th Bn. R. West Kent Regt.) withdrew from advanced posts near Rouvroy (about 10 km. S.W. of Chaulnes) and went into cellars ar Warvillers at 02.00 hours. The front of the 72nd Inf. Bde. was then held by the 15th and 19th Entrenching Battns. and was withdrawn before dawn to the eastern outskirts of Warvillers.

At 09.00 hours the enemy shelled the village with 4.2's and 77's, the bombardment lasting about an hour. About 09.30 the troops on both flanks were observed to be retiring and the village came under enfilade machine-gun fire.

28th March (cont'd.)

At 10.00 hours the outpost troops were withdrawn and the brigade commenced a general retirement to the Caix - Le Quesnel line (about 4 km. W. of Warvillers). The retirement was conducted in an orderly manner and the enemy, who was making steady progress on both flanks, advanced very cautiously opposite the Brigade front. During the retirement the brigade came under artillery and M.G. fire, the latter both from the ground and the air, but casualties were very light. A battery of 18-pdrs. located about 2 km. W. of Warvillers, retired and took up a position about 400 yards behind the Caix - Le Quesnel line. The brigade reached this line about 14.00 hours. It proved to be a strong line with a good field of fire and well wired. It was occupied by troops of the 72nd and 73rd Inf. Bdes., 103rd Field Coy., R.E., 12th Sherwood Foresters and various Composite companies of personnel from Reception Camps, leave trains, etc.

Men of the R.H.A., R.F.A. and Tank Corps were observed holding the line with the infantry.

Units having become somewhat mixed on reaching the Caix - Le Quesnel line, the 1st Battn. North Staffordshire Regt., (under 2/Lt. A. Peacock) came temporarily under the orders of Lt.-Col. Hain, commdg. the 7th Battn., Northamptonshire Regt.

The battery of 18-pdrs. previously mentioned gave a very fine display of shooting at almost point-blank range, the enemy being obviously uncomfortable and it was later ascertained from a prisoner that they suffered heavy casualties. An artillery officer and signaller stood in an exposed position observing the shoot and controlling the fire by means of visual signalling, excellent results being obtained. This splendid piece of work greatly impressed the infantry, especially as the guns were in a very exposed position, concealment being impossible. The enemy artillery was evidently not in position as this shoot drew no reply but later the line was shelled by an enemy field gun, no casualties being caused.

During the afternoon heavy fighting was taking place in the village of Le Quesnel (on our right) and it was evident from the Very lights sent up by the enemy's advanced troops that he was still making rapid progress on both flanks, though he made no attempt to attack the Caix - Le Quesnel line which was a good position strongly held. About 17.00 hours orders were received for the line to be evacuated. Troops of the 72nd and 73rd Inf. Bdes. received the following order:-

"Retire through the French lines to Villers-
"aux-Erables where lorries will meet you and convey
"you to Castel".

The order to abandon the line caused some disappointment as the troops were confident in their ability to hold up the enemy, but the withdrawal was rendered necessary by the enemy's encircling movement.

The route followed was via Beaucourt & Mezieres. The roads were very congested with retiring infantry and artillery. The battalion came under intermittent shell-fire and M.G. fire at long range but without suffering casualties.

28th March (cont'd).

At Beaucourt the troops of the West Kent's, North Staffords, and East Surrey's were collected together and marched to Villers - aux - Erables under the command of Lt.-Col. H.J.Winyon, D.S.O. On arrival at Villers the promised lorries did not appear and the troops of the brigade were given a 3 hours' rest in a barn.

During the withdrawal it became evident that the garrison of the Caix line had narrowly escaped being surrounded by the enemy who had nearly reached Mezieres when his advance ceased at dusk. The line was held by a small number of French infantry who had no organised positions but were supported by some batteries of 75's as well as British artillery.

About 22.00 hours the 72nd Bde. left Villers under the command of Br.-General R.W.Morgan, DSO., and marched across country to Castel, a distance of about 9 kilometres. Finally the Brigade Transport Lines were reached about 01.00 hours on the 29th. These were situated at the Western end of the Bois de Senecat (about 3 km. W. of Castel.) A hot meal was served, which was very welcome to the troops after a tiring day.

29th March.

A party of 27 men of the Battalion under 2/Lieut. Peirson, was detailed by General Morgan to proceed to Castel and take up two posts covering the crossings of the river Avre; sentries were in position at 03.45 hours and the remainder of the men were billetted in a barn near by. At 12.00 hours orders were received for the posts to be withdrawn and for the party to rejoin at the transport lines. Castel was about 4 or 5 miles behind the line and was not under fire. Preparations were being made for the destruction of the bridge over the Avre in the event of a further enemy advance.

During the afternoon Lt.-Col. Winyon held a conference of officers of the West Kent's, North Stafford's, and East Surrey's. He informed us of the latest news of the general situation, which was still critical, the fall of Montdidier having just been reported. He also stated that the promised rest had been postponed and that in view of the seriousness of the situation, the 24th Division had been ordered to take up a reserve line covering Amiens. The remnants of the Brigade were then re-organised as one Battalion as follows:-

C.O.   Lt.-Col. H.J.Winyon, D.S.O.
Adjt. Lieut. G.S.Bowen.

A. Coy. R.W.Kent's	under	Lieut. Selfe.
C. " " "	"	Capt. S.G.Thompson.
North Stafford Coy.	"	2/Lieut. A. Peacock.
East Surrey Coy.	"	2/Lieut. Lefort.

The strength was then as follows:-

West Kent's.	7 officers	189	other ranks.
North Stafford's.	2 "	71	" "
East Surrey's.	2 "	90	" "

About 15.00 hours the Battn moved northward from Bois de Senecat via Hailles to Thezy and spent the night in a field near Thezy Station. The transport moved N.W. to Cottenchy.

30th March.

Shortly before dawn a position was taken up on the high ground to the N. of Thezy and posts were duly dug. About 12.00 hours the battalion was withdrawn and billetted in Thezy, which had been evacuated by the civilians. At this time the front line ran approximately from Hangard - Moreuil. Thezy being some 3 miles from the nearest points.

31st March.

The Battalion moved up to the posts at 04.00 hours and stood to till 09.00 hours when it was again withdrawn to billets in the village, one Coy. remaining in the posts. At about 15.00 hours the enemy commenced a general attack on the line Hangard - Moreuil and the battn. was called out of billets to 'stand to' in the posts. The enemy's attack was beaten off by the British and French. The battn. remained in the posts all night and was relieved at dawn on 1st April by the 15th Entrenching Battalion, under Lt.-Col. E.A.Cameron, D.S.O.

1st April.

The battalion spent a quiet day in billets in Thezy.

2nd April.

The battalion again spent the day in billets.

3rd April.

The battalion relieved the 19th Entrenching Battalion in the posts at dawn. An officer was sent forward to Domart- sur-la-Luce to ascertain the situation in the forward area. He discovered that the line was beingheld by the 29th French Division who had succeeded in holding up the enemy.

A large number of French batteries, chiefly of 75's, had been brought up and these did good work continually, and British 60-pdrs. also showed considerable activity.

Squadrons of British and French cavalry occasionally went forward and did good work in local actions.

4th April.

The battalion was relieved at dawn by the 24th Divl. Depot Battn., under the command of 2/Lieut. J.D.MacLaren. Orders were received to move to the S.W. corner of Bois L'Abbe (W. of Villers-Bretonneux). The march was carried out under heavy shelling with both H.E. and gas shells, the West Kent's suffering some casualties whilst passing through the village of Gentelles, but the North Stafford Coy. fortunately escaped loss. An enemy attack was in progress and there was considerable artillery activity all day. After spending about 4 hours in Bois L'Abbe in a heavy downpour of rain, the battn. moved to a wood about 1½ miles N.W. of Gentelles, where the night was spent in the open. During the evening the wood was bombed and machine-gunned by an aeroplane with British markings. No casualties occurred.

5th April.

At dawn the North Stafford Coy. moved out about 1 mile from the main position and dug posts near a small copse. After a short time orders were received to move to the Bois de Blangy, about ½ mile further north. During the day the back areas were harassed by enemy H.V. guns.

Orders were received that the Battalion would be relieved at dusk by troops of the 3rd Australian Division. This relief was carried out about 20.00 hours.

.. ..

72nd Brigade.

24th Division.

1st BATTALION

NORTH STAFFORDSHIRE REGIMENT

APRIL 1918

War Diary

Summary of Events

Date & Place	Summary of Events	Remarks
NIEBAS 9.4.18	Day spent by Companies in refitting – clothing etc. Capt. Q.D.B. Oxley took over duties of Adjutant.	
9.4.18	Lieut. Col. H.V.R. Hobson took over Command of the Battalion and the following officers joined from units as below: Lieut. A. Crew from 11th R. Warwicks. Regt. " C.J. Mansell " 3/5th " " " A.E. Jackson " 1/5th 2 James. Regt. " J.D. Menwick " " " " " J.H. Dostrell " " " " " H.J. Keble joined from 12th Royal Fusiliers took over duties as transport Officer Capt: C.N. Coad M.C. R.A.M.C. joined & took over duties of Medical Officer to the Battalion.	
10.4.18	"B" Coy took over billets in OCHANCOURT	
11.4.18	The commanding Officer made a recce of the respective Billet Areas.	
12.4.18	Lieut. D.C. Butterworth arrived, going from hospital & Convalescent Camp. Lieut. F. Pullan joined the Battalion. Lieut. H.J. Keble took H.T. strength joined M.T. depot at ABBEVILLE.	

War Diary

Summary of Events

NEBAS

13.4.18 — Day passed in having a General reorganisation. Commanding Officer took the Battalion on parade in afternoon.

14.4.18. — Battalion took part in Brigade Route march to AULT where it was intended to hold a Church service, the however was impossible owing to the inclemency of the weather, after a short stay in AULT the Battalion marched home arriving at NEBAS at 5pm

15.4.18 — Day spend in Battalion & Company training.

16.4.18. — Provisional orders regarding move of Division to 1st Army Area received. The Strength of the Bn this day was reduced to 900 of all ranks men.

17.4.18 — Left the Battalion at 10pm for Etaples.
At 3am the Battalion marched out of NEBAS to FEUQUIERES where it entrained after several hours waiting at 12.30pm 17th. travelling via ABBEVILLE, ETAPLES, ST.Pol. The Battalion arrived at BRIAS at 12 midnight marched to billets at B Coy at HUCLIER & C & D coys at VALHUON a distance of 14 kilos away. The Battalion was formed part of G.H.Q Reserve in that army. area. Bn. Hqrs. were in Huclier.

18.4.18 — Day spent in organising & preparation for training.

19.4.18 — Day spent in training, all leave guards fires, much was carried out on improvised basis at Huclier.

Remarks

War Diary

HUCLIER
20.4.18 — Day spent in Battalion & Company training in valley S.W. of HUCLIER. Lewis gun classes for teams & NCOs were commenced under Capt. Johnston, an instructors from the XIII Corps Lewis Gun School.

21.4.18 — The Battalion spent the day at PERNES. A full day's training was carried out from. was cooked to the Battalion reached home at about 6 p.m. 25 Officer reinforcements arrived under the charge of Capt. B. Morley, 2/Lts Kay were posted to Coys. A Subterranean class for officers without definite employment were formed. Lieut. W.P. Brigstone took over the duties of Signalling Officer, 2/Lieut. R.H. Blore took over duties of Lewis Gun Officer. Lieut. G.N. Adams took over command of "C" Coy. & 2/Lieut. A. Green became Asst. Adjutant. Lieut. G.F. Hannbrough went over as B.T.O. was temporarily in charge of the Bn. Transport, 2/Lieut. J.F. Pearson went on leave for a Course of Scouting & Sniping with Lieut. Shuck to Pernes. Proceeded the duties of Intelligence Officer.

22.4.18 — A Church Parade was held in the valley S.W. of Huclier. The Bn. had held since Brigade Parade in A.3.C. After Church Parade one Coys training was carried out. When a heat wait the afternoon when training was resumed.

23.4.18 — Day spent in training in valley S.W. of HUCLIER. Lieut. Shutt & 2/Lieut. Pearson returned from leave, the Infantry Course having been broken up at short notice.

24.4.18 — The Battalion spent the day at PERNES. A full day's training was carried out on the shooting ground of the Canadian Corps School. Range practice and firing from firing over cover at men were carried out. The Battalion arrived back in billets about 7 p.m.

WAR DIARY

Summary of Events

HULLIER

25.4.18 — The day was spent in training at HULLIER. Regimental Sports arranged for the afternoon were postponed for the following day owing to inclement weather. The band of the Garrison Arty Regt gave a few selections outside Bn. H.Q. Lieut. P.S.W. SHUTE, M.C. Arrived to Bn. from 3rd Bn. Headquarters as Brigade Intelligence Officer, & 2/Lieut. A.E. JACKSON was transferred to Bn. L.T.M. Battery.

26.4.18 — Training was carried out at HULLIER during the morning. During the afternoon Regimental Sports, which were held on the R. called S.W. of HULLIER, 15-swept being carried out with great success. The 24th Divisional Band was in attendance.

27.4.18 — Training was carried out by A & B Coys at HULLIER, & by C & D Coys the hands as PERNES. Special attention was paid to SECTION SCHEMES.

28.4.18 — Divine Service was arranged but owing to inclement weather had to be abandoned. Lieuts G.N. Lomax, E.R.C. Wood, S.E. Steeley opened the Bn. from England. Various units of the Battalion took part in the Brigade Rifle meeting at PERNES. No. 5 Platoon "B" Coy under 2/Lt. Denerell representing the Battalion in the inter platoon contest. Lt-Col. Hodson, Lt. G.H. Hussbotham, May Coy SSO Capt Peacock, Lt & Qm Elsegood, Sheuts Crawford & Sorater Kent, Q.N. Komas all shot-for the Battalion in various competitions both Revolver & Rifle.

No. 8 Section A. Company represented the Bn. in the inter section competition.

30.4.18 — Day spent in training. Provisional orders received for 24th Division to relieve 3rd Canadian Division.

W. Hodson Lieut. Col.
Comdg. 1st Bn North Staffordshire Regiment.

From March 31st to April 3rd the Brigade were in Reserve and units in rotation were either manning these positions or billetted in the town of THEZY. During the afternoon of the 31st a stand-to was ordered owing to heavy enemy attacks on the HANGARD- MOREUIL Front. A position was taken up 1 mile N.E. of THEZY and occupied during the night of 31st March/1st April, the battalion returning to billets in THEZY on the morning of the 1st.

On April 4th the Brigade moved to the BOIS DE BLANGY & BOIS L&ABBE in outpost positions where it remained till relieved by Australian troops on the night 5/6th April.

The troops were taken by motor lorry to SALEUX where the night was spent, entraining on the afternoon of 6th for ST. BLIMONT, moving the Seaforths marched to ST. VALERY, where the following day (8th April) to NIBAS. Here the work of re-organising the battalion was begun.

Operation Order No 1.
1st North Staffordshire Regt.

1. The Bn less "B" Coy will parade on "A" Coy's parade ground in full marching order with blankets at 3. a.m. 17th inst.

   "B" Coy will parade at 4.15 p.m. 16th inst with Cooker & march to FEUQUIERES reporting on arrival to the R.T.O for entrainment duty.

2. The Bn will entrain at FEUQUIERES as under
   - Bn. H.Q
   - A. Coy
   - C. "   } At 4/30 a.m. 17th inst.
   - D. "

   Transport less B. Cooker & Team 3. a.m. 17th inst.
   "B" Coy with Cooker & Team 10.30 a.m. 17th inst.

3. (a) H.Q Officers' kits ck — Ord Room material — will be stacked at Bn H.Q.ors by 10 p.m. 16th inst
   (b) Coy Officers Kits less those of "B" Coy will be stacked outside Officers Mess by 10 p.m. 16th inst.
   (c) All Lewis Guns, Magazines & Officers Kits of "B" Coy will be collected before 4 p.m. 16th inst.
   Transport Officer will arrange to collect the whole

4. The Q.M will issue Rations for 17th inst which will be cooked & issued to men before 6 p.m. 16th inst.
   O.C. B. Coy will draw Rations for 17th & cook same under Coy arrangements.

5. O.C. Coys are held responsible for the cleanliness of their billets on quitting them.

6. (a) O.C. Coys & T.O. will render to O.R. by 5 p.m. 16th final marching out state
   (b) T.O. will obtain from Orderly Room Bath marching out state & hand same to R.T.O. FEUQUIERES on arrival there

7. Acknowledge.

Issued at 12 Noon.

16/4/18.

(Sgd) E.D.B. Oxley Capt & A/Adjt.
1st Nth Staffordshire Regt.

Copies to
No 1 C.O
2 O.C. A Coy
3 O.C. B "
4 O.C. C "
5 O.C. D "
6 T.O
7 Q.M
8 R.S.M.
9 File
10 War diary

WAR DIARY

1st Bn. North Staffordshire Regt.

Month of May 1918.

W. Norton LIEUT.-COLONEL,
CMDG. 1st NORTH STAFFORDSHIRE REGT.

WAR DIARY or INTELLIGENCE SUMMARY

Army Form C. 2118.

1st Battn. North Staffordshire Regiment

Place	Date	Hour	Summary of Events and Information	Remarks and references to Appendices
	1918 May 1st		Battalion marched from HUCLIER to LES BREBIS. Billeted for the night at LES BREBIS.	1348.
	2nd		Battn. took over front line positions from the 58th Bn. Canadian Troops in the ST EMILE Sector, North of LENS. A certain proportion of officers and other Ranks remained with the Transport at FOSSE 10 (SAINS EN GOHELLE) under the command of Major G.O. Way DSO. Lieut. D.C. Butterworth assumes duties of Adjutant vice Capt. E.D.B. Oxley, attached to Brigade as "G" Learner this date. 2nd Lieut. E.T. Pearson assumes duties of Asst. Adjt. from this date.	1348.
	3rd 4th		Training of troops taken in hand at FOSSE 10. "Riding class for Officers started by Major G.O. Way, D.S.O.	1348.
	5th	11.15 a.m.	Divine Service at Church Army Hut, FOSSE 10. Battalion relieves the 8th West Kent Regiment, returning to Support line at CITE ST. PIERRE. The 9th East Surrey Regiment holds the front line, and the 8th West Kent get into Reserve at BULLY GRENAY.	1348.
	6th		Nothing of interest to report	1348.
	7th		Lieut. E.M.W. Higginbotham proceeded to G.H.Q. Lewis Gun School on a Lewis Gun Course.	1348.
	8th		Battalion takes over front line positions from 9th East Surrey Regt. Support line handed over by us to 8th West Kent Regt. Major G.O. Way DSO takes command of the Battalion in the line. Lieut. Alcock Hollom appe. Batts. to Transport lines. Special precautions taken by the Battalion.	O.O. 310 to atta'd list 1348.
	Night of 9th/10th		Enemy attack repulsed. Battalion attacks in all night. But attack does not materialise.	1348.
	10th 11th		Two platoons of "B" Company affected by gas from Lewsy gas shell bombardment this morning. The whole of No 6 Platoon and a number of men from No 6 Platoon had to be evacuated to C.C.S. Most of these casualties have proved fatal. Three officers viz., Lieut. Catt, 2/Lt Mackend, and 2/Lt. Kennedy, all of B Company, were also affected by gas, and had to leave the line.	1348.
	12th		Lieut G.M. Lomax assumes duties of Transport Officer from this date.	1348.

Army Form C. 2118.

WAR DIARY
or
INTELLIGENCE SUMMARY.

(Erase heading not required.)

1st Battalion
North Staffordshire Regiment

Instructions regarding War Diaries and Intelligence Summaries are contained in F. S. Regs., Part II. and the Staff Manual respectively. Title pages will be prepared in manuscript.

Place	Date	Hour	Summary of Events and Information	Remarks and references to Appendices
	1918 May 13th		Nothing of interest to report	
	14th		2nd Lieut W.R Goodwin takes over the duties of Intelligence Officer from this date. Two deserters from the German lines (131st Regt, 42nd Divn.) were brought in.	
	15th		Enemy attempted a raid on our Left Company front (near MASON'S HOUSE) which was repulsed. There were no casualties.	
	16th		Battn. came back into Brigade Reserve at BULLY GRENAY, being relieved by the 9th East Surrey Regiment.	O.O. No 25 attached
	17th		Time spent in cleaning up equipment etc. and resting.	
	18th		Training resumed. All rifles and Lewis guns inspected by Armourer Sergeant. Each man in future to fire 5 rounds per day	
	19th		Church Parade. Address in the afternoon to all officers by Brig General R.W.Morgan, D.S.O.	
	20th		Nothing of interest to report.	
	21st		Battalion Sports, everyone very keen and weather perfect. The Divisional Band in front	
	22nd		Battalion up into Support at CITÉ ST PIERRE, relieving the 8th West Kent Regt, who go to front line position.	O.O. No 6 attached
	23rd		Quiet day. Nothing of interest to report.	
	24th			
	25th		Promotion to Acting Captain of Lieut D.C. Butterworth (Adjutant) and of Lieut Q.M. Lemon (Transport Officer) is announced.	
	26th		Nothing of interest to report	
	27th		Nothing of interest to report.	
	28th		Battalion moves up to front line, relieving West Kent Regt.	O.O. No 3 attached
	29th		2/Lieut N.C. Kidwell (casualty owing to gas) to England and struck off strength of Battalion. 25/5/18.	
	30th		Left front heavily bombarded early this morning, but no casualties.	
	31st		Into Company Relief	

W. Hodson
Lieut Colonel
Commanding 1st North Staffordshire Regt.

SECRET.   COPY No. 8

OPERATION ORDER No. 4.

1st. Bn. North Staffordshire Regiment.

Ref. Map 36 c S.W.1.

1. The Battalion will relieve the 9th. Bn. East Surrey Regt. in the Line on the night of the 8th./9th. inst.

2. ORDER of RELIEF.

   "A" Coy. 1st. North Staffords will relieve "B" Coy. 9th. East Surrey Rgt.
   "B"   "   "   "   "   "   "   "C" "   "   "   "   "
   "C"   "   "   "   "   "   "   "D" "   "   "   "   "
   "D"   "   "   "   "   "   "   "A" "   "   "   "   "

3. ADVANCE PARTIES.

   Advance parties consisting of one Officer per Coy. and one NCO. per platoon will report to respective Coy. Hd.Qrs. of the 9th. East Surrey Regt. by 2.30 p.m. The Intelligence Officer, Sergt Lappage, Sergt. Tunstall, Sergt. Rutter and Headquarters Scouts will report to Battn. Hd.Qrs., 9th. East Surrey Regt at 2.30 p.m. Sergt. Tunstall will take over all Stores etc. at Battn. Hd. Qrs.

4. GUIDES.

   Guides consisting of 1 per Coy. Hd. Qrs. and 1 per Platoon will be provided by the 9th. East Surrey Regt as follows:-
   Guide for "D" Coy. 1st.N.Staffs. will be at Junction N.7.c.0290 at 9.15 pm.
     "   " "A" Coy.   "   "   "   " "   "A" Coy. Hd.Qrs. at 9.15 pm.
     "   " "B" Coy.   "   "   "   " "   "B" Coy. "   "   " "   "
     "   " "C" Coy.   "   "   "   " xxxx&xx will be "arranged" between O.C. Coys. concerned.

5. RATIONS.

   Companies will take over Ration and Water arrangements from Coys. they relieve.

6. CERTIFICATES.
   Handing over certificates will be handed over to O.R. by 9.0 a.m. 9th. inst.
   Certificates to the effect that all billets have been left clean to be rendered with the above.

7. O.C. Coys. will notify completion of relief by wiring word "BRONCHO"

8. ACKNOWLEDGE.

   Issued at 9.0 p.m. Date 7/5/18.

   COPIES to 1. C.O.
              2. O.C., 9th. Bn. East Surrey Rgt.
              3. O.C. "A" Coy.
              4. O.C. "B" Coy.
              5. O.C. "C" Coy.
              6. O.C. "D" Coy.
              7. Quartermaster.
              8. War Diary.

                                              J.C.Butterworth.
                                              Lieut. & A/Adjt.
                                         1st. North Staffordshire Regt.

S E C R E T.   COPY No. 2

OPERATION ORDER No. 5.
1st. Bn. North Staffordshire Regt.

Ref. LENS 36 c. S.W.1.

1. **GENERAL.**

   The Battalion will be relieved on the night of the 16/17th. inst. by the 9th. East Surrey Regt.

2. **ORDER OF RELIEF.**

   "A" Coy. 1st. North Staffs. Regt. will be relieved by "C" Coy. 9th. East Surrey Regt.
   "B" Coy.   "   "   "   "   "   "   "   "B"   "   "
   "C" Coy.   "   "   "   "   "   "   "   "D"   "   "
   "D" Coy.   "   "   "   "   "   "   "   "A"   "   "

3. **DISPOSITION.**

   On relief the Battalion will proceed into reserve.
   Headquarters "A", "B", and "C" Coys. at BULLY GRENAY and "D" Coy. at CITE CALONNE.

4. **ADVANCE PARTIES.**

   Will consist of 1 Officer, and 1 N.C.O. per Coy. and 1 N.C.O. per platoon who will proceed in parties of 3 only leaving Coy. Hd.Qrs at 9 a.m. 16th. inst. They will take over billets and Battle Positions of opposite Coys. of Reserve Battn. The Quarter Masters will arrange for the taking over of Bn. Hd. Qrs. personnel.

5. **GUIDES.**

   Will be arranged between Coy. Commanders concerned.

6. **TRANSPORT.**

   The Transport Officer will arrange for Coy. limbers to meet their respective Coys. at Junction of CHURCH STREET and BETHUNE ROAD (M.12.b. 03.70.) at about 11.30 p.m. 16th., Maltese cart and one limber will meet Hd. Qrs. personnel at this point at 10.30 p.m.
   Lewis Guns, magazines, Officers' Trench Kits, Mess utensils etc will be loaded and limber will proceed to reserve billets with respective units.

7. **HANDING OVER.**

   O.C. Coys. will hand over all Battle Positions to relieving Companies.
   Handing over certificates will be rendered to O.R. by 2.0 p.m. on 17/5/18.

8. O.C. Companies will report completion of relief by wiring Coy. Commanders name only, also their arrival in reserve billets by word " IN."

9. **ACKNOWLEDGE.**

   Issued on 15/5/18

   COPIES to:-   1. C.O.   2. War Diary
                    3. O.C. 9th. E.Surrey Regt.   4. Transport Officer
                    5. O.C. 8th.R.W.Kent Regt. 6. Quartermaster.
                    7. O.C., "A" Coy.   8. O.C. "B" Coy.
                    9. O.C., "C" Coy.   10. O.C. "D" Coy.

                                                            A.C.Butterworth
                                                             Lieut. & A/Adjt.
                                             1st. Bn. North Staffordshire Regt.

S E C R E T.

OPERATION ORDER No. 6 by
Lieut. Colonel H.V.R.Hodson, Commanding 1st.Bn. North Staffordshire Regiment.

Ref. LENS.36 c S.W.1   1/10,000

1. **GENERAL.** The Battalion will relieve the 8th. Bn. Royal West Kent Regt. in Support on the night of the 22nd./23rd. inst.

2. **ORDER OF RELIEF.** "A" Coy. 1st. Bn.N.Staffs.Regt will relieve "A" Coy 8th. Bn. R.W.Kent Rgt.
   "B" "   "   "   "   "   "   "   "   "B" Coy.   "   "
   "C" "   "   "   "   "   "   "   "   "C" Coy.   "   "
   "D" "   "   "   "   "   "   "   "   "D" Coy.   "   "

3. **ADVANCE PARTIES.** Advance parties consisting of 1 Officer per company, and 1 N.C.O. per Platoon will report to Bn. Hd.Qrs., 8th. Bn. R.W. Kent Rgt. at 2.0 p.m.
   Advance party from Bn. Hd.Qrs. will consist of the Intelligence Officer, Sergt. Tunstall and 1 Signaller. The above parties will proceed in batches of 3 at 200 yards interval. Advance parties will take over all Water and Ration arrangements.

4. **ORDER OF MARCH** "A", "B" and "C" Coys. will move in above order, Platoons at 200 yards interval. First Platoon of "A" Coy. will not pass Fosse 11 (M.8.d.) before 9.45 p.m.
   "D" Coy. will move independenaly from CITE CALONNE leaving at 9.45 p.m. by "S" Track.

5. **TRANSPORT.** All Lewis Guns, Magazines, Officer's Trench kits, cooking utensils etc. will be loaded on Coy. limbers which will march with their respective Coys. as far as Church CITE ST.PIERRE (M.11.d.) One limber and Maltese Cart will be at Bn. Hd.Qrs. at 9.15 p.m. to carry H.Q. Trench goods. "D" Coy. limber will be at "D" Coy. H.Q. at 9.30 p.m.

6. **DRESS.** Fighting Order for all ranks. Box Respirators in "Alert" position.

7. **RELIEF.** Companies will wire completion of relief by using word "HIGGY"

8. ACKNOWLEDGE.

Issued 22nd. May, 1918.

COPIES to :- 1. C.O.
2. War Diary
3. O.C. "A" Coy.
4. O.C. "B" Coy.
5. O.C. "C" Coy.
6. O.C. "D" Coy.
7. Q.M.
8. Transport Officer.
9. O.C. 8th. Bn. R.W.Kent Regt.

(Sd) D.C. Butterworth. Lieut. & A/Adjt.
for Lieut. Colonel.
Commdg. 1st. Bn. North Staffordshire Regiment.

SECRET.   Copy No. 7?

Operation Order No. 8. B.

Lieut. & Col. H. V. R. Hodson,

Comdg. 1st. Bn. North Staffordshire Regt.

GENERAL.

(1). The Battalion will relieve the 8th. Bn. Royal West Kent Regt. in the line on night of 28/29th May 1918.

(2). ORDER OF RELIEF.

'A' Coy 1st. Bn. N. Staffords will relieve 'C' Coy. 8th. R.W. Kents.
'B' '   '   '   '   '   '   '   'D' '   '   '   '
'C' '   '   '   '   '   '   '   'A' '   '   '   '
'D' '   '   '   '   '   '   '   'B' '   '   '   '

ADVANCE PARTIES.

(3). Usual advance parties will proceed to respective companies of 8th. Bn. R.W. Kents at 2 p.m. 28th inst.

GUIDES.

(4). Guides where necessary will be arranged by O.C. Coys. concerned.

TIMES OF RELIEF.

(5). Times for commencement of relief will be arranged by O.C. Coys. concerned but no relief will commence before 10 p.m.

HANDING OVER.

(6). O.C. Coys. will take over all trench stores, maps etc., together with Battle positions. Above as far as positions in Support are concerned will be handed over to advance parties of 9th. Bn. E. Surrey Regt. Usual handing over certificates will be rendered to Bn. Hd. Qrs. by noon 29th inst.

(7). Completion of relief will be notified by wiring word 'SHARPEY'.

(8). Acknowledge.

                                                ACButterworth
                                            Captain & Adjutant.
                                    1st. Bn. North Staffordshire Regiment.

Copies to:-
    (1). C. O.   (2). 2nd. in Command.
    (3). O.C. 8th.Bn.R.W.Kent Regt.   (4). O.C. 'A' Coy.
    (5). O.C. 'B' Coy.   (6). O.C. 'C' Coy.
    (7). O.C. 'D' Coy.   (8) & (9) War Diary.
    (10). O.C. 9th. E. Surrey Regt.

        Issued at 10 a.m. 28-5-18.

WAR DIARY

1st to 30th June 1918.

1st Bn. North Staffordshire Regt.

WAR DIARY or INTELLIGENCE SUMMARY

Army Form C. 2118.

1st Battn., North Staffordshire Regiment

Place	Date	Hour	Summary of Events and Information	Remarks and references to Appendices
	1918 June 1st		Battalion in the front line. Quiet day.	
	2nd		A raid was carried out by 2/Lt Harper, one Platoon, and 4 R.E. officers who entered the enemy lines at 12.0 midnight. A few barrage had been arranged which was very efficient and was in full swing when our troops went over. An enemy machine gun opened fire on the raiding party. No M.G. was found, but on the arrival of the raiders the gun was back silenced their effort one. The Machine Gun was captured, and two dug-outs were destroyed. None of the enemy were encountered in the section of trench entered, and our party retired without having sustained any casualties.	
	3rd		Battalion goes back into reserve at BULLY GRENAY, being relieved by the 7th East Surrey Regiment.	O.O. No.9 attached
	4th		Day devoted to cleaning up equipment, arms etc. No parades.	
	5th		Lieut. S. Mrs Hippisthorn appointed Acting Captain from this date — Authority: 24 Div. A.90/2391 dated 5/6/18.	
	6th		Band of 1st N. Middlesex Regt. plays in front of Battalion Headquarters.	
	7th		All Officers and NCO's attend a Lecture on "Liaison between R.A.F. and Infantry" by an officer of the R.A.F. at The Cinema, LES BREBIS.	
	8th		Lieut. Shute, Brigade Intelligence Officer lectures to the officers of the Battalion on "Scouting and Observation Duties". The Battalion Scouts were present. The Band of the 13th Middlesex was in attendance.	
	9th		A. P.T. and Bayonet Fighting Competition was arranged. The Band of the 13th Middlesex was in attendance.	
	10th		Battalion relieves 8th West Kent Regiment in support at CITE ST PIERRE. Capt. Renner "A" Company the Camp, & Divisional Reception Camp. Lieut N.M.Taft arrives at Don Reserve Camp and posted to "C" Company. O.O. No. 10 attached	
	11th		Nothing of interest to report.	
	12th		Captain S.N.W. Hippisthorn wounded and evacuated as casualty.	
	13th		Quiet day.	
			—do—	

WAR DIARY or INTELLIGENCE SUMMARY

Army Form C. 2118.

Place	Date	Hour	Summary of Events and Information	Remarks and references to Appendices
	June 14th		Battalion relieved 8th West Kent Regt. in front line. Relief passed off without incident.	O.O. No.11 attached
	15th		35 O.R. became casualties owing to Ryenne	W.D.
	16th		18 O.R. —do—	W.D.
	17th		35 O.R. —do—	W.D.
	18th		Capt. G.G.T. Roman, 2/Lt. [?] Harper, 2/Lt. R.B. Hughes and 31 O.R. down with Pyrexia.	W.D.
	19th		Lt. E.B.Q. Wood, 2/Lt. W.P. Bridgett, 2/Lt. Hemingham and 30 O.R.	W.D.
	20th		On this date an enemy trench mortar bombardment by 2/Lt. Pullam. No engagement in sector gained. On the return of the Raiding Party to our lines 2/Lt. Pullam was killed by a bomb, and unfortunately RQMS, CSM Liddle being slightly wounded went 1/Lt Clarke affected. 2nd L. TRH was not the casualty. 2/Lt. W.R. Goulburn, 2/Lt. H.L. Buckley and 16 O.R. down with Pyrexia. Battalion came into reserve at BULLY GRENAY, being relieved by 9 East Surrey Regt.	O.O. No.13 attached W.D.
	21st		Major Way D.S.O. and Capt. Buttonworth (Adjutant) sick in billet. 20 O.R. down with Pyrexia.	W.D.
	22nd		2/Lt. Warburton gone on leave to England. 11 O.R. down with Pyrexia	W.D.
	23rd		1 Case of Pyrexia	W.D.
	24th		Lt. M.M.T.P., 2/Lt. E.C. Haley and 8 O.R. Pyrexia cases.	W.D.
	25th		2 Cases of Pyrexia	W.D.
	26th		Major Way D.S.O. gone on leave to England. Battalion sent up supports at CITE ST.PIERRE, relieving Royal West Kent.	W.D. O.O. No.14 attached
	27th		4 Cases of Pyrexia	W.D.
	28th		1 Case of Pyrexia	W.D.
	29th		—do—	W.D.
	30th		2nd Lt. Harper "A" Company, evacuated to Military Cas. Total number of casualties through Pyrexia during the month: 10 Officers, 229 O.R.	W.D.

Commanding 1st Bn. North Staffordshire Regiment

SECRET.   COPY No.........   2

OPERATION ORDER No. 9 by
Lieut. Colonel E.V.R. Hodson.
Commanding, 1st. Battalion, North Staffordshire Regiment.

Ref. LENS 36 c. S.W.1.

1. **GENERAL.** The Battalion will be relieved in the Front Line on the night of the 3rd./4th. June by the 9th. Battn. East Surrey Regt. On relief the Battalion, less "C" Coy. who will proceed to CITE CALONNE, will proceed to reserve billets at BULLY GRENAY.

2. **ORDER OF RELIEF.**
   "A" Coy. 1st. North Staffs. will be relieved by "C" Coy. 9th. Battn. E. Surrey Regt.
   "B" Coy.   "   "   "   by "B" Coy   "
   "C" Coy.   "   "   "   by "A" Coy   "
   "D" Coy.   "   "   "   by "D" Coy. "

3. **ADVANCE PARTIES.**
   The usual advance parties will proceed to take over reserve billets leaving the Line at 10.30 a.m. They will proceed in parties of not more than 2 at 200 yards interval.

4. **GUIDES.** Will be arranged by O's C. Coys. concerned. Time of commencement of relief will be 10.0 p.m.

5. **TRANSPORT.** Coy. limbers, Maltese carts, and Headquarters limbers will be at the junction of CHURCH STREET and BETHUNE ROAD - (M.12.b.02.70 by 11.30 p.m. approximately. Lewis Guns, magazines, Trench bundles etc. will be loaded here and limbers will proceed with their respective units to reserve billets.

6. **HANDING OVER.**
   All Trench Stores etc. will be carefully handed over - Battle Positions carefully explained and counter attack routes.

7. O.C. Companies will report relief complete by wiring the word "EVA" and their arrival in reserve billets by runner.

8. ACKNOWLEDGE.

   ISSUED at   2nd. June, 1918.

   COPIES to :-   1. C.O.
                   2/3 War Diary.
                   4. O.C., 9th. Bn. East Surrey Regt.
                   5. O.C., 8th. Bn. R.W. Kent Regt.
                   6. O.C., "A" Coy.
                   7. O.C., "B" Coy.
                   8. OC., "C" Coy.
                   9. O.C., "D" Coy.
                  10. Transport Officer.
                  11. Quartermaster.

                                            Capt. & A/Adjt.
                                            for Lieut. Colonel.
                                Commdg. 1st. Battn. North Staffordshire Regt.

SECRET.   Copy No. 2

OPERATION ORDER No. 10
By Lieut. Colonel H.V.R.Hodson, Comdg. 1st. Bn. North Staffordshire
Regiment.

Ref. MAP 44. S.W.

1. GENERAL.   The Bn. will relieve the 8th. Bn. Royal West Kent
                   Regt. in Support on the night of 9/10th. June.

2. ORDER OF   "A" Coy. — Lt. H.Smith —— will relieve "D" Coy. 8th. ...
   RELIEF.   R.W.K. Coy.
                   "B"   "   "   "   "   "D" "
                   "C"   "   "   "   "   "C" "
                   "D"   "   "   "   "   "A" "

3. ADVANCE   The usual advance parties will report to Bn. Hq. Coy.,
   PARTIES.   8th. Bn. Royal West Kent Regt. by 5.0 p.m. They will
                   proceed in parties of 2 at 200 yards interval to POST 11
                   and will use Trac. NORTH of POST 16 to Brigade Hq. Bde.,
                   thence proceeding by the usual Route.

4. GUIDES.   Guides, if required will be found from Advance Parties.

5. ORDER OF   "A", "B" and "D" Coys. will move in above order, Platoons
   MARCH.   at 200 yards interval. First platoon of "A" will not pass
                   POST 17 (Bds.) before 10 p.m.
                   "C" Coy. will move independently via "B" Track.
                   No personnel of "C" Coy. other than Advance Parties and
                   personnel for Divisional XXXX Reception Camp will leave
                   CITE GALONNE before 10.15 p.m.

6. TRANSPORT.   All L.vis Guns, Magazines etc. of "A", "B" and "D" Coys.
                   will be loaded on Limbers in B. Sgt. Mjrs. "D" Coy. Billets
                   Limbers will be collected by respective Coys. at Eng. de
                   Church, CITE ST-PIERRE.
                   Hollowa Coy. and the Limber will collect Bomb. Grenade
                   Bombs at 9.30 p.m. All pick, axe & packs etc. of personnel
                   proceeding to Divisional Reception Camp will be stacked at
                   Bn. Hq. at 5.0 p.m.
                   Transport Officer will arrange for transport.
                   All Officer's kits, mess packs etc. of "A", "B" and "D"
                   Coys. plus Bn. Hq. & Guides, to be sent to Transport, will be
                   stacked outside Bn. Hq. Orp. by 8.30 p.m.
                   Transport Officer will arrange for transport
                   All kits of "C" Coy. for trans. it. will be collected by
                   Transport Officer at 11.15 p.m.

7. DETAILS.   All personnel for Divisional Reception Camp will parade
                   under Captain C.W.Simpson, M.C. at Bn. Hq. Orp. 4.30 p.m.

                                                                     H.T.S.

Operation Orders (continued)

8. HANDING OVER — All practice wiring material, fatigues, tools etc, will be carefully handed over.

9. Companies will wire arrival in Support billets by the word "LADDIE"

10. ACKNOWLEDGE

Issued at 6.0 p.m. 8th. June, 1918.

ACButterworth
Captain & A/Adjt.
1st. North Staffordshire Regiment.

COPIES to :—
1. C.O.
2.) War Diary.
3.)
4. O.C. 8th. Bn. Royal West Kent Rgt.
5. T.O.
6. O.C. "A" Coy.
7. O.C. "B" Coy.
8. O.C. "C" Coy.
9. O.C. "D" Coy.

SECRET   Copy No. .....2.....

OPERATION ORDER NO. II.
BY LIEUT. COL. H.V.R. HODSON
COMMANDING 1ST. BATTALION NORTH STAFFORDSHIRE REGIMENT.

1. **GENERAL**

    The Battalion will relieve the 8th. Bn. Royal West Kent Regt. in the line on night of 14/15th. inst. Relief will commence at 10.15p.m.

2. **ORDER OF RELIEF.**

    "A" Coy. 1st. Bn. N. Staffords. will relieve "D" Coy. 8th. Bn. R. W. Kent Regt.
    "B" "   —   —   —   —   —   —   "C" "   —   —   —
    "C" "   —   —   —   —   —   —   "A" "   —   —   —
    "D" "   —   —   —   —   —   —   "B" "   —   —   —

3. **ADVANCE PARTIES.**

    Will leave support billets at 5.0p.m. They will use Trench Routes invariably.

4. **GUIDES.**

    Will be arranged by O's. C. Coys. concerned.

5.   Usual certificates will be rendered to Battn. Hd. Qrs. at usual times.

6.   Completion of relief will be notified by wiring word "MAC"

7.   Acknowledge.

    Issued at.. 11-20am 14-6-18

                                      (Sgd.) D.C. Butterworth, Captain & A/Adjt.
                                        1st. Battalion North Staffordshire Regiment.

Copies to:-
  1. C. O.   ✓2. War Diary.
  3. War Diary   4. O. C. 8th, Bn. Royal West Kent Rgt.
  5. O. C. "A" Coy.   6. O. C. "B" Coy.
  7. O. C. "C" Coy.   8. O. C. "D" Coy.
  9. Qr. Mr.

SECRET   Copy No. ...7...

OPERATION ORDER NO. 12.
BY LIEUT. COL. H. V. R. HODSON
COMMANDING 1ST. BATTALION NORTH STAFFORDSHIRE REGIMENT.

1. A Raid will be carried out by "B" Coy 1st. Bn. North Staffordshire Regt. on the enemy trenches from N.14.b.1.7. to N.14.b 35.90. on the night of 15/16th. June 1918.
   O.C. Raid Captain R.W. Sharp.
   The Raid will be a silent one unless the Officer in Command of the Raiding Party requires Artillery support, in which case he will fire a single Green Very Light, on the Signal being given the O.C. 107 Bde. R.F.A. will give the Artillery support as arranged in Attached Artillery programme.

2. The object of the Raid is to capture prisoners and destroy enemy dug-outs. The Raiding Party after having entered the enemy trenches, should not withdraw till they have secured prisoners and indentification.

3. The Raiding Party will consist of 1 Officer, 1 Platoon 1 Section ("B" Coy.) and 4 Sappers of 103rd. Coy. R. E. and will be devided into 5 Parties. i.e.
   Right Blocking Party.
   Left   "   "
   Conductor comminication trench Blocking Party.
   Clearing Party.
   Rear Party.

4. The Raiding Party will be assembled at N.8.c.65.05. by 11.15pm
   The Raiding Party will leave our trenches from this point at 11.30.p.m.

5. The Signal for withdrawal will be a Red Very Light fired low in the direction of the enemy support line.

6. Watches will be synchronised at Bn. Hd. Qrs. (~~COMMON~~ CAMERON CASTLE) N.7.c.00.70. by all units concerned at 8p.m. 15th. inst.

7. The O.C. Raid (Capt. R.W. Sharp.) will personally supervise the arrangements for the assembly of the Raiding Party, at the point of departure from our trenches and see that all necessary equipment and details for the above are complete.
   The Artillery F.O.O. will be with the O.C. Raid at N.8.c.65.05 to take action should artillery support be called for as arranged

8. The Medical Officer 1st. Bn. N. Staffird Regt. will make all necessary arrangements for the collection and evacuation of wounded.

9. Advanced ~~Command~~ Bn. Gd. Qrs. will be established at Left support Coy. H. Q. N.7.b.7.1. at 10.p.m. Messages will be sent up to 2.a.m.

Operation Orders Continued.

10. The following code will be used for the purpose of the Raid:-
  Raiders entered   BULL.
  Raiders returned   COW
  Prisoners captured   PIG
  Casualties   STAG.
  Green Very Light being sent up the Artillery F.O.O. would send word back "BARRAGE" upon which Artillery will carry out programme as arranged.

14/6/18.

H Hodson Lieut. Col.
Commanding 1st. Battalion North Staffordshire Regt.

Copies to.
1. C. O.   2. O.C. Raid.
3. 72nd. Infantry Brigade.   4. 107 Brigade R.F.A.
5. 103rd. Coy R. E.   6. 2/Lieut, F. Pullam,
7. War Diary   8. War Diary.

ORDERS IN CONTINUATION OF OPERATION ORDER NO. 12.

BY LIEUT COL. H. V. R. HODSON.

COMMANDING 1ST. BATTALION NORTH STAFFORDSHIRE REGIMENT

---

1. The Raiding Party under 2/Lieut. PULLAN will leave our trenches at N.8.c.65.05. at 11.30.p.m. and move along Conductor Sap to the enemy trenches at N.14.b.1.8.

2. The formation the Raiding Party will adopt as soon as clear of our wire will be 3 Sections abreast each in single file. i.e. Right Blocking Party. Conductor Communication Trench Blocking Party. Left Blocking Party. These will be followed by the Clearing Party, followed by the Rear Party.
   The O.C. Raiding Party will lead the advance across "No Mans Land" together with the attached R.E's. to destroy the wire if necessary with a Bangalore Torpedo.

3. Should the Raiding Party meet with strong opposition it is left to the discretion of the Officer I/C of Raiding Party to fire a single Green Very Light when Artillery support will be given as arranged.

4. On getting through the enemy wire the Right blocking party will form a block at N.14.b.05.65. the Left blocking party will work up to the left and form a block at N.14.b.2.95. the Conductor communication trench blocking party will work down Conductor Trench and form a block at N.14.b.2.6.
   The Clearing Party with attacged R.E's. will work up CINNABAR TRENCH as far as N.14.b.35.90. The Rear Party will remain at the point of entry and conduct any prisoners captured back to our trenches.

5. The Blocking Parties will be armed with Rifle and Bayonet, Bandolier (50rds. S.A.A.)
   Two men in each of these parties will carry a Bucket containing 6 MILLS Bombs and two pairs of strong Wire Cutters.
   The Clearing Party will be armed with Rifle and Bayonet, Pea Bombs. Rear Party Rifle and Bayonet and 50rds. S.A.A.

6. When the Signal for withdrawal is given the Clearing Party will withdraw first followed by Conductor communication trench party then Right and Left Blocking Parties lastly the Rear Party.

H Hodson Lieut. Col.
Commanding 1st. Battalion North Staffordshire Regt.

Copies to.
1. O.C.O.
2. 2/Lieut. Pullan
3. War Diary
4. War Diary.

SECRET   Ref. 44.A. S.W.I.   Copy No. 9

OPERATION ORDER NO. 13.

BY MAJOR G.C. WAY. D.S.O.

COMMANDING 1ST. BATTALION NORTH STAFFORDSHIRE REGIMENT.

1. GENERAL.

The Battalion will be relieved in the front line on night of 20/21st. June, by 9th. Battalion East Surrey Regt. On relief the Bn. less "B" Coy. will proceed into reserve billets at BULLY GRENAY. "B" Coy. will proceed to CITE CALONNE.

2. TRANSPORT.

All trench goods less Lewis Guns and Magazines of All Coy's. and Bn. Hd. Qrs. will be at COLONY DUMP by 10.45p.m. Companies will detail 1. N.C.O. and 2 men per Coy. to be responsible for loading and unloading of their respective goods on Light Railway. Trench goods of "B" Coy. will be unloaded at CITE CALONNE. Transport Officer will arrange for transport of goods of "A" "C" & "D" Coy's. from point of detrainment of goods of these Coy's. to their respective billets, he will also arrange for transport of Lewis Guns and Magazines of "A" "C" & "D" Coy's. from FOSSE 16 de LENS. to which point they will be carried by Companies.

3. ADVANCE PARTIES.

Usual advance parties will leave the line at 2p.m. and will travel in all cases by the trench routes.

4.   Completion of relief will be notified by wiring word "HOPPY" and Coy's will report their arrival in billets.

5.   Acknowledge.

Issued at. 3.30a.m.   20 - 6 - 18.

E.J.Rimson 2/Lt. for Captain & A/Adjt.
1st. Battalion North Staffordshire Regiment.

Copies to.

1. C. O.   2. 8th. Bn. Royal West Kent Regt.
3. 9th. Bn. East Surrey Regt.   4. T.O. & Tr. Mr.
5. O.C. "A" Coy.   6. O.C. "B" Coy.
7. O.C. "C" Coy.   8. O.C. "D" Coy.
9. & 10. War Diary.

S E C R E T.

Ref. Sheet 44a. S.W.1.

OPERATION ORDER No. 14 by,

Lieut. Col. H. V. R. HODSON,

Comdg. 1st. BN NORTH STAFFORDSHIRE REGIMENT.

(1). GENERAL.
ABattn. will relieve the 8th. Bn. Royal West Kent. Regt. in Support on night of 26th-27th inst.

(2). ORDER OF RELIEF.
Companies will relieve opposite Companies of 8th. Bn. Royal West Kents.

(3). ADVANCE PARTIES & GUIDES.
Usual advance parties will report at Bn. Hd. Qrs. 8th. Bn. R.W. Kents by 4.30 p.m., they will supply guides where necessary and will carefully take over all Battle positions. Trench routes will be used in all cases by these parties.

(4). ORDER OF MARCH.
Coys. will move in Alphabetical order - Platoons at 200 yds. interval, first Platoon "A" Coy. will not pass FOSSE 11 (M.8.d) before 10.15 p.m. "B" Coy. will proceed independently from CITE CALONNE but will not leave before 10.15 p.m.

(5). TRANSPORT.
(a). All goods for Transport of "A" "C" "D" Coys. and Bn. Hd Qrs. will be stacked outside various Hd. Qrs. by 2.30 p.m. Transport Officer will arrange transport.
(b). All goods for Trenches of "A" "C" "D" Coys. and Bn. Hd. Qrs. will be stacked outside various Hd. Qrs. by 7.0 p.m. Coys. & Bn. Hd. Qrs. will detail 1 N.C.O. and 2 men to remain with these goods during transmission to Support billets. These parties will be with goods at 7.0 p.m.
(c). Lewis Guns and Magazines of "A" "C" & "D" Coys. will be loaded on Coy. limbers by 9.30 p.m. These will proceed with Coys. as far as FOSSE 16 (M.10.c.)
(d). Transport for remainder of Bn. Hd. Qrs. material for transport will be at Bn. Hd. Qrs. by 9.0 p.m.
(e). Transport Officer will arrange for transport of "B" Coy's goods.

(6). Coys. will wire time of arrival in Support billets.

(7). Acknowledge.

Issued at Date. 25/6/18

(Sgd). D.C. Butterworth. Capt. & A/Adjt.
1st. Bn. North Staffordshire Regiment.

Copies to:-
(1). C. O. (2) O.C. 8th. Bn. Royal West Kents.
(3 & 4). War Diary. (5).Transport Offr. & Qr. Mr.
(6). O.C. "A" Coy. (7).O.C. "B" Coy.
(8). O.C. "C" Coy. (9).O.C. "D" Coy.

CONFIDENTIAL.

W A R   D I A R Y.

OF

1st Bn. NORTH STAFFORDSHIRE REGIMENT.

FROM JULY 1st TO JULY 31st.

1918.

1st North Staffordshire Regiment

Army Form C. 2118.

WAR DIARY
or
INTELLIGENCE SUMMARY.

July 1918

Place	Date	Hour	Summary of Events and Information	Remarks and references to Appendices
CITE ST. PIERRE	1918 July 1st		Battalion in support at CITE ST. PIERRE. Captain D.C. Butterworth to England on leave.	
Front Line	2nd		Captain W.D. Stewart M.C. arrives from England and takes over duties of Adjutant from this date. Battalion relieves 2nd Royal West Kent Regt. in front line positions	
"	3rd		Quiet day. Nothing of interest to report	
"	4th		Enemy artillery activity very pronounced	
"	5th		Nothing to report.	
"	6th		Intr. Company Relief. (C. Company relieved B in present zone)	
"	7th		Unusual enemy artillery activity. One of our Wiring Parties dispersed (1 Casn Officer from M.G. fire; 1 Killed, 3 wounded)	
BULLY GRENAY	8th		Battalion goes into Reserve at BULLY GRENAY, being relieved by 9th Bn. East Surrey Regt.	
"	9th		Resting, cleaning up, etc.	
"	10th		Training resumed	
"	11th		Training continues.	
"	12th		—do—	
"	13th		Battalion visited by Corps Commander (General Sir Aylmer Hunter Weston). Winning of Battle postponed out on a Test One.	
"	14th		Battalion relieves 8th Bn. Royal West Kent Regt. in support at CITE ST PIERRE	
CITE ST.PIERRE	15th		Quiet day	
"	16th		—do—	

1st Bn North Staffordshire Regiment

Army Form C. 2118.

WAR DIARY
or
INTELLIGENCE SUMMARY.
(Erase heading not required.)

July 1918 (continued)

Instructions regarding War Diaries and Intelligence Summaries are contained in F. S. Regs., Part II. and the Staff Manual respectively. Title pages will be prepared in manuscript.

Place	Date	Hour	Summary of Events and Information	Remarks and references to Appendices
CITE ST. PIERRE	1918 July 17th		Batt. O.i.n H.Q. moved from HODSON'S HOUSE to MORGAN MANSION (formerly Brigade H.Q.)	
"	18th		Quiet day	
"	19th		-do-	
"	20th		Battn. relieved 8th Royal Wt. Kent Regt. in front line positions. Lieut. E.R.G. Wood wounded in his quarters at 3 p.m. shot through the R lid with his own rifle, and rumours all pointed to the fact that he shot himself on purpose. (The matter is being investigated)	See OO No 19 attd
Front Line	21st		Quiet day	
"	22nd		A certain amount of artillery retaliation on our front, consequent on raids carried out by Divisions on our right	
"	23rd		Gas Projector attack made from our front (400 Projectors used)	
"	24th		Inter-Company Relief ("A" Company relieved "D" in forward zone)	See OO No 20 attd
"	25th		A Raiding party of the 9th East Surrey Regiment went over from our front. They captured a light machine gun	
"	26th		Battalion goes into Reserve at BULLY GRENAY, being relieved by 9th East Surrey Regiment	See OO No 21 attd
BULLY GRENAY	27th		Resting, cleaning up, etc.	
"	28th		Holiday. No working parties sent out, and no parades.	
"	29th		Battalion visited by Corps Commander.	
"	30th		Training carried on	
"	31st		-do-	

G.A. Trentham
for Lieut. Colonel
Commanding
(1st North Staffordshire Regiment)

SECRET.   COPY No. 9

OPERATION ORDERS No. 15 by
Lieut. Colonel H.V.R.Hudson, Commanding,
1st. Battalion North Staffordshire Regiment.

1. **GENERAL.** The Battalion will relieve the 8th. Bn. Royal West Kent Regt. in the line on the night of the 2/3rd. inst.
Relief will commence at 10.0 p.m. Support billets and Battle positions will be handed over to the 9th. Bn East Surrey Regt.

2. **DISPOS-ITIONS**
   "B" Coy. 1st.Bn.North Staffordshire Regt. in the Front Line.
   "A" Coy.   "   "   "   "   "   "   "BLACK LINE(Left)
   "C" Coy.   "   "   "   "   "   "   "BLACK LINE(Centre)
   "D" Coy.   "   "   "   "   "   "   "BLACK LINE(Right)

3. **ADVANCE PARTIES.** These will be constituted as usual. They will leave Support billets at 5.0 p.m. and use trench routes invariably. "B" Coy. will take over from "C" and "D" Coys. 8th. Bn. Royal West Kent Regt.(joint Coy. Hd.Qrs. N.7.b.62.07) ; "A" "C" and "D" Coys. will take over from their respective sectors from "A" and "B" Coys. 8th.Bn. Royal West Kent Regt.(joint Coy.Hd.Qrs N.12.d.65.95.)

4. O's C Coys. are responsible for the allotment of dug-out and cellar accommodation to their men in the new positions, and will make necessary arrangements for guiding them there.

5. The usual certificates (Trench Stores Returns etc) will be rendered at the usual times. A certificate stating that dug-outs, cellars etc have been left clean, and that sanitary arrangements were satisfactory (or otherwise) will be rendered at the same time as the other certificates.

6. Completion of relief will be notified by wiring the words "ZILLAH"

7. ACKNOWLEDGE.

ISSUED at 1.15 p.m.   DATED. 2nd. JULY 1918.

E.T.Beirson 2/Lt
& A/Adjt.
1st. Battn. North Staffordshire Regiment.

COPIES to :-
1. Commanding Officer.   6. O.C. "B" Coy.
2. O.C., 8th. R.West Kent Regt.   7. O.C. "C" Coy.
3. O.C., 9th. East Surrey Regt.   8. O.C. "D" Coy.
4. Quartermaster.   9.)
5. O.C., "A" Coy.   10.) War Diary.

SECRET.   Copy No. 8

1st. BATTALION NORTH STAFFORDSHIRE REGT.

OPERATION ORDER No. 16.

1. **GENERAL.** "C" Coy. will relieve "B" Coy. in the Front Line on the night of the 5/6th. inst.
   Relief will commence at dusk.
   On relief "B" Coy. will move back to the billets vacated by "C" Coy. in the BLACK LINE (Centre Company).

2. All arrangements XXXX regarding advance parties, guides, etc will be made by O.C. Coys. concerned.

3. Usual certificates and returns will be rendered at the usual times.

4. Completion of relief will be notified by wiring the word "CIPHER"; "B" Coy. will report arrival in Support billets by wire or runner using the word "ARTHUR".

5. ACKNOWLEDGE.

Issued at 3.30 p.m.   Dated 5th. July, 1918.

Copies to :-   1. Commanding Officer.
               2. O.C. "A" Coy.
               3. O.C. "B" Coy.
               4. O.C. "C" Coy.
               5. O.C. "D" Coy.
               6. O.C., 8th. Bn. Queen's Regt.
               7.)
               8.) War Diary.
               9. File.

                                    Capt. & Adjt.
                              1st. Bn. North Staffordshire Regiment.

SECRET.

Copy No. 10.

1st. Battalion North Staffordshire Regiment.
OPERATION ORDER No. 17.

1. GENERAL. The Battalion will be relieved in the Front Line on the night of 8/9th. July, by the 9th. Bn. East Surrey Regt. On relief the Battalion less "A" Coy. will proceed to BULLY GRENAY.
"A" Coy. will proceed to CITE CALONNE.

2. ORDER OF RELIEF. "A" Coy. 1st. Bn. North Staffordshire Regt. will be relieved by
                                        "B" Coy. 9th. Bn. East Surrey Regt.
    "B" Coy.   "   "   "D" Coy.   "   "
    "C" Coy.   "   "   "A" Coy.   "   "
    "D" Coy.   "   "   "C" Coy.   "   "

3. ADVANCE PARTIES. Usual advance parties will leave the line at 2-30 p.m. and will travel in all cases by the trench route.

4. TRANSPORT. All trench goods (less Lewis Guns and Magazines) of all Coys. and Battn. H.Q. will be at COLONY DUMP by 10-45 p.m. Companies will detail 1 N.C.O. and 2 men per coy. to be responsible for loading and unloading of their respective goods on the Light Railway.

Trench goods of "A" Coy. will be unloaded at CITE CALONNE.

Transport Officer will arrange for transport of goods of "B", "C" & "D" Coys. from detraining point to respective Coy. billets. He will also arrange for transport of Lewis Guns and Magazines of "B", "C" & "D" Coys. from FOSSE 16 de LENS, to which point they will be carried by Coys. "A" Coy. will carry Guns and Magazines direct to CITE CALONNE.

5. HANDING OVER All trench stores will be carefully handed over and receipts obtained. Battle positions will be carefully explained and handed over.

6. CONDITION OF BILLETS. Certificates that all dug-outs etc. were handed over and reserve billets taken over in a clean and sanitary condition will be rendered to Orderly Room by 9 a.m., 9th. inst.

(continued.)

Operation Order No. 17 (continued)

Completion of relief will be notified by wiring the word "CLARA". Coys. will report arrival in Reserve Billets by runner or wire using the word "HERE".

8. ACKNOWLEDGE.

W.D. Stamer

Capt. & Adjt.
1st. Battn. North Staffordshire Regiment.

ISSUED at 10.30 A.M. Dated 7-7-18.

Copies to :—
1. C.O.
2. O.C., 8th. Battn. R.West Kent Regt.
3. O.C., 9th. Battn. East Surrey Regt.
4. T.O. and Q.M.
5. O.C., "A" Coy.
6. O.C., "B" Coy.
7. O.C., "C" Coy.
8. O.C., "D" Coy.
9.) War Diary.
10.)
11. R.S.M.
12. R.Q.Mess.

Secret

Copy VIII.

1st. Battalion North Staffordshire Regiment.

OPERATION ORDER No. 18.

1. The Battalion will relieve the 3th. Bn. Royal West Kent Regt. in Support on the night of the 14/15th. July.

2. Companies will occupy the same areas as during the last tour in Support.

3. Order of March and times of starting as follows:-

    "A" Coy.   ....   10-15 p.m.
    "C" Coy.   ....   10-0 p.m.
    "B" Coy.   ....   10-15 p.m.
    "D" Coy.   ....   10-30 p.m.

4. Companies will leave 200 yards interval between platoons.

5. Advance parties consisting of One Officer per company and one N.C.O. per platoon will leave present billets at 4-0 p.m. Trench routes will be used in all cases.

6. All trench stores, cooking utensils etc. for "B", "C" & "D" Coys. and Hd.Qrs. will be stacked outside various Hd.Qrs. by 7-0 p.m. A guard of 1 N.C.O. and 2 men per company will remain with this kit during transmission.

7. Officers' valises, men's packs and all kit for storing will be stacked outside Coy. billets by 2-30 p.m. Transport Officer will arrange to collect these.

8. Lewis Guns and Magazines of "B" "C" & "D" Coy's. will be loaded on Coy. Limbers by 9-45 p.m. These will proceed with Coy's.s far as FOSSE 16.

9. Transport Officer will arrange for transport of "A" Coy's. stor

10. Coy's. will wire time of arrival in Support Area.

11. "A" Coy. will carry Lewis Guns and Magazines.

P.T.O.

2.

12. ACKNOWLEDGE.

Issued at 12.20 A.M.   Dated:- 14. 7. 18.

                                                              Captain & Adjt.
                          1st. Battalion North Staffordshire Regiment.

Copies to :-

       No. 1. Commanding Officer.
           2. O.C., "A" Coy.
           3. O.C., "B" Coy.
           4. O.C. "C" Coy.
           5. O.C. "D" Coy.
           6. O.C., 8th. Battn. Royal West Kent Regt.
           7. War Diary.
           8. War Diary.
           9. R.S.M.
          10. Bn. Hd.Qrs.Mess.
          11. Transport Officer.
          12. Quartermaster.

SECRET.

Copy 4.

OPERATION ORDER No. 19
1st. Battalion North Staffordshire Regiment.

1. The Battalion will relieve the 8th. Bn. Royal West Kent Regt. in the line on the night of 20/21st. inst.

2. "D" Coy. 1st. Bn. North Staffordshire Regt. will relieve "B" Coy. 8th. Bn. R.W.Kent Regt.
   "A" Coy.   "   "   "A" Coy.   "   "
   "B" Coy.   "   "   "C" Coy.   "   "
   "C" Coy.   "   "   "D" Coy.   "   "

3. Usual advance parties will leave support billets at 3-0 p.m. and will take over all trench stores and reconnoitre all battle positions etc. They will use trench routes in all cases. Advance party of "A" Coy. will take over arrangements for carrying of meals for "D" Coy.

4. Completion of Relief will be notified by wiring time only.

5. ACKNOWLEDGE.

ISSUED at 9.50 pm   Dated:- 19.7.18

Capt. & Adjt.
1st. Bn. North Staffordshire Regt.

Copies to :-
1. Commanding Officer.   7. O.C. "C" Coy.
2. O.C. 8th. R.W.Kent Regt.   8. O.C. "D" Coy.
3. War Diary.   9. T.S.M.
4. War Diary.   10. Bn. H.Q. Mess.
5. O.C. "A" Coy.   11. T.O.
6. O.C. "B" Coy.   12. Quartermaster.

SECRET.

OPERATION ORDER No.20   Copy No. 7

1st. Bn. North Staffordshire Regiment.

1. "A" Coy. will relieve "D" Coy. in the front line on the night of 23/24th. July, 1918.

2. On relief "D" Coy. will take over the accommodation now occupied by "A" Coy. and will become Right Support Coy.

3. O.C., "D" Coy. will arrange to provide ration carrying parties for "A" Coy. on relief.

4. "Handing over" and "Taking over" Certificates will be sent to Orderly Room by 12 noon day after relief.

5. All further arrangements will be made by O's C. Coys. concerned.

6. O.C. Coys. will notify Bn. H.Q. of completion of relief by wiring the time only.

7. If the wind is favourable to-night for a Gas Projectile attack, this relief will be postponed 24 hours. The following Code Words will be used :-
   Relief will take place .... "PINK"
   Relief will not take place......... "BLUE"

8. ACKNOWLEDGE.

   Issued at 12.15 p.m.   Dated 23rd. July, 1918.

   [signature]

   Capt. & Adjt.
   1st. Bn. North Staffordshire Regt.

Copies to :-
1. Commanding Officer.
2. O.C. "A" Coy.
3. O.C. "B" Coy.
4. O.C. "C" Coy.
5. O.C. "D" Coy.
6. War Diary.
7. War Diary.
8. R.S.M.
9. Transport Officer & Quartermaster.
10. O.C., 3rd. Bn. The Rifle Brigade.

12.30 pm   26.7.18

W.J. Stamer

Army Form C. 2118.

WAR DIARY
or
INTELLIGENCE SUMMARY.
(Erase heading not required.)

Instructions regarding War Diaries and Intelligence Summaries are contained in F. S. Regs., Part II. and the Staff Manual respectively. Title pages will be prepared in manuscript.

Place	Date	Hour	Summary of Events and Information	Remarks and references to Appendices

C O N F I D E N T I A L.

WAR DIARY

of

1st. BN. NORTH STAFFORDSHIRE REGIMENT.

From August 1st. 1918 To August 31st. 1918.

Vol.

Army Form C. 2118.

WAR DIARY
or
INTELLIGENCE SUMMARY.
(Erase heading not required.)

Instructions regarding War Diaries and Intelligence Summaries are contained in F. S. Regs., Part II. and the Staff Manual respectively. Title pages will be prepared in manuscript.

Place	Date	Hour	Summary of Events and Information	Remarks and references to Appendices
BULLY GRENAY	Aug 1st		Battalion relieves 7th Battalion Loyal West Kent Regiment in Support. No casualties. 3 platoons of "D" Company who are returning to do a minor enterprise proceeded to the 34th Divisional Reception Camp. Also 2/Lieut. Wright and 95 O.R's. who are a surplus to establishment. BULLY GRENAY received considerable attention from hostile artillery. A considerable number of Gas Shells being fired. 2/Lieut. Kinsall returned from leave. Also 2/Lieut. Peacock, who from this date becomes Battalion Bombing Officer. O.O. No. 32 attached.	6/8
SUPPORT CITE ST-PIERRE	2		"A" & "B" Coys. front Coys. "D" & "B" Coys. in Support. 72nd. Infantry Brigade Horse Show cancelled on account of inclement weather. Major G.C.T.W. Greville 2nd. Battalion Leinster Regiment attached to the Battalion from this date as Second in Command. Major G.C.T.W. G.S.O. proceeded to England for 14 days.	6/8
-Do-	3		Quiet day. nothing of interest occurred.	6/8
-Do-	4		2/Lt. L.T. Pattison returned from Musketry Course at 1st Army School. Colonel Hodgson proceeded to FOSSE 10 for two nights.	6/8
-Do-	5		Brigade Horse Show. The Battalion won first prize in:- (1) Transport Turnout (11) Heavy Draught. (111) Light Draught. (iv) Tug-of-war. "A" Bowl Rd. (Pl.) Bullets fell bw G.9's. Officers Mess Bn. Coolhouses and Bomb and S.A.A. Store blown up.	6/8
-Do-	6		Relief took place normally. Nothing very noteworthy. All Wire entanglements with Colonel Gaillly. Opens. 107 Group R.F.A. re. "B" Coy's. minor enterprise.	6/8
FRONT LINE	7		Battalion relieved the 8th Royal West Kent Regiment in the front line. Colonel S.V.P. Hodson. proceeded on leave. Major Greville takes over command of the Battalion. "B" Coy. front line. "A" Coy. right (rear) Left Black line (ex. Santha Black line for "B" Coy. (only a slight row) Left Black line low. No casualties during relief. O.O. 35 attached.	6/8
-Do-	8		No casualties during relief. Considerable snelling of forward area during the night and early morning. Liason with Battalion on our left.	6/8
-Do-	9		Divisional Horse Show. Arrivals in Transport Turn-out and Light Draught. 2nd. in Pug-o-war. 3rd. in Quarter Mile. Two prisoners taken in raid of Battalion on our right. 3 platoons "B" Coy.	6/8

Army Form C. 2118.

WAR DIARY
or
INTELLIGENCE SUMMARY.
(Erase heading not required.)

Instructions regarding War Diaries and Intelligence Summaries are contained in F. S. Regs., Part II. and the Staff Manual respectively. Title pages will be prepared in manuscript.

Place	Date Aug	Hour	Summary of Events and Information	Remarks and references to Appendices
FRONT LINE	10		Rejoined Battalion from 24th Divisional Reception Camp. "B" Coy. relieved "D" Coy. in the Front line, "B" Coy. on relief proceeded to Left Coy. Sector Black line.	108
-Do-	11		Conference at Brigade Hd. Qrs. to decide on new dispositions. Considerable hostile artillery activity.	108
-Do-	12		Very hot day. Quieter than usual. Gas projectiles discharged from Brigade front at midnight. No hurrah, slight retaliation.	108
-Do-	13		Battalion relieved by 9th Bat Alton East Surrey Regiment. On relief Battalion proceeded to BULLY GRENAY and became Battalion in Reserve. Relief over early and without casualties.	108
BULLY GRENAY	14		Cleaning up. C.O. attended lecture by the Inspector General of Training.	108
			Performance by the Brigade Concert Party in the evening.	
-Do-	15		Visit of the Corps Commander, General Sir Aylmer Hunter Weston. He was very pleased with all he saw, and conveyed his congratulations to the Battalion.	108
-Do-	16		The Battalion practised the usual for open warfare on the MARQUEFFLE Training area. Cookers went with the Battalion. Three cases of men sleeping on their posts remand for F.G.C.M. by the C.O.	108
-Do-	17		Battalion spent the day on the rifle range at LE QUESNOY. Cookers were taken. Orders received that we are to relieve the 7th Battalion Somerset Light Infantry in the front line in a new Section on 19th.	108
-Do-	18		C.O. Adjutant and Company Commanders to reconnoitre new front. Transport moved to MAZINGARBE. Pltes. Platt and Ridge tried by F.G.C.M. for sleeping on their posts. No training. Voluntary Church Service.	108
-Do-	19		Billets and Bivouacs inspected by the B.G.C. No training. Battalion relieves the 7th Battalion Somerset Light Infantry in the LENS Section. "A" Coy. Front line, "B" & "D" Coy's. Black line, "B" Coy. in reserve. C.O. 25 Inches.	108
RIGHT SUBSECTION	20		Considerable front line hostile artillery activity at 5.30 A.M. Enemy bombardment and relief was completed at 12.30 A.M.	108

Army Form C. 2118.

WAR DIARY
or
INTELLIGENCE SUMMARY.

(Erase heading not required.)

Instructions regarding War Diaries and Intelligence Summaries are contained in F. S. Regs., Part II. and the Staff Manual respectively. Title pages will be prepared in manuscript.

Place	Date	Hour	Summary of Events and Information	Remarks and references to Appendices
Right Sub-Section	21		Very hot day. Considerable hostile artillery activity during the afternoon. Pte Sims tried by F.G.C.M. for sleeping on his post.	
do	22		Very hot day. Hostile artillery activity normal. Two sections of 7th Battalion Somerset Light Infantry raided hostile trenches on our front in conjunction with a raid by the Kings Liverpool Regiment on our right. Identification obtained.	
do Front Line	23		Two Poles deserted to the Battalion on the right. Very quiet day.	
do	24		Visit Corps Horse Show. Our Transport got second prize in general Turn-out. 90 men went to the Show from front line area. Lorry Transport arranged by Brigade.	
do	25		Colonel H.V.M. Hodson returned from leave. 2/Lieut. MacInrdy returned from Gas Course. 11.30 a.m. Conference re. minor operation we are to carry out this tour. Capt. Stamer to Transport Lines. "D" Coy. relieves "A" Coy. in front line, relief over at 10.50 p.m. No casualties.	
do	26		Quiet day.	
do	27		Enemy artillery active. "B" Coy's. area heavily shelled between 1 and 2 p.m. and again about 6 p.m. A few very slight casualties occurred. LiaVIN was heavily shelled with H.E. and Gas about midnight, fully 1,000 shells being fired.	
do	28		Very quiet day. 2/Lieut. Goodwin with the Scouting Sergt. and Corpl. spent 24 hours in MOSSs 1 within 50 yards of a Boche post. They took up a position inside an old Roller and gained useful information regarding the enemy's line. "C" Coy. carried out a practice counter-attack on the JEANNE D'ARC locality.	

(A500) Wt. W2771/M691 5/17 750,000 Sch. 52 Forms/C2118/4

D. D. & L., London, E.C.

WAR DIARY
or
INTELLIGENCE SUMMARY.

Army Form C. 2118.

Instructions regarding War Diaries and Intelligence Summaries are contained in F. S. Regs., Part II. and the Staff Manual respectively. Title pages will be prepared in manuscript.

(Erase heading not required.)

Place	Date Aug.	Hour	Summary of Events and Information	Remarks and references to Appendices
RIGHT SUB-SECTION	29		Day appears to be very ordinary, and was increased its early evening bombardment.	WD/S
-do-	30		Considerable artillery activity ceased on B.M. and a new H.Q. Inspected all night parties at 11 a.m. Major Greville proceeded to Transport Lines. Two Platoons "D" Coy. raided enemy trenches, no identification was got them. 3/4 A/2's. Crawford and Newton part 1/3 of the party. Our Artillery barrage fell short and inflicted men we [illegible]. Casualties 3 killed, 1 missing, 4 wounded. O.C. "B" Coy wounded.	WD/S
-do-	31		Battalion relieved by 8th Batt. N.S.Fus. and proceeded to Reserve billets at HULLY GREEN. Were subjected to heavy bombardment from time to time, but nothing which we last one week suffered. O.C. "D" Coy. 2/Lieut [illegible] Wounded.	WD/S

N. Hodson

Bat. 1st Battalion North Staffordshire Regt.

1st. BN. NORTH STAFFORDSHIRE REGIMENT.

Copy No. 13

S E C R E T.   OPERATION ORDER NO. 22.

1. The Battalion will relieve the 8th. Bn. Royal West Kent Regt. in support on the night 1st/2nd August.

2. Coys. will occupy the same areas as during the last tour in Support.

3. Order of march and times as follows:-
    - "A" Coy.   9.45 p.m.
    - "C" "   9.30 p.m.
    - "B" "   9.45 p.m.
    - "D" "   10.0 p.m.

4. 200 yards interval will be kept between platoons.

5. Advance parties consisting of one officer per Coy. and 1 N.C.O. per platoon, will leave present billets at 6.0 p.m. Trench Routes will be used where possible.

6. All Trench Stores, Cooking utensils etc., for "B" "C" and "D" Coys. and Hd. Qrs. to be stacked outside the various Hd.Qrs. at 8.0 p.m. A guard of 1 N.C.O. and 2 men per Coy. and Bn.Hd. Qrs. will remain with this kit during transmission.

7. Lewis Guns and magazines of "B" "C" and "D" Coys. will be loaded on Coy. limbers by 9.45 p.m. these will proceed with Coys as far as FOSSE 10.

8. Officers' valises, men's packs, etc., and all kit for storing will be stacked outside Coy. billets by 4.0 p.m. Transport Officer will arrange to collect these.

9. Transport Officer will arrange for transport of "A" Coy's Stores.

10. "A" Coy. will carry Lewis Guns and magazines.

11. Coys. will wire time only on arrival in Support area.

12. All Trench Stores, Battle positions etc., must be carefully taken over by advance parties.

13. O's.C. Coys. will render a certificate by 9.0 a.m. August 2nd. to the effect that all Trenches and accommodation taken over were in a clean state, and that the correct establishment of full boxes of S.A.A. were taken over or otherwise.

14. Acknowledge.

Issued at 10.0 p.m.

Date 31st. July 1918.

W. D. Stamer
Capt. & Adjt.
1st. Bn. North Staffordshire Regt.

Copies to:-
- No. 1. C.O.
- " 2. O.C. "A" Coy.
- " 3. O.C. "B" Coy.
- " 4. O.C. "C" Coy.
- " 5. O.C. "D" Coy.
- " 6. O.C. 8th.R.W.Kents.
- " 7. R.S.M.
- " 8. Transport Officer
- " 9. Quarter Master.
- " 10. Hd.Qrs.Mess.
- " 11. Signalling Officer.
- " 12. War Diary.
- No. 13. War Diary. ✓

OPERATION ORDER No. 23.   Copy No 12

1st. Bn. North Staffordshire Regiment.

1. The Battalion will relieve the 8th. Bn. Royal West Kent Regt in the line on the night of 7/8th. August, 1918.

2. "A" Coy. 1st. North Staffs. Rgt. will relieve "B" Coy. 8th. R.W.Kent R
   (Right Coy. BLACK LINE)
   "B" Coy.   "   "   "   will relieve "D" Coy. in Front Line.
   "C" Coy.   "   "   "   "   "   "A" Coy.
   (Left Coy. BLACK LINE.)
   "D" Coy.   "   "   "   will relieve "C" Coy.
   (Centre BLACK LINE Coy)

3. Usual Advance Parties will leave present billets at 3 p.m. They will take over all trench stores and reconnoitre battle positions. Advance Parties of "A" Coy. will take over arrangements for carrying meals for "B" Coy.

4. Usual certificates will be sent to Orderly Room by Noon on August 8th.

5. O.C. Coys. will notify Bn. H.Q. on completion of relief by wiring time only.

6. Acknowledge.

Issued at 10.15 pM.   Dated August 6th. 1918.

(signed) G.D. Stamer

Capt. & Adjt.
1st. Bn. North Staffordshire Regt.

Copies to :-
1. Commanding Officer.
2. O.C., 8th. Bn. Royal West Kent Regt.
3. O.C. "A" Coy.
4. O.C. "B" Coy.
5. O.C. "C" Coy.
6. O.C. "D" Coy.
7. Transport Officer.
8. Quartermaster.
9. R.S.M.
10. H.Q.Mess.
11. Signal Officer.
12. War Diary.
13. War Diary.

SECRET   OPERATION ORDER No. 24.   Copy No. 12.

SECRET.   1st. Battalion North Staffordshire Regiment.

1. "C" Coy. will relieve "B" Coy. in the Front Line on the night of 10/11th. August.

2. On relief, "B" Coy. will move into accommodation at present occupied by "C" Coy. and will become Left Support Coy.

3. O.C. "B" Coy. will arrange to find ration carrying parties for "C" Coy. on relief.

4. Handing over and taking over certificates will be sent to Orderly Room by 12 noon, August 11th.

5. All further arrangements will be made between O's C. Coys. concerned.

6. O's C. Coys. will notify Bn. H.d. on completion of relief by wiring the time only.

7. ACKNOWLEDGE.

Issued at 12 noon.   Date :- 10.8.18.

W.J. Stamer

Captain & Adjt.
1st. Bn. North Staffordshire Regt.

Copies to :-
1. Commanding Officer.
2. O.C. "A" Coy.
3. O.C. "B" Coy.
4. O.C. "C" Coy.
5. O.C. "D" Coy.
6. 8th. Bn. The Queen's Regt.
7. 11th. Bn. The Rifle Brigade.
8. R.S.M.
9. Qr.Mr.
10. T.O.
11. War Diary.
12. War Diary.
13. Signal Officer.

SECRET.   OPERATION ORDER No. 25.   Copy No. 12

1st. Battalion North Staffordshire Regiment.

1. The Battalion will be relieved by the 9th. Bn. East Surrey Regt. on the night of 13/14th. August.

2. On relief the Battalion, less "A" Coy. will proceed to BULLY GRENAY.

3. "A" Coy. will proceed to CALONNE.

4. Usual advance parties will leave present billets at 5 p.m.

5. Coys. will take over same billets in reserve as before.

6. All officers' trench kits, cooking utensils etc. will be stacked on Coy. Dumps by 10-30 p.m.
O's C. Coys. will detail 1 N.C.O. & 2 men to load this kit.

7. Trench Goods of "A" Coy. will be unloaded at CITE CALONNE.

8. T.O. will arrange transport for Trench Goods of "B" C"&"D" Coys. from unloading point to billets.

9. Lewis Guns of "B", "C", & "D" Coys. will be met by transport at Water Tower, on the FOSSE 16 Road. T.O. will arrange this.

10. "A" Coy. will carry Lewis Guns & Magazines to CALONNE.

11. All handing over certificates to be sent to Orderly Room by 12 Noon, August 14th.

12. O's C. Coys. will notify Bn. H.Q. on completion of relief by wiring time only.

13. ACKNOWLEDGE.

Issued at 9.30 AM   Date :- 13th. August.1918.

W.D. Stamer

Capt. & Adjt.
1st. Bn. North Staffordshire Regt.

Copies to :-
1. Commanding Officer.
2. O.C. "A" Coy.
3. O.C. "B" Coy.
4. O.C. "C" Coy.
5. O.C. "D" Coy.
6. O.C., 9th. Bn. East Surrey Regt.
7. R.S.M.
8. Signal Officer.
9. Quartermaster.
10. Transport Officer.
11. War Diary.
12. War Diary.
13. Medical Officer.

SECRET.   OPERATION ORDER No. 26.   Coy No. A

1st. Bn. North Staffordshire Regiment.

1. The Battalion will relieve the 7th. Bn. Somerset Light Infantry in the right sub-section front line on the night 19/20th. August.

2. "A" Coy. will leave present billets at 10 p.m. and take over the Front Line Coy. area.
   "B" Coy. will leave present billets at 9-30 p.m. and take over Left BLACK LINE Coy. Area.
   "D" Coy. will leave present billets at 9-45 p.m. and take over Right BLACK LINE Coy. Area.
   "C" Coy. will leave present billets at 10 p.m. and take over Reserve Coy. Area.

3. Guides will be arranged between O.C. Coys. concerned.

4. Advance parties of 1 Officer per Coy. and 1 N.C.O. per Platoon (except "A" Coy.) will leave present billets at 1.30 p.m. and report at Bn. H.Q. at N.17.c.75.50. for guides.

5. The Bn. Intelligence Officer, a percentage of Scouts and Runners will leave present billets at 1.30 p.m. and report at Bn. H.Q. at N.17.c.75.50.
   The Intelligence Officer will be in charge of this party.

6. All Trench Stores, S.O.S. Rockets etc. will be carefully taken over.

7. All stores for the Line will be dumped outside various H.Q's at 2.0 p.m.
   A guard of 1 N.C.O. and 2 men per Coy. and Bn. H.Q. will remain with this kit during transmission.

8. "A", "B" & "D" Coys. will use COUNTRY SPUR Dump. "C" Coy. & Bn. H.Q. will use END Dump.

9. Arrangements for Water will be as taken over. Quartermaster will send up Petrol Tins to Coys. as under.
   "A" Coy.   16 Tins. Empty.
   "B" Coy.   8   "   "
   "C" Coy.   8 Tins Full nightly.
   "D" Coy.   8 Tins Empty.
   Bn. H.Q.   8 Tins full nightly.

10. "A" Coy. will carry Lewis Guns and Magazines.

11. Lewis Guns & Magazines "B", "C" & "D" Coys will be loaded on Coy Limbers by 9.45 p.m. These will proceed with Coys. as far as possible.

12. Officers' valises, mens' packs etc, will be stacked outside Coy. Billets by 2.0 p.m. Transport Officer will arrange to collect these.

13. Transport Officer will arrange with O.C. "A" Coy. to transport "A" Coy's Goods to the line. Transport for this purpose will be at "A" Coys'. H.Q. at 10 p.m.

14. 200 yards interval will be kept between Platoons on the march.

15. Quartermaster will arrange to send up sufficient utensils for cooking purposes for each Coy. on the train.

T.O.

Copies to:-

1. File.
2. War Diary.
3. War Diary.
4. O.C. "A" Company.
5. O.C. "B" Company.
6. O.C. "C" Company.
7. O.C. "D" Company.
8. Transport Mess.
9. Headquarters' Mess.
10. O.C., 1st. North Staffordshire Regiment.
11. O.C., 9th. E. Surrey Regt.,
12. A/R.S.Major.

Operation Order No. 26. Cont.

16. Officers Commanding Coys. will report completion of relief to Bn. H.Q. by wiring the time only.

17. ACKNOWLEDGE.

Issued at 9.50 A.M. Dated:- 19th. August, 1918.

W.J. Stamer
Capt. & Adjt.
1st. Bn. North Staffordshire Regt.

Copies to :-
1. Commanding Officer.
2. O.C., "A" Coy.
3. O.C., "B" Coy.
4. O.C., "C" Coy.
5. O.C., "D" Coy.
6. Transport Officer.
7. Quartermaster.
8. R.S.M.
9. Signal Officer.
10. O.C., 7th. Somerset Light Infantry.
11. War Diary.
12. War Diary.
13. Intelligence Officer.

SECRET.　　　　　　　　　　　　　　　　　　　　　　　Copy No...14..........

OPERATION ORDER No.27.
1st. Bn. NORTH STAFFORDSHIRE REGIMENT.

1. "D" Coy. will relieve "A" Coy. in the Front Line on the night 25th/26th inst.

2. On relief "A" Coy. will move into accomodation at present occupied by "D" Coy. and will become Right Support Coy.

3. Handing over and taking over certificates will be sent to Orderly Room by 12.0 noon August 26th.

4. All further arrangements will be made between O'sn. C. Coys. concerned.

5. O's. C. Coys. will notify Battn. Hd. Qrs. on completion of relief by wiring time only.

6. Acknowledge.

Issued at 11.50 a.m.　　　　　　　　　　　　　　　Late Pr – d –13.

　　　G.Binson 2/Lt for　　　Capt. & Adjt.
　　　　　　　　　　　　　　1st. Bn. North Staffordshire Regt.

Copies to:-
　No. 1. C.O.　　　　　　　　　　　No. 2. O.C. "A" Coy.
　"   3. O.C. "B" Coy.　　　　　　"   4. O.C. "C" Coy.
　"   5. O.C. "D" Coy.　　　　　　"   6. 6th.Bn.E.Kent Kent Regt.
　"   7. 12th.Bn.The Kings Regt.　"   8. T.M.B.
　"   9. Q.M.　　　　　　　　　　　" 10. Transport Officer.
　" 11. War Diary.　　　　　　　　" 12. War Diary.
　" 13. Signalling Officer.

for War
Diary

1st. Bn. North Staffordshire Regt.

OPERATION ORDER No. 28   Copy No. 10

Ref. Sheet 44A. S.W.1.   29th. August. 1918.

1.   A Raid will be carried out by "C" Coy. 1st. North Staffordshire Regt. on the night of the 30/31st. August, on the enemy trenches between N.8.d.3.5 to N.8.d.15.05 also penetrating to the Support Line from N.8.d.55.35 to N.14.b.35.95.
      O.C. Raid - Captain Steeley, Commanding "C" Coy. 1st. Bn. North Staffordshire Regt.

2.   The object of the raid is to capture prisoners, secure identification, kill Germans and destroy enemy dug-outs.

3.   Strength of Raiding Party will be two Platoons divided into four Sections under the command of 2/Lieut. Crawford and 2/Lieut. Cowden respectively.

4.   The Raiding Party will be assembled by 12 Midnight about 30 yards in front of our wire moving slowly forward to within about 120 yards of the enemy's wire opposite the three proposed points of entry at N.8.d.20.50., N.8.d.15.25., and N.8.d.15.05.
      At ZERO hour i.e. 12.15 a.m., an intense barrage lasting two minutes will open on the enemy Front Line from N.8.d.40.60 to N.14.a.85.95. At Zero plus 2 minutes, this barrage will lift onto CINNABAR TRENCH from N.8.d.55.35 to N.14.b.35.95.
      At ZERO plus 7 minutes this barrage will again lift from CINNABAR TRENCH on to the CITE ST.AUGUSTE Road where it will remain till "Stop" or 15 minutes after the withdrawal signal is given. As soon as the barrage lifts at ZERO plus 2, the Raiding Party will advance following up the barrage as closely as possible and enter the enemy's trenches. In addition a Box Barrage will be formed round the area being raided in which the Medium and Light Trench Mortars will co-operate.(vide attached Artillery Barrage table.)
      A feint bombardment with smoke will be opened at ZERO minus 3 minutes on the German Trenches in the vicinity of POTMAN STACKS, to draw the enemy's fire, if possible, from the point actually being raided.
      Detailed action of each Platoon is attached on a separate sheet.

5.   The signal for withdrawal will be a rocket Golden Rain and Coloured Stars followed by another similar signal fired from the enemy's Front Line trench. The Raiding Party will on no account withdraw from the enemy's trenches until atleast a quarter of an hour after the trench has been entered and dug-outs searched, as many as possible being destroyed with mobile charges, carried by the R.E. Party attached.

6.   The Officer Commanding the raid will personally supervise the arrangements for the assembly of the Raiding Party at the point from which it will leave our trenches, i.e. N.8.c.90.50. and also the assembly of the Party in NO MAN'S LAND.

7.   The Medical Officer, 1st. Bn. North Staffordshire Regt. will make the necessary arrangements for the collection and evacuation of wounded.

Operation Orders No. 28.   Continued.

8. The following Code will be used for the purposes of the Raid.

  Raiders entered .... BULL.
  " Returned .... COW.
  Prisoners Captured .... PIG.
   (Nos. may be given e.g. 3 PIGS.)
  Casualties .... STAG.

9. Watches will synchronised at Bn. H.Q. CONSTITUTION HILL, M.17.c.75.45. by all units concerned, each sending a representative there for this purpose at 6.0 p.m. 30th. August 1918. The greatest care will be exercised in seeing that watches are accurately synchronised.

10. Advanced Bn. H.Q. will be established at Old Coy. H.Q., N.7.b.62.07. by 10.0 p.m. and will remain there till the close of operations

        T. Hodson Lieut. Colonel.
     Cmdg. 1st. Bn. North Staffordshire Regt.

Copies to :-

1. O.C. 1st. Bn. North Staffordshire Regt.
2. O.C., "C" Coy.
3. 72nd. Infantry Brigade.
4. O.C., Medium T.M.Battery.
5. O.C., 72nd. Light T.M.Battery.
6. O.C., 107th. Brigade. R.F.A.
7. O.C., "B" Coy. 24th. M.G.Battn.
8. 17th. Infantry Brigade.
9. O.C., 9th. Bn. East Surrey Regt.
10. War Diary.
11. War Diary.

S E C R E T.   Copy No. 14

OPERATION ORDER No. 29

1st. BN. NORTH STAFFORDSHIRE REGIMENT.

1. The Battalion will be relieved by the 8th. Bn. Royal West Kent Regiment in the right Sub Section on the night 31/1st Sept. 1918.
2. On relief the Battalion less "A" Coy. will proceed to BULLY GRENAY and become Battalion in Reserve.
3. "A" Coy. will proceed to CALONNE.
4. Usual advanced parties will leave present billets at 6.0 p.m.
5. All Trench goods, officers' kits, cooking utensils, etc., will be stacked at house at M.17.b.65.35. by 10.0 p.m. by "A", "B" and "D" Coys.
6. "C" Coy. and Battalion Headquarters will stack their Trench goods on the Road outside Battalion Headquarters by 10.0 p.m.
7. Transport Officer will arrange to send one limber per Company and one limber for Battalion Headquarters to these dumps to collect this kit at 10.0 p.m.
8. A Guard of 1 N.C.O. and 2 men per Company and Battalion Headquarters will remain with this kit as loading and unloading party.
9. Transport Officer will arrange for one limber to be at the Water Tower at FOSSE 16 at 11.0 p.m. to carry Lewis Guns and magazines of "D" Company and "B" Company.
10. "A" and "C" Coys. will carry Lewis Guns and magazines.
11. All Battle Positions, Trench Stores, etc., will be carefully handed over to incoming Unit, including petrol tins.
12. All handing over Certificates, etc., will reach Battalion Headquarters by 12.0 noon Sept. 1st.
13. O's.C. Coys. will inform Battalion Headquarters on completion of relief by wiring time only.
14. Acknowledge.

Issued at 11.45 A.M.   Date 31 - 8 - 18.

(Sgd). Stamer.

Capt. & Adjt.
1st. Bn. North Staffordshire Regt.

NOTE.
Further information as to guides will be notified later.

Copies to:-

No 1.	C.O.	No. 2.	2nd. In Command.
" 3.	O.C. "A" Coy.	" 4.	O.C. "B" Coy.
" 5.	O.C. "C" Coy.	" 6.	O.C. "D" Coy.
" 7.	O.C.8th.Royal West Kent.Regt.	" 8.	O.C.9th.Royal Sussex Regt.
" 9.	Transport Officer.	" 10.	Quarter-Master.
" 11.	R.S.M.	" 12.	O.C.9th.East Surrey Regt.
" 13.	Signalling Officer.	" 14.& 15.	War Diary.

Secret.
9/8 43

WAR DIARY
of
1st Bn. North Staffordshire Regt.

September
1918

Army Form C. 2118.

WAR DIARY
or
INTELLIGENCE SUMMARY.
(Erase heading not required.)

Instructions regarding War Diaries and Intelligence Summaries are contained in F. S. Regs., Part II. and the Staff Manual respectively. Title pages will be prepared in manuscript.

Place	Date Sept.	Hour	Summary of Events and Information	Remarks and references to Appendices
BULLY GRENAY	1		Day spent in cleaning up. "D" Coy. did not arrive in Billets until 7 a.m. after very late relief. 2/Lieut. R.W.Clift joined the Batt.	DCB
- Do -	2		Battalion less "A" & "C" Coy's. spent the day on MARQUEFFLES Range & Commanding Officer to 8th Corps School at FRESSIN for tour of inspection.	DCB
- Do -	3		Battalion less "B" & "D" Coy's. to Range at MARQUEFFLES. Colonel Hodson returned from FRESSIN. Performance by the Brigade Concert party in the evening.	DCB
- Do -	4		Inspection by Major General Hoare Nairne Commanding 24th Div. at 10 a.m. on Brigade Horse Show ground, special attention paid to new organisation. Corps Commander General Sir Aylmer Hunter Weston to witness a conference preparatory to a to a tactical exercise on MARQUEFFLES Training area.	DCA
- Do -	5		"B" & "D" Coy's. carried out the Tactical exercise "A" & "C" Coy's. continued with usual Training. Concert in the evening by Brigade Concert party in aid of the North Staffordshire Regt. Prisoners of War fund. Money collected Francs.	DCB
- Do -	6		Battalion relieved 9th Battalion East Surrey Regt. innRight Sub Section: Several posts have been established in the old German Front Line. Relief complete 1 a.m. No casualties. O.O. No: 30 attached.	DCB
LEFT SUB SECTION CITE ST PIERRE.	7		"B" & "C" Coy's. in Front line. "A" & "D" Coy's. in the Black line. Working parties busy wiring and consolidating the new line. Very heavy Thunder showers Trenches mostly under water.	DCB
- Do -	8		Sgt. Rutter, (N.C.O. I/c. Scouts) sniped in forward Jack-in-Box	DCB

Army Form C. 2118.

WAR DIARY
or
INTELLIGENCE SUMMARY.
(Erase heading not required.)

Instructions regarding War Diaries and Intelligence Summaries are contained in F. S. Regs., Part II. and the Staff Manual respectively. Title pages will be prepared in manuscript.

Place	Date SEPT.	Hour	Summary of Events and Information	Remarks and references to Appendices
LEFT Sub Section CITE ST PIERRE	9		In CANTEEN ALLEY. Germans attempted to raid our two left forward posts "B" Coy. but were driven off by Lewis Gun fire, and casualties inflicted. 9.2 Shoot of 200 rounds on enemy forward system opposite Nos: 5 & 6 posts.	DCB
— Do —	10		Enemy attempted to raid Lewis Gun post CANTEEN ALLEY, two of our men wounded. Poured with rain. 2/Lieut. Dunk rejoined Battn. Captain Steely, rejoined from Course.	DCB
— Do —	11		Enemy attempted to raid "B" Coy's. left posts at 2.15 a.m. Six of our men wounded. Enemy driven off and casualties believed to have been inflicted on them, by our artillery protective barrage. Very wet again. Considerable hostile artillery activity during the 24 hours.	DCB
— Do —	12		Conference of Commanding Officers at Brigade H.Q. at 8 a.m. Weather very bad and the Trenches are beginning to get into an appalling state. Conference of Coy. Commanders at Battalion H.Q. 3.30 p.m. Considerable hostile artillery activity on right Coy. area.	DCB
— Do —	12		Hostile artillery active. Enemy working party located and fired on. This resulted in our Trenches undergoing considerable hostile artillery activity harassing fire during the morning. Poured with rain in the afternoon. Inter-Coy. relief. "A" Coy. relieved "C" Coy. "D" Coy. relieved "B" Coy. Relief complete at 10.40 p.m. O.O. No: 31 attached.	DCB
— Do —	13		Hostile artillery active harassing our working parties. Forward area fairly quiet. Weather improving.	DCB
— Do —	14		Hostile party of 40 or 50 attempted to raid two right posts of "D" Coy. but were driven off by Lewis Gun and rifle fire. One wounded German surrendered to 9th Batt. East Surrey Regt on our	DCB

Army Form C. 2118.

WAR DIARY
or
INTELLIGENCE SUMMARY.
(Erase heading not required.)

Instructions regarding War Diaries and Intelligence Summaries are contained in F. S. Regs., Part II. and the Staff Manual respectively. Title pages will be prepared in manuscript.

Place	Date SEPT	Hour	Summary of Events and Information	Remarks and references to Appendices
LEFT SUB-SECTION			immediate right. Our casualties 3 O.R's. wounded. Considerable hostile artillery activity throughout the day, shelling all movement.	DCR
~Do~	15		Weather improved. Hostile artillery less active during the day. Demonstration by TANKS on MARQUEFFLES Training area. Percentage of Officers and N.C.O's. attended. Moonlight night, Bombing in back areas.	DCA
~Do~	16		Hostile artillery active. Battalion relieved by 9th Battalion East Surrey Regt. Sideslips to the North and relieves one Company and 2 platoons 8th Queens (R.W.S.) Regt. O.O. 32 attached. Casualties 1 killed 5 wounded.	DCR
~Do~	17		Hostile artillery active in bursts, no casualties. Duties of Adjutant taken over by Lieut. D.C. Butterwoth, duties of 2nd in Command taken over by Capt. W.D. Stamer, M.C. Patrols sent out by "B" and "C" Coy's. to see if enemy had evacuated his front line, negative results were obtained.	DCA
~Do~	18		Relieved by 9th Battalion East Surrey Regt. and Battalion proceeded into reserve at BULLY GRENAY and CITE CALONNE, casualties nil.	DCR
~Do~	19		Battalion witnessed demonstration of attack with co-operation between Infantry and Tanks at MARQUEFFLES. 2/Lieut's. MACKIE and PORTER joined the Battalion and joined "A" and "B" Coy's. respectively. Major G.G.F. Greville proceeded to join 50th Division, Lieut. W.H. Hubball to M.G.C. England, 2/Lieut. W.P. Brighton to R.A.F. England.	DCR

Army Form C. 2118

WAR DIARY
or
INTELLIGENCE SUMMARY

(Erase heading not required.)

Instructions regarding War Diaries and Intelligence Summaries are contained in F. S. Regs., Part II. and the Staff Manual respectively. Title Pages will be prepared in manuscript.

Place	Date Sept.	Hour	Summary of Events and Information	Remarks and references to Appendices
RESERVE BULLY GRENAY	20th		Day spent in cleaning up scrubbing equipment.	JCD
~do~	21st		Battalion carried out Training at MARQUEFFLES in conjunction with Tanks of 10th Batt. Tank Corps. Training comprising overcoming of Outpost zones and main lines of resistance. Platoons given 200 yards frontage on which to attack. Demonstration was witnessed by contingents of the 73rd Brigade.	DCk
~do~	22nd		Very wet day - Day observed as a rest day, no parades took place. Football matches between "B" & "D" Coy's. "C" Coy's. H.Qrs. & "D" Coy. "A" & "B" Coy's. winners were "B" Coy's. & H.Qrs. later in the day "A" Coy. drew with "B" Coy. Nil points being the score.	DCk
~do~	23rd		Day spent in Training at BULLY GRENAY and CALONNE. Commanding Officer inspected "B" "C" & "D" Coy's. during the morning. "A" Coy. drew with Batt. H.Qrs. in Football match and Sergts. beat the Officers' team by 4 points - 2. Major General A.C. Daly. C.B. dined at Battalion Mess.	DCk
LEFT SUBSECTION	24th		Battalion relieved 9th Battalion East Surrey Regt. in line "A" & Coy's. front line and "C" & in Support, relief complete 10.35 p.m. casualties nil. copy of O.O. 34 attached. Night was quiet, patrols went to reconnoitre enemy's wire.	DCA
~do~	25th		Very wet in early morning. Quiet day with exception of 5.9"s on "A" Coy's. area for which retaliation was obtained. Very quiet night.	DCk
~do~	26th		Weather clearer. Post of 8th Kent's raided at 11.30 a.m. our right post helped to repulse this raid we suffered no casualties West Kents had 1 Officer and 2 O.R's. wounded. Intermittent shelling of front line all day - weather good quiet night.	DCk

1875 Wt. W593/826 1,000,000 4/15 J.B.C. & A. A.D.S.S./Forms/C. 2118.

Army Form C. 2118.

WAR DIARY
or
INTELLIGENCE SUMMARY.
(*Erase heading not required.*)

Instructions regarding War Diaries and Intelligence
Summaries are contained in F. S. Regs., Part II.
and the Staff Manual respectively. Title pages
will be prepared in manuscript.

Place	Date	Hour	Summary of Events and Information	Remarks and references to Appendices
LEFT SUB SECTION	SEPT. 27th		Artillery demonstration on whole of Divisional front with a view to leading Hun to expect an attack, retaliation poor. Following appointments to acting ranks authorized Capt. W.D. Stamer M.C. to be Major Lieut. D.C. Butterworth to be Captain, quiet day, casualties nil.	DCK
-do-	28th		Wet morning, advance parties from 58th Div. arrived to take over line. Day continued to be wet. Casualties 1 killed 3 wounded.	DCK
-do-	29th		Battalion was relieved in the line by 2/2 London Regt. 58th Div. and embussed at BULLY GRENAY proceeding to COUPIGNY. (Relief complete 12 midnight.	DCK
-do-	30th		Battalion entrained at HERSIN at 2.30 p.m. for BOUQUEMAISON arrived at BOUQUEMAISON at 6 p.m. and marched to billets in SUS-ST-LEDGER - The day was very cold and wet - billets consisted of barns. Battalion was present in billets at 10 p.m.	DCK

2/10/18

N.P. Hodson Lieut-Colonel
Cmdg. 1st Bn. North Staffordshire Regt.

SECRET.   Copy No. 12

1st. BN. NORTH STAFFORDSHIRE REGT.

OPERATION ORDER No. 31.

1. Inter-Company reliefs as follows will be carried out on the night 12/13th September.
   "D" Company relieves "B" Company in the Right Coy. Sector.
   "A"   "   "   "C"   "   "   " Left   "   "
   On relief "B" and "C" Coys. will occupy billets vacated by "D" and "A" Coys. respectively.
2. All arrangements as to Advance Parties, guides etc., will be made by O's. C. Coys. concerned.
3. On relief O.C. "B" Company will send 2 Sections to CAMERON CASTLE to carry for "D" Company. Carrying parties for the Left Sector will continue under existing arrangements.
4. Usual certificates will be rendered to Battalion Headquarters by 12.0 noon, Sept. 13th.
5. Battalion Headquarters will be notified on completion of relief by wiring time only.
6. ACKNOWLEDGE.

Issued at 12.0 noon.   Date 12-9-18.

                                                                    Capt. & Adjt.
                                                            1st. Bn. North Staffordshire Regt.

Copies to:-
    No. 1.   C.O.
     " 2.   O.C. 8th. Bn. R.W. Kent Regt.
     " 3.   O.C. 8th. Bn. The Queen's Regt.
     " 4.   O.C. "A" Coy.
     " 5.   O.C. "B" "
     " 6.   O.C. "C" "
     " 7.   O.C. "D" "
     " 8.   Transport Officer.
     " 9.   R.Q.M.S.
     " 10. Signalling Officer.
     " 11. R.S.M.
     " 12. & 13. War Diary.

SECRET.   Copy No........

1st. Bn. NORTH STAFFORDSHIRE REGIMENT.
OPERATION ORDER No. 32.

1. "B" and "C" Companies will leave their present accommodation during the afternoon of Sept. 16th. and relieve "C" Company 8th Bn. The Queens (R.W.S.) Regt. Dispositions as previously laid down.

2. "A" and "D" Companies will be relieved by the 9th. Bn. East Surrey Regt. on the night 16/17th Sept. On relief they will move into BLACK LINE area.

3. All Stores will be carried.

4. "A" and "D" Companies Cook houses will move from CAMERON CASTLE into positions to be selected by O's. C. Companies concerned.
"B" and "C" Companies Cook houses will move into positions in NASH TRENCH which will be vacated by the 8th Bn. The Queens Regt.

5. Rations etc., for "A" "B" and "C" Companies will be dumped at EDDY DUMP, "D" Company COLONY DUMP, Battalion Hd. Qrs. OSLER DUMP. Transport Officer will arrange this commencing night 16/17th Sept.

6. O's. C. Companies will forward to Battalion Hd. Qrs. by 12 noon 17-9-18 a sketch map showing new dispositions by Sections.

7. Battalion Hd. Qrs. will remain in present position.

8. O's. C. Companies will notify Battalion Hd. Qrs. on completion of relief by wiring the time only.

9. ACKNOWLEDGE.

Issued at 10.30 p.m.   Date 15.9.18

(W.J) Stainer

Capt. & Adjt.
1st. Bn. North Staffordshire Regt.

Copies to:-
```
No.  1.  C. O.
"    2.  O.C. "A" Coy.
"    3.  O.C. "B"  "
"    4.  O.C. "C"  "
"    5.  O.C. "D"  "
"    6.  Transport Officer.
"    7.  Quarter Master.
"    8.  R. S. M.
"    9.  O.C. 9th. Bn. E. Surrey Regt.
"   10.  O.C. 7th. Bn. Queens (R.W.S.) Regt.
"   11. & 12. War Diary.
"   13.  Signalling Officer.
```

SECRET.   Copy No. 11

1st. Bn. NORTH STAFFORDSHIRE REGIMENT.

OPERATION ORDER No. 33.

1. The Battalion will be relieved in the left sub section on the night of 18/19th. inst. by the 9th. Bn. East Surrey Regt. On relief the Battalion less "A" Coy. will proceed to BULLY GRENAY, "A" Coy to CITE CALONNE. Relief will commence at dusk.

2. "A" Coy. 1st. Bn. North Staffordshire Regt. will be relieved by "C" Coy. 9th. Bn. East Surrey Regt.
   "B" Coy. 1st. Bn. North Staffordshire Regt. will be relieved by "B" Coy. 9th. Bn. East Surrey Regt.
   "C" Coy. 1st. Bn. North Staffordshire Regt. will be relieved by "D" Coy. 9th. Bn. East Surrey Regt.
   "D" Coy. 1st. Bn. North Staffordshire Regt. will be relieved by "A" Coy. 9th. Bn. East Surrey Regt.
   Guides will be arranged by O's.C.Coys. concerned.

3. Usual advance parties will leave present positions at 3.30 p.m. Trench routes will be used.

4. All Trench goods, Officers' Kit. etc., will be stacked on EDDY DUMP by 8.30 p.m. One N.C.O. and two men per Coy. will be detailed to load and unload these goods from train. Transport Officer will arrange to transport these goods from unloading point to Coys.'Billets. One limber will be at Battalion Hd. Qrs. at 9.0 p.m. to collect Battalion Hd. Qrs. Trench goods.

5. Lewis Guns and magazines of "B", "C", and "D" Coys. will be carried to FOSSE 16. Transport Officer will arrange for transport for these from FOSSE 16 at 10.30 p.m.
   "A" Coy. will carry Lewis Guns and magazines.

6. All Battle Positions, Trench Stores, etc., will be carefully handed over and usual certificates rendered to Battalion Hd. Qrs. by 12.0 noon 19th. inst.

7. Completion of relief will be notified to Battalion Hd. Qrs. by wire only. O's.C. Coys. will report arrival into Rest Billets.

8. ACKNOWLEDGE.

Issued at 10.0 p.m.   Dated 17-9-18.

                                    D.C.Butterworth
                                    Lieut. & A/Adjt.
                                    1st. Bn. North Staffordshire Regt.

Copies to :-
 No. 1. Commanding Officer.   No. 2. O.C. "A" Coy.
  "   3. O.C. "B" Coy.   "   4. O.C. "C" Coy.
  "   5. O.C. "D" Coy.   "   6. Transport Officer.
  "   7. Quarter-Master.   "   8. O.C. 9th. East Surrey Regt.
  "   9. Signal Officer.   " 10. & 11. War Diary.
  " 12. R.S.M.

SECRET.   Copy No. 9

1st. BN. NORTH STAFFORDSHIRE REGT.
OPERATION ORDER No. 34.

1. The Battalion will relieve the 9th. Bn. East Surrey Regt. in the left sub section on the night of the 24th/25th inst.

2. Coys. will be disposed as follows:-
    "A" Coy.   Left Front Line Coy.
    "D" "   Right "   "   "
    "C" "   Left Black Line "
    "B" "   Right "   "   "

3. Usual advance parties will leave present billets at 2.0 p.m. Trench routes will be used where possible.

4. Officers valises, mens packs, etc., and all kit for storing and for Divisional Wing will be stacked outside Coy. billets at 11.0 a.m.
    Goods for transmission by rail to the line will be stacked outside Coy. billets by 6.0 pm. Transport Officer will arrange transmission and Coys. will detail usual guards over these goods.
    Coys. will use EDDY DUMP.
    Bn. Hd. Qrs. will use OSLER DUMP.
    "B", "C" and "D" Coys. limbers will be at Coy. billets at 7.0 p.m. to carry Lewis guns and magazines and Officers Mess utensils as far as CHURCH, CITE ST PIERRE.
    "A" Coy. will carry Lewis guns and magazines.
    Battalion Hd. Qrs. limber and Maltese cart will be at Bn. Hd. Qrs. at 7.0 p.m. to carry Bn. Hd. Qrs. and R.A.P. trench goods to forward Bn. Hd. Qrs. (MAIN STREET).

5. "D", "C" and "B" Coys. will pass "OSS" 11 in this order at 7.30 p.m.
    "A" Coy. will march independently from CALONNE.

6. Usual certificates will be rendered to Bn. Hd. Qrs. by 12.0 noon 25th. inst.

7. Notification of relief will be by wire only.

8. ACKNOWLEDGE.

Issued at 8.0 p.m.   Sept. 23rd. 1918.

                                        D. Butterworth
                                        Lieut. & A/Adjt.
                                        1st. Bn. North Staffordshire Regt.

Copies to:-
    No. 1. Commanding Officer.   No. 2. Second in Command.
    "   3. O.C. "A" Coy.   "   4. O.C. "B" Coy.
    "   5. O.C. "C" "   "   6. O.C. "D" "
    "   7. Transport Officer.   "   8. Quarter Master.
    "   9.& 10. War Diary.   " 11. O.C. 9th. Bn. East
    " 12. R.S.M.   Surrey Regt.

SECRET.   Copy No. 8

1st. BN. NORTH STAFFORDSHIRE REGT.

OPERATION ORDER NO. 35.

1. The Battalion will be relieved in the Left Sub Sector on the night of 29th/30th., by the 2/2 Londons (R.F.). On relief the Battalion will embus at BULLY GRENAY and proceed to COUPIGNY Huts.

2. An advance party as under will leave the line at 9.0 a.m. 29th. inst. and take over huts at COUPIGNY.
   Bn.Hd.Qrs. Lieut. C.N. Adams and 1 N.C.O.
   1 Officer and 1 N.C.O. per Coy.
   This advance party will be under command of Lieut. C.N. Adams and will rendezvous at Bn.Hd.Qrs. at 9.0 a.m.

3. Guides of one N.C.O. per platoon and 1 N.C.O. for Bn.Hd.Qrs. will will rendezvous at Bn.Hd.Qrs. at 3.30. p.m. 29th. and will proceed under command of 2/Lieut. Peacock to BULLY GRENAY, reporting at Bn.Hd. Qrs. 2/2 Londons at 5.0 p.m. These guides will guide respective units of 2/2 Londons to line.
   Trench routes will be invariably used by all advance parties and guides.

4. Lorries to carry Battalion to COUPIGNY will arrive in Square BULLY at 7.30 p.m. Companies will report their arrival in BULLY GRENAY to the Adjutant at Reserve Bn.Hd.Qrs. BULLY GRENAY when busses will be detailed.

5. Transport arrangements will be as follows:-
   (a) All Lewis guns and magazines will be carried to busses.
   (b) Officers Trench Kits, cooking utensils, etc., of "A", "B", "C" and "D" Coys. will be stacked at Junction of CHURCH STREET and BETHUNE Road, M.12.b.03.70. by 8.0 p.m. Transport Officer will arrange for transport of these goods to COUPIGNY. Guards of one N.C.O. and one man per Coy. will remain with these goods during transmission.
   (c) Bn.Hd.Qrs. Trench goods including R.A.P goods will be stacked at Bn.Hd.Qrs. at 8.0.p.m. Transport Officer will transport these to COUPIGNY. Regtl. Sergt. Major will detail one N.C.O. and 2 men to remain with these goods during transmission.
   (d) Mens Packs and blankets, will be sent direct to COUPIGNY.
   (e) Transport Officer will arrange to transport Officers Kits and mens rations only from Divisional Wing.
   (f) Transport and Quarter Masters Stores will move to COUPIGNY Huts under arrangements to be made by Transport Officer.

6. All Defence Schemes, Aeroplane photographs, Trench Stores and S.O.S. Rockets will be carefully handed over. Battle Positions carefully explained and usual receipts and certificates rendered to Bn.Hd. Qrs. by 12.0 noon 30th. inst.

7. Completion of relief will be notified to Bn.Hd.Qrs. by wiring time only and Coys. will report their arrival both in BULLY GRENAY as in para. 4 and into huts at COUPIGNY.

8. ACKNOWLEDGE.

Issued at 2.0 p.m.   DCButterworth   Date 28.9.18.
                                  Capt. & A/Adjt.
                                  1st. Bn. North Staffordshire Regt.

Copies to:-
No. 1. Commanding Officer.   No. 2. Second in Command.
"   3. O.C. 2/2 Londons.   "   4. O.C. "A" Coy.
"   5. O.C. "B" Coy.   "   6. O.C. "C" Coy.
"   7. O.C. "D" Coy.   "   8. & 9. War Diary.
" 10. Transport Officer.   " 11. Quarter Master.
No. 12. Bn. Sig. Offr. No. 13. I.O. No. 14. M.O. No. 15. R.S.M.

TO,
Hd. Qrs.,
72nd. Inf. Bde.

Herewith War Diary for the month of September.
Please acknowledge receipt.

H. Hodson Lieut. Col.
Comdg. 1st. Bn. North Staffordshire Regt.

ORDERLY ROOM.
DATE 2-10-18
No. F666.
1ST NORTH STAFFORDSHIRE REGT

Army Form C. 2118.

WAR DIARY
or
INTELLIGENCE SUMMARY.
(Erase heading not required.)

1st Bn NORTH STAFFORDSHIRE REGIMENT.

Month ending 31st OCTOBER 1918.

WAR DIARY:-

Army Form C. 2118.

WAR DIARY
or
INTELLIGENCE SUMMARY.
(Erase heading not required.)

Instructions regarding War Diaries and Intelligence Summaries are contained in F. S. Regs., Part II. and the Staff Manual respectively. Title pages will be prepared in manuscript.

Place	Date	Hour	Summary of Events and Information	Remarks and references to Appendices
SUS ST LEDGER	1.10.18		Day spent in cleaning of equipment etc. Day was fine and cold. Kitbags of men upon inspection proved to be for the most part good.	DCB
	2.10.18		Battalion training was carried out in large field outside SUS ST LEDGER. Weather was fine. R.O. spoke to the battalion on good work already done by the Brigade and the results he hoped for in the future. G.O.C. 34th Division also saw the battalion in training. Inter Coy Final Football match was played, B.H.Q. versus A Coy which resulted in a win for B.H.Q. by 3 goals to 2.	DCB
	3.10.18		Battalion took part in Brigade exercise in and around SUS ST LEDGER. Bn's part consist of of manning of an outpost line and in taking of a final objective of 3 objectives.	DCB
	4.10.18		Morning was spent in training on battalion training field and the afternoon in games and recreation. A lecture was given by B.S. Collins Grade 78th TPs on recent operations by 17th Division. Officers of the battalion attended and the lecture was thoroughly enjoyed.	DCB

WAR DIARY
or
INTELLIGENCE SUMMARY.

Army Form C. 2118.

Place	Date	Hour	Summary of Events and Information	Remarks and references to Appendices
SUS St LEGER	5/10/18		Appreciated. Orders for 1st.Line Transport to move were received.	
	6.10.18		Battalion left SUS ST.LEGER and marching via HUMBERCOURT entrained at MONDICOURT for RIBECOURT at 09.30.hrs. RIBECOURT was reached at about 06.30.hrs.without event and the Bn. was met by guides who guided Coys via "LESQUIERES to bivouaced camp South of GRAINCOURT These were reached safely, and the men settled down for the night. Great interest was displayed owing to the fact that the Bn.was bivouaced immediately west of BOURLON WOOD.	DCR
GRAINCOURT	7.10.18		Battle surplus was dispatched this day to 24th.D.R.C. at MOROHIES and the Bn. prepared to move with 73nd.Bde into support of 63rd Div. on 7th.October. The strength of the Bn.less battle surplus was 21 Officers and 622.O.R. Minimum strength of Section; was 1 N.C.O. and 6 men. C.O. and Company Commanders with R.G.C.went to reconnoitre routes by which the Brigade would move into support of 63rd.Division At 13.30 hrs.the Bn.left their bivouacs to proceed to CANTAING into further bivouacs and trenches. - Here Greatcoats and Haversacks were	DCR

Army Form C. 2118.

WAR DIARY
or
INTELLIGENCE SUMMARY.
(Erase heading not required.)

Instructions regarding War Diaries and Intelligence Summaries are contained in F. S. Regs., Part II. and the Staff Manual respectively. Title pages will be prepared in manuscript.

Place	Date	Hour	Summary of Events and Information	Remarks and references to Appendices
			dumped and every man was fitted out with fighting order, packs being carried instead of haversacks, each man carried 170 rounds of S.A.A.	
CANTAING	8.10.18		Bn. with 72nd. Inf. Bde. moved into support of 63rd. Div. and occupied positions in RUMILLY TRENCH, S.W. of RUMILLY. ZERO for attack on NIERGNIES by 63rd. Div. was 04.30. hrs. 8th. October and the Bn. left CANTAING for RUMILLY TRENCH at 06.30. hrs crossing river L'ESCAUT by NOYELLES. Up to this point the Bn. sustained no casualties although hostile shelling on RUMILLY TRENCHES was at times exceedingly heavy. The village of NIERGNIES was taken by 63rd. Div. at about 11.00 hrs. and the 72nd. Bde. was called upon to hold and consolidate positions in and around the village the left flank being allotted to the 1st. N. Staffords. A.B. & C. Coys moved at 16.30 hrs to take up these positions and on the way up came under very heavy shell fire. Casualties were sustained as follows. Killed 2. Other Ranks. Wounded 11. Other Ranks. Eventually a line was established with 1st. North Staffords on the left, 8th. R. East Surreys on the right and 8th. R.W. Kents in reserve.	DCB

Army Form C. 2118.

WAR DIARY
or
INTELLIGENCE SUMMARY.
(Erase heading not required.)

Instructions regarding War Diaries and Intelligence Summaries are contained in F. S. Regs., Part II. and the Staff Manual respectively. Title pages will be prepared in manuscript.

Place	Date	Hour	Summary of Events and Information	Remarks and references to Appendices
NEIRGNIES	9.10.18		The 24th.Division now held the line with 72nd.Bde.forward,73rd Bde.in support and 17th.Bde. in reserve.	
			Orders were received that 8th.West Kents in conjunction with Guards Division on our right would attack the village of AWOINGT at 6.20 hrs. as zero. - 1st.North Staffords would remain in present positions and the 9th.East Surreys would form a defensive flank to the North.	
			The village was taken successfully by the West Kents with 36 prisoners and information was received that the enemy had withdrawn. The En. pushed out reconnaissance patrols - 2/Lt RIDER'S platoon of "A"Coy. 2/Lt CLIFT'S of "C"Coy. went into CAMBRAI and "scout hands" with troops of 57th.Div. and Canadians. Cavalry patrols were pushed out from 6th D.G and the village of CAUROIR was reported clear of the enemy. 72nd Bde. now became reserve Bde. of the Div. and spent the night concentrated around NeIRGNIES. The troops were exceedingly cheerful and spent a long time hunting for souvenirs left by the Hun in his hasty retreat. 2/Lt.NEILSON was hit this day and 2/Lt.HILL M.M. took over command of	bcR

Army Form C. 2118.

WAR DIARY
or
INTELLIGENCE SUMMARY.

(Erase heading not required.)

Instructions regarding War Diaries and Intelligence Summaries are contained in F. S. Regs., Part II. and the Staff Manual respectively. Title pages will be prepared in manuscript.

Place	Date	Hour	Summary of Events and Information	Remarks and references to Appendices
NIERGNIES	10.10.18		"D"Coy. The enemy shelled NEIRGNIES and the precincts heavily during the night and casualties resulted as follows - Wounded Other Ranks 2.	
		At 07.00 hrs. the Division moved forward and the Bn. moved as leading Bn. of 72nd.Inf.Bde. via NEIRGNIES - AWOIGNT - CAUROIR to CAGNOCLES across country reaching CAGNOCLES at about 17.30hrs and the Bn. went into billets for the night in the village "A" echelon transport being billeted just outside the village. Altogether this day was entirely pleasant, the weather was exceptionally good and a long halt for dinners outside CAUROIR was verymuch appreciated by the men. Billets in CAGNOCLES were good. Casualties NIL.	DCK
CAGNOCLES	11.10.18		The advance was continued at 06.30.hrs upon AVESNES, 72nd.Bde.now became support Bde. to 17th.Bde.who were attacking. The Bn. left CAGNOCLES at 06.30 hrs and moved as leading Bn. of 72nd.Bde.towards AVESNES. It was soon apparent that the 17th.Bde.had met with strong opposition, this proved to be so and that the 3rd. R.B's and 1st.R.FS had sustained serious casualties on the open ground between AVESNES	DCK

(A9473) Wt W2355/P360 600,000 12/7 D. D. & L. Sch. 53a. Forms/C2118/15

WAR DIARY
or
INTELLIGENCE SUMMARY.

(Erase heading not required.)

Army Form C. 2118.

Place	Date	Hour	Summary of Events and Information	Remarks and references to Appendices
			and ST.AUBERT the enemy being strongly positioned with good machine gun positions in the houses in the latter village especially in the TOWER of ST.AUBERT. Orders were given for the men to dig in on the slope in rear of Railway from AVESNES to RIEUX, this was done and B.T.Q. was established in the Railway embankment - these positions we were occupied for the night and the Bn. area was subjected to considerable hostile shelling, with the result that casualties as follows were sustained. Wounded,4.Other Ranks. During the day the Bn was placed at the disposal of B.G.C. 17th.Inf.Bde. and "A"Coy were sent forward to occupy a position on the open ground N.N.E. of AVESNES they were eventually withdrawn at about 14.00 hrs to the Bn. area and remained with the Bn. during the night. The night was without event but very cold and damp. Total casualties, Killed,1.Other rank, Wounded,4.Other Ranks - 2/Lt.Goodwin proceeded on leave.	
Rly Embankment 12.10.18 S.W of AVESNES -LEZ-AUBERT			The Bn. sideslipped during the morning of Bn.inst further along the embankment in a Westerly direction until its left flank :	

WAR DIARY
or
INTELLIGENCE SUMMARY.

(Erase heading not required.)

Army Form C. 2118.

Place	Date	Hour	Summary of Events and Information	Remarks and references to Appendices
			rested in front of RIEUX on the Railway – at 15.00 hrs the Bn. moved forward in support of the 8th.Bn.Queens Regt. and after crossing Rail Way embankment swung round and advanced across the open ground leaving the AVESNES on the right and having the CAMBRAI VILLERS – N – CHAUCHIES road as left boundary, orders were received that the Bn. we would spend the night in billets in AVESNES but these were cancelled and the Bn. eventually dug itself in on the reverse slopes of the hill on which ST.AUBERT stands – A miserable downpour set in and the night spent was extremely uncomfortable – Capt. Left arrived to command "D" Coy. 2/Lts. SPERRATT and HIGGINBOTTAM joined the Bn from ENGLAND and were posted to "B" & "A" Coys respectively. 2/Lt. CURTIS proceeded on leave.	
ST.AUBERT	16.10.18		The Bn. left its bivouacs outside ST AUBERT at 04.30.hrs on the morning of the 13th.October to take over positions occupied by 1st.RFs in front of ST AUBERT and the outpost positions in front of MONTRECOURT, river guarding bridges thrown across the river Selle. The enemy held	DCB

Army Form C. 2118.

WAR DIARY
or
INTELLIGENCE SUMMARY.

(Erase heading not required.)

Instructions regarding War Diaries and Intelligence Summaries are contained in F. S. Regs., Part II. and the Staff Manual respectively. Title pages will be prepared in manuscript.

Place	Date	Hour	Summary of Events and Information	Remarks and references to Appendices
			the railway embankment on the eastern side of the river in considerable strength and from now onward the task allotted to the Bn. gradually increased in its difficulties, as no cover of any description was available and the enemy had excellent observation over the whole Bn. area. During the whole period in which the Bn. occupied the area they were subjected to heavy bombardments the whole of the time, at guns of all calibres and in abnormally heavy gas concentration in and around the whole area. Positions as follows were taken up on the morning of the 13th. "D" Coy left forward Coy with outposts in front of MONTRECOURT WOOD and remainder of Coy dug in rear of Wood. "B" Coy occupied similar positions on the right en-the-piece of the Bn.front and "A" & "C" Coys were in support dug in in echelon about 1000 yds in rear astride the road from ST AUBERT to MONTRECOURT. Lt.Col. Hodgson was wounded at 11.00 hours this morning and went down the line MAJOR W.D.STANSFELD.C. took over command of the Bn. Orders were received during the afternoon that three platoons of "A" Coy would proceed at	

WAR DIARY
or
INTELLIGENCE SUMMARY.
(Erase heading not required.)

Army Form C. 2118.

20.00 hrs to relieve a similar party of the 8th. Bn. Queens Regt. in
the village of MONTRECOURT that they would also attempt to establish
posts on the Railway embankment across the river Selle. At 20.00 hrs a
barrage was put down and "A" Coy less 1 platoon which was left in reserve crossed the river and attacked the embankment - their effort was
completely successful and three M.G's and ten prisoners were captured
seven of whom were killed by an enemy shell. Unfortunately operations
on their right did not succeed and they were counter-attacked and forced
to withdraw. They did great damage to the enemy as was testified by
one of the prisoners voluntarily the next day. Casualties were 1 killed
and eight wounded Lieut.E.R.BYAS commanded the party and 2/Lt. W.I.
HARPER.M.C. and 2/Lt.A.A.RIDER assisted him. The three platoons of the
Queens Regt. were relieved and the Bn. now held MONTRECOURT on the
western bank of the river Selle and "B" Coy remained in reserve.
B.H.Q. was removed during the night from MONTRECOURT WOOD to "B" Coys
Headquarters in a farmhouse on the outskirts of ST AUBERT. The

Army Form C. 2118.

WAR DIARY
or
INTELLIGENCE SUMMARY.
(Erase heading not required.)

Instructions regarding War Diaries and Intelligence Summaries are contained in F. S. Regs., Part II. and the Staff Manual respectively. Title pages will be prepared in manuscript.

Place	Date	Hour	Summary of Events and Information	Remarks and references to Appendices
MONTRECOURT WOOD	14.10.18		disregulations were maintained throughout the night. - Total casualties sustained on 13th.October.were. Killed,2.Other Ranks. Wounded,Officers 1. Other Ranks 13. Orders were received after a conference of C.O's at 72nd.Bde H.Q. that the 72nd Bde.would attack at 06.10 hours on the 16th.October the attack to be carried out by two Covs. of 1st. North Staffords and 2.Covs.of 8th. Bn. R.W.Kents and the 8th.East Surreys to be in reserve. "A" & "D" Covs. were selected to attack for this Bn. The aim of the attack was to obtain a footing for and attack on a large scale at a later date by the 19th. Division. The objectives given to the Bn. were two, the first to be taken by "A" Coy was the Railway embankment east of the town and the second, to be taken by "D" Coy was a sunken road beyond, about 500.yds from the embankment. A Company Commanders conference was held and details of the attack settled. At this period "A" Coy. was unfortunate and were heavily shelled 8 men being killed in one small track. CAPT.STUBLEY and 2/Lt. GOWDEN were gassed 2/Lt.HILL. was wounded and 2/Lt.CRAWFORD	DCB

WAR DIARY
or
INTELLIGENCE SUMMARY

(Erase heading not required.)

Army Form C. 2118.

Instructions regarding War Diaries and Intelligence Summaries are contained in F. S. Regs., Part II. and the Staff Manual respectively. Title pages will be prepared in manuscript.

Place	Date	Hour	Summary of Events and Information	Remarks and references to Appendices
MONTRECOURT	15/6/18		took over command of "B" Coy. "A" Coy were relieved by "B" Coy and also	
Wood			brought into village companies to lie in touch with C.O. and in	DCR
			command of left Company. Night was—1st. Lt. Ewing was wounded and	
			command of left Company was taken over by Capt. Wilson. 6 hostile bombs of	
			the 2nd 1st Bn and one A.P.M. had been sent over last night two platoons to hold	
			trench at C.6.d and C.12.d. Our Co's and C.O.'s were sent up to the	
			line during the night but were not used in positions of assembly and we have	
MONTRECOURT	1/10/18		no mishap. C.O.'s and O.C's had been up at the complete of two small wood	DCR
Wood			on "G" & the 57th and also had gone out during the afternoon and made	
			a reconnaissance (word) of a strong point found at the south of this wood	

WAR DIARY or INTELLIGENCE SUMMARY.

Army Form C. 2118.

(Erase heading not required.)

Instructions regarding War Diaries and Intelligence Summaries are contained in F. S. Regs., Part II. and the Staff Manual respectively. Title pages will be prepared in manuscript.

Place	Date	Hour	Summary of Events and Information	Remarks and references to Appendices
MONTRECOURT	17.10.18		Our first attack at 20.00 hrs on 16th & 17th was clear to Australia under orders not to allow another attack if the decided however on 17th and that the casualties already suffered by the Bn were such that it would not be advisable for a further attempt to be made — the Bde had been pushing forward during such & held the bottom of HAUSSY RIDGE fire and exposure since the early morning of 13th October. We were then brigaded to St AUBERT Bde. ("Walcourt") and held the bottom of the ridge Nos 1 & 2 Coys front of CAPELLETTE WOOD.	BCB
			We took up these forward positions on the left of CAPELLETTE WOOD. 1 Bn on the right with 1 platoon of B Coy to MONTRECOURT. It was then arranged that the 7th Bn N Fusiliers just could about 2.30 hrs on 18th — 19th when the Bn arrived at fresh Bn H.Q. Nos 3 & 4 Coys were relieved in the support of their position HAUSSY and our lone Coy fell back to bottom side of the river settled. S/Major RIDGE was posted and left wing of Battn. At 2.40 hrs on 18th the Battalion was relieved by the 1/4th	BCB

WAR DIARY
or
INTELLIGENCE SUMMARY.

(Erase heading not required.)

Army Form C. 2118.

Place	Date	Hour	Summary of Events and Information	Remarks and references to Appendices
ST AUBERT	18.10.18		On the 17/10/18 orders to the 10th Bn. were published that at 20.00 hrs and forward formations were to pass in 3rd Army area to and in turn the 10th Bn. were directed to a table of strength establishment.	
			October 18. 10th Battalion suffered the following casualties: killed 31 O.R., wounded 7 O.R., demised 7 Officers, 127 O.R. Sick 33 O.R. The 10th Bn. Battalion marched from its work and the war in which it took part and under the best of conditions.	
			The Battalion arrived out of ST AUBERT & billets in outskirts of same. At about 8 hours - AVESNES - 8 hours - LAST AL entered.	BCB
			Weather fair 50 on 10th Oct. In the afternoon of October 18th reached positions recommended.	
			AI.	
			The 11th Bn. War Diary and Intelligence Lost Battle of Mons.	
CAMPEAU	19.10.18		Very fine weather and new horses. Division in Reserve to VIII Corps.	BCB
			At 12.15 to 20.30 hrs.	

Army Form C. 2118.

WAR DIARY
or
INTELLIGENCE SUMMARY.
(Erase heading not required.)

Instructions regarding War Diaries and Intelligence Summaries are contained in F. S. Regs., Part II. and the Staff Manual respectively. Title pages will be prepared in manuscript.

Place	Date	Hour	Summary of Events and Information	Remarks and references to Appendices
CAMBRAI	20.10.18.		Day spent in resting and cleaning of billets.	DCK
do	21.10.18.		Day spent in billets and clearing up - ground reconnoitred for Coy and Bn tactical schemes. Capt G.N.JONAS proceeded on leave.	DCK
do	22.10.18		Day spent by Coys in training and tactical schemes on open ground west of CAMBRAI. - Day was wet and cold.	DCK
do	23.10.18		Battalion scheme, east of CAMBRAI. A & C Coys attacked position held by A Coy on ground immediately west of CAMBRAI. Scheme proved both interesting and enjoyable as the battalion had advanced over the identical ground under war conditions so recently. 2/Lieut SOUSTER rejoined from leave. Lieut M.K. was to be acting CAPTAIN whilst commanding a Company.	DCK
do	24.10.18.		Battalion spent day on training area in Company training and inspections. R.S.O. inspected Company billets.	DCK
do	25.10.18		Battalion took part in Bde exercise on open ground east of CAMBRAI. 1st objective being hills east of TANKTON. Lieut. C. MULLINS U.S.M.G. took over duties of R.O. from Capt Taylor to leave.	DCK

WAR DIARY
or
INTELLIGENCE SUMMARY.

(Erase heading not required.)

Army Form C. 2118.

Instructions regarding War Diaries and Intelligence Summaries are contained in F. S. Regs., Part II. and the Staff Manual respectively. Title pages will be prepared in manuscript.

Place	Date	Hour	Summary of Events and Information	Remarks and references to Appendices
AVESNES LEZ AUBERT	26.10.18.		Battalion moved with 72nd Infy Bde into billets in AVESNES.- 24th Division now becomes support division to 61st division in line.- Billets were far better than those in RUMILLY. Gov Commanders conference at 17.30 hrs. 2/Lieut J.J.CRUIKSHANK rejoined from 6 months tour of duty at home.	DCK
do	27.10.18.		Brigade Church Parade held in Gaman Cinema at AVESNES. PM attended.	DCK
do	28.10.18.		Training carried out by Coys on open ground outside AVESNES. "B"Coy beat H.Qs Coy by 2 goals to Nil.	DCK
do	29.10.18.		Training carried out under Coy arrangements during morning. Bn took part in Bde cross-country run during afternoon taking 2nd place in the Brigade, the run being won by 9th R.W.Fants.	DCK
do	30.10.18.		Training carried out under Coy arrangements. C.O. Adjutant and Coy Commanders met C.O.24th Div at FAUSSY Station and a tour of the scene of the operations carried out by the Division on Oct 16/18 was made including the counter attack which developed on the Divisions right flank, taking of sand-pits by 8th K.R.Rents-bridging of SELLE	DCK

Army Form C. 2118.

WAR DIARY
or
INTELLIGENCE SUMMARY.

(Erase heading not required.)

Place	Date	Hour	Summary of Events and Information	Remarks and references to Appendices
AVESNES-LES-AUBERT	31/10/18		river by 9th E.Surrey Regt and operations carried out by the Battalion in and around MONTRECOURT.2/Lt W.R.Goodwin rejoined from leave. Training was carried out under Coy arrangements. Bn cross-country run took place this afternoon. 2/Lt Curtis rejoined from leave. Weather broke in the afternoon. The Battalion received orders to prepare to move to forward areas. A scheme was this day set on foot for helping French civilians in the Bn area in the way of food etc.	

31.10.18

(W.D.Slocum.)
Major
Cmdg 1st Bn North Staffordshire Regt.

Army Form C. 2118.

WAR DIARY
or
INTELLIGENCE SUMMARY.
(Erase heading not required.)

CONFIDENTIAL

1st Battn North Staffordshire Regiment.

W A R   D I A R Y.

Month ending 30th NOVEMBER 1918.

Army Form C. 2118.

WAR DIARY
or
INTELLIGENCE SUMMARY.
(Erase heading not required.)

Instructions regarding War Diaries and Intelligence Summaries are contained in F. S. Regs., Part II. and the Staff Manual respectively. Title pages will be prepared in manuscript.

Place	Date	Hour	Summary of Events and Information	Remarks and references to Appendices
MESNES LE HURLUS	1/11/18		Day spent by Companies in training under Company arrangements.	
			Demonstrations were carried out in the attack with smoke barrage	
			from No 87 Coy.M.Gs. Battle surplus including 2nd I.O., Coys. 2nd Lt.	
			Pascoe, and 69 other ranks left for 31st D.R.C. Onzebih.	
			Trench strength of Battalion is now 17 Officers and 433 other ranks.	
			Major J. Stewart M.C. to be A/Lieutenant Colonel.	
			Orders received that Battn. would move to TAUSSY November 2nd.	
-do-	2/11/18		Battn. moved with 73rd Bde. into Bde. in reserve to 31st Division who	
			took over part of the line from 61st Division in front of PREUX-AU-BOIS.	
			COPY O.O.80 ATTACHED.	
			Battalion to TAUSSY.	
TAUSSY	3/11/18		Officers reconnoitred assembly position and routes to same. These	
			positions were to be between B.5.c.3. & B.5.a.4.6. in PREUX-AU-BOIS.	
TAUSSY	4/11/18		Battn. left billets at TAUSSY at 07.30 hours and proceeded in	

Army Form C. 2118.

WAR DIARY
or
INTELLIGENCE SUMMARY.
(Erase heading not required.)

Instructions regarding War Diaries and Intelligence Summaries are contained in F. S. Regs., Part II. and the Staff Manual respectively. Title pages will be prepared in manuscript.

Place	Date	Hour	Summary of Events and Information	Remarks and references to Appendices
			reserve to 73rd Bde. via RIEUX FARM to Eastern outskirts of	
			BOHAIN. No time was spent here however and the Batn advanced	
			across the open ground in a N.E. direction towards Rly. embankment South	
			of SEPMERIES. News of the advance by 73rd Bde. was good, the village	
			of MARESCHES having fallen into their hands, and later JENLAIN and	
			the JENLAIN-LE QUESNOY ROAD. The Batn. moved into billets in	
			SEPMERIES at 13.00 hours. Great interest was displayed in the booty	
			prisoners taken by 73rd Bde. who numbered over 520. Officers went	
			forward during the afternoon to reconnoitre ground in front of	
			MARESCHES. Night was spent in SEPMERIES. Lieut Cooke rejoined	
			from leave and took over Command of 'D' Company.	
SEPMERIES			The Batn. left SEPMERIES at 13.30 hours still in reserve to	
			73rd Bde. and proceeded without event into billets in MARESCHES-	
			LE-GRAND. Billeting was extremely close and weather was bad.	
			The troops were heartily received by the civilians who had been	
			six hours of the Boche up to 06.30 hours on 24 October the last.	

Army Form C. 2118.

WAR DIARY
or
INTELLIGENCE SUMMARY.
(Erase heading not required.)

Instructions regarding War Diaries and Intelligence
Summaries are contained in F. S. Regs., Part II.
and the Staff Manual respectively. Title pages
will be prepared in manuscript.

Place	Date	Hour	Summary of Events and Information	Remarks and references to Appendices
WARGNIES LE GRAND	5/11/18		Batn. was ordered to be prepared to move into support with 73rd Bde. on morning of 6th inst. - 'B' Echelon was formed and the Batn. equipped in fighting order.	
			Came to the 19th Division being held up at RUTHECHIES, the advance of 24th Division was held up for a time in front of ST MAAST la VALLEE on the western bank of river GAMPRON and 73rd Bde. did not move from WARGNIES le GRAND on 6th inst. 73rd Bde. however moved into Reserve and 72nd Bde. became Support Bde. 1st North Staffords in reserve to the Bde.	
-do-	7/11/18		The 17th Bde. attacked across River GAMPRON at 06.00 hours took ST.MAAST and the high ground to N.E. of river. The Bn. moved to LA BOIS CRETTE in Reserve to 72nd Bde at 04.30 hours. After 17th Bde. had captured high ground N.E. of ST.MAAST the 72nd Bde. became front line Bde. 8th N.W.Kants on right 8th G.Surreys on left 1st North Staffords in Reserve. The leading Battalions continued	

Army Form C. 2118.

WAR DIARY
or
INTELLIGENCE SUMMARY.

(Erase heading not required.)

Instructions regarding War Diaries and Intelligence Summaries are contained in F. S. Regs., Part II. and the Staff Manual respectively. Title pages will be prepared in manuscript.

Place	Date	Hour	Summary of Events and Information	Remarks and references to Appendices
			the advance and captured BAVAY without difficulty at about 14 hours.	
			The Batln moved to ST WAAST la VALLEE. The men were again heartily	
			welcomed by the civilians as the enemy had been in their midst at	
			dawn the same day and in many cases civilians were still found	
			locked in their cellars. Everywhere evidence of the brutality and	
			looting of the enemy was apparent - linen - furniture- crockery	
			had been stolen and houses ransacked in every direction. Surplus	
			stores were now held then ground East of BAVAY with 19th Division on	
			left and Guards Division on right, and 1st Batn. moved from ST.	
			WAAST to billets in BAVAY which were occupied at about 16.30 hours.	
			Here again the civilians received the troops with open arms.	
			The roads had been blown up in many places the bridges over the	
			bad shute. Orders were received during the morning of 8th inst. by	
			which would be carried out on the morning of 9th inst. by	
			2nd R.W.Kents on left and 1st North Staffords on right. 1st	
			Line held by the 1st Surreys behind Staff Headquarters.	

Army Form C. 2118.

WAR DIARY
or
INTELLIGENCE SUMMARY.
(Erase heading not required.)

Instructions regarding War Diaries and Intelligence Summaries are contained in F. S. Regs., Part II. and the Staff Manual respectively. Title pages will be prepared in manuscript.

Place	Date	Hour	Summary of Events and Information	Remarks and references to Appendices
BAVAY	7/11/18		At 03.30 hours the Batln. left BAVAY to proceed to assembly positions occupied by Sth U.S.Engrs. West of River HOGNEAU. The Line was taken over at about 05 30 hours. Under M.G.fire from enemy M.Gs.on Eastern bank of River HOGNEAU. 'A' Coy. suffered the following casualties. 5 killed 7 wounded. 'B' Coy were right front-line commanded by Capt L.M.Sharp. 'C' Coy.left front line commanded by Lieut.W.R.Lawton. 'D' Coy. support Coy. commanded by Lieut. N.F.Cooke. 'A' Coy. in reserve at B.H.Q. in La GRASCOYS. commanded by 2nd Lt.R.R.Schuster. The morning was misty to begin with and inclined to be rainy. The ground was very heavy and there was considerable M.G.fire from enemy line and it appeared probable that opposition might be strong. At 06.00 hours the Bn. advanced upon the first objective which was the high ground East of River HOGNEAU. Opposition was first met with a little East of 'B' Coy. the form of M.G. fire. This was successfully dealt with by 'B' Coy. and eventually the village of La GROGNIES was captured by the Bn. 'B' & 'C' Coys then passed on towards southern portion of	

(A9259) Wt W4355/P360 600,000 12/17 D. D. & L. Sch. 50a. Forms/C2118/15

WAR DIARY
or
INTELLIGENCE SUMMARY.
(Erase heading not required.)

Army Form C. 2118.

Instructions regarding War Diaries and Intelligence Summaries are contained in F. S. Regs., Part II. and the Staff Manual respectively. Title pages will be prepared in manuscript.

Place	Date	Hour	Summary of Events and Information	Remarks and references to Appendices
			BOIS DE LA LANIERE, were considerable M.G.fire was encountered but eventually dealt with and the wood in front of the village fell into our hands at approx.08.00 hours. On the leading platoons of B & C Coys attempting to leave the BOIS DE LA LANIERE on its eastern side, they were met by very considerable M.G. fire from the direction of ETIGNIES. This was persistent and was intermingled with sniping from direction of CHAUSSE PRUNEAUT. The advance was temporarily held up on both Kents front and Guards front and the Battn. temporarily consolidated a line in front of the wood. The enemy now commenced to shell heavily the BOIS DE LA LANIERE and the wood further through it also fields in rear and it was realised that the enemy meant to hold the line of MAUBEUGE-MONS RAILWAY immediately east of ETIGNIES. Harassing fire from 18-pdrs. (1 Section 107 Bde.R.F.A. was under the command of Lt.Col.Stamer M.C throughout the whole operation) was brought to bear on suspected M.G.posts in ETIGNIES and on the Rly. and an attempt was made to push forward. 'B' Coy were partially successful but McKenna and	

(39475) Wt W3355/P256 60,000 12/7 D. D. & L. Sch 53a. Forms/C2118/13

Army Form C. 2118.

WAR DIARY
or
INTELLIGENCE SUMMARY.
(Erase heading not required.)

Place	Date	Hour	Summary of Events and Information	Remarks and references to Appendices
BOIS-DE-LA-HAUT LANIERE 2/A	14-17		'C' Coy and Guards Division could not get forward owing to persistent M.G. fire and heavy shelling of forward areas and eventually a line about 500X East of BOIS DE LA LANIERE was consolidated by B & C Coys - 'D' Coy was withdrawn into support and 'A' Coy to X reserve in houses in LE GROS THENE. 'A' echelon of transport was brought up to western outskirts of LONGUEVILLE. During the night 'D' Coy pushed forward patrols down CHAUSSEE BRUNEHAUT to attempt to clear up the M.G. situation, it was however impossible to get into the village as the M.G. fire was enfilade and although four separate patrols attempted to reach FEIGNIES during the night none succeeded. The 9th.N.Y.Yorks however succeeded in establishing their line on the MONS-MAUBEUGE RAILWAY North of FEIGNIES and the 2nd Grenadier Guards dug in South of FEIGNIES. At 05.00 hours our patrols succeeded in establishing posts on the MONS-MAUBEUGE RAILWAY East of FEIGNIES.	
FRONT OF FEIGNIES			During the night of 8/9th Nov. the 24th Division took over the	

WAR DIARY or INTELLIGENCE SUMMARY.

Army Form C. 2118.

Corps frontage having 72nd & 73rd Bdes. in line and 17th in support, this meant that the relief promised the 72nd Bde. at dawn on 9th was impossible and in addition they were given five objectives covering a total distance of 7000 yards. Zero was 07.45 hours and the Bn. commenced to advance on FRAMERIES village at this hour. The Bn. completed the capture of the village at about 09.00 hours. The advance was continued to the final objective through L'OUVRAGE, South of BOIS des SARTS, FBG. des SARTS and the Batn. consolidated on the high ground East of MONS-MAUBEUGE Road at about 11.30 hours 9th Nov. During the afternoon orders were received that 'A' Coy were to go and hold part of an outpost line running from POISSOIS to BLUGIES which was to act as a support to Cavalry who were endeavouring to find touch with the enemy. During the night of 9/10th Nov. this outpost line was shelled also billets in FBG. de MONS which resulted in following casualties.3 killed 7 wounded.

Army Form C. 2118.

WAR DIARY
or
INTELLIGENCE SUMMARY.
(Erase heading not required.)

Instructions regarding War Diaries and Intelligence Summaries are contained in F. S. Regs., Part II. and the Staff Manual respectively. Title pages will be prepared in manuscript.

Place	Date	Hour	Summary of Events and Information	Remarks and references to Appendices
FBG DE MONS	10/11/18		Battalion was relieved in line by 13th Bn.60th Rifles and proceeded to billets in EUGIERS. This ended the Bns second tour of open fighting during which as a front line Battalion they had advanced over a distance of over 16000x in 48 hours. The men were very tired but in the best possible spirits. Total casualties were 10 killed 30 wounded. Officer casualties nil. A draft of 85 other ranks joined the Bn. this day. 'B' Echelon rejoin the Bn.	
FEIGNIES	11/11/18		At 06.00 hours the Bn. marched out of EUGIERS (0.0.58 attached) and proceeding via LONGUEVILLE – BAVAY, went into billets in BUVIGNIES S.W. of BAVAY. During the march news was received that hostilities would cease at 11.00 hours Nov.11th and on the Bns' arrival in billets this was confirmed.	
BUVIGNIES	12/11/18		Bn. moved by march route 2 billets in ST MARIE LA VALLEE during the afternoon. Capt W.J.T. Oxley M.C. rejoined the Bn. from employment as A/G.S. Officer 5 with 24th Division.	

Army Form C. 2118.

WAR DIARY
or
INTELLIGENCE SUMMARY.
(*Erase heading not required.*)

Instructions regarding War Diaries and Intelligence Summaries are contained in F.S. Regs., Part II. and the Staff Manual respectively. Title pages will be prepared in manuscript.

Place	Date	Hour	Summary of Events and Information	Remarks and references to Appendices
STWAAST	8/11/18		Day spent in clearing up of equipment and in kit inspections. Capt.K.F.H.Murray rejoined the Batn.	
-do-	9/11/18		Batn.paraded at 08.35 hours and was addressed by M.G.C. 73rd Bde. who expressed his appreciation of the good work accomplished by all ranks of the Batn. during recent successful operations. Remainder of day spent in cleaning equipment etc. Capt.D.C.Butterworth proceeded on leave. Capt.J.Lawler M.C. & C. rejoined from leave.	
-do-	10/11/18		A short training recconnaisance was carried out in the morning. A Sports Committee was formed under Capt.K.F.H.Murray who is in charge of all Recreational Training and Sports Competitions. An Inter-Platoon Football Competition commenced to-day.	
-do-	11/11/18		Thanksgiving Services were held in the Parish Church in commemoration of the termination of hostilities. Covs.B.H.Q.and Transport attended as strong as possible. Services were conducted by Rev.F.G.M.Kennedy C.F. Capt.N.M. left rejoined from leave.	

Army Form C. 2118.

WAR DIARY
or
INTELLIGENCE SUMMARY.
(Erase heading not required.)

Instructions regarding War Diaries and Intelligence Summaries are contained in F. S. Regs., Part II. and the Staff Manual respectively. Title pages will be prepared in manuscript.

Place	Date	Hour	Summary of Events and Information	Remarks and references to Appendices
ST. WAAST	7/11/18		The Batn. moved to MARESCHES marching off at 08.25 hours and proceeding via LA BOIS CRETEE and VILLERS POL, a march of about 8½ miles. Billets in MARESCHES were poor, the village having suffered considerably from small-fire. O.O. No.40 attached.	
MARESCHES	9/11/18		The Bn. moved to CITE DESSEMER (DENAIN) marching off at 08.10 hours and proceeding via SEPMERIES – ARTRES – MING – THIANT –DOUCHY – NEUVILLE. The march was about 17 miles long, a detour of about 4 miles being necessary owing to a bridge over the canal de l'escaut being broken. The Bn. arrived in billets about 14.30 hours. Billets were excellent, nearly all the men having beds for the night. The civilians were very friendly and did all they could to make Officers and men comfortable. O.O. No.41 attached.	
CITE DESSEMER	10/11/18		The Bn. moved to ESAILLON, marching off at 09.30 hours. The distance was about 9 miles, the route followed being ROUEIX – HASPAING – AUBERCHICOURT. Billets in ESAILLON were in a very dirty condition, but after being cleaned up they were fairly good.	

WAR DIARY
or
INTELLIGENCE SUMMARY.
(Erase heading not required.)

Army Form C. 2118.

Instructions regarding War Diaries and Intelligence Summaries are contained in F. S. Regs., Part II. and the Staff Manual respectively. Title pages will be prepared in manuscript.

Place	Date	Hour	Summary of Events and Information	Remarks and references to Appendices
ECHELON.	19/4/19		Major The Hon. W.H.Littleton and 2nd Lieut. G.Sulberg joined the Battn. this day, and 2nd Lieut. W.H.Wright left to join the M.G.C. Grantham. O.C.No.13 attached.	
			Two hours training was carried out under Company Commanders. A Company Commander's Conference was held at B.H.Q. at 12.00 hours at which the Educational and Recreational Schemes were discussed.	
-do-	21/4/19		The Battalion paraded on the Square at 10.00 hours and proceeded for a short route march, marching past Lieut.Col.Cameron D.S.O. Acting Brigade Commander. The inter-platoon football competition was continued and some keen games took place.	
-do-	22/4/19		Battalion drill was carried out at 10.00 hours. An excellent lecture on 'Demobilization' was delivered at 11.30 hours by Capt.Books. Divisional Education Officer. Further games in the football competition took place. The weather was fine but frosty. Lieuts. H.S.Emery and W.H.Robinson joined the Battalion.	

Army Form C. 2118.

WAR DIARY
or
INTELLIGENCE SUMMARY.
(Erase heading not required.)

Place	Date	Hour	Summary of Events and Information	Remarks and references to Appendices
ECAILLON	23/11/18		A short Battalion Drill Parade was held at 10.00 hours. The remainder of the day was devoted to Recreational Training.	
do-	24/11/18		No training was carried out. The Divisional Band played in the Square during the afternoon, this was much appreciated. Three lorries left at 08.00 hours for the LENS AREA, 75 Officers and other ranks taking advantage of this opportunity to revisit this area where the Battalion had spent many months of Trench warfare. Lieut. G.W.Gibson joined this day.	
ECAILLON	25/11/18		The Bn. moved to the LANDAS AREA, marching off at 08.30 hours. The route followed was VILLERS CAMPEAU - MARCHIENNES - BEUVRY. Billets were reached about 13.00 hours. They were good for the most part, but very scattered, the Battn. Billeting Area being 6 kilometre in length. 2nd Lieuts.A.A.Rider and N.E.Jaques joined the Battalion. O. C. No. 43 attached.	

Army Form C. 2118.

WAR DIARY
or
INTELLIGENCE SUMMARY.
(Erase heading not required.)

Instructions regarding War Diaries and Intelligence Summaries are contained in F. S. Regs., Part II. and the Staff Manual respectively. Title pages will be prepared in manuscript.

Place	Date	Hour	Summary of Events and Information	Remarks and references to Appendices
LANDAS	26.11.18		The Battalion moved to the NOMAIN Area,marching off at 11.10 hours, and arriving in billets about 13.00 hours. Billets were good but scattered. The Battalion was complimented by the Acting Brigade Commander on it's smart turnout and good march discipline. (Operation Order No.4 attached)	
NOMAIN	27.11.18		2/Lt.J.W.Cock returned from 6 months duty in England. Training was carried out by Companies from 09.00 - 13.00 hours. The Football Competition and Educational Classes were continued. 2/Lt.W.Collins (Sherwood Foresters) joined the Battalion.	
NOMAIN	28.11.18		Outdoor training was interfered with by bad weather.	
NOMAIN	29.11.18		Training was carried out during the morning.The Commanding Officer inspected the recent drafts,a total of 140 Other Ranks being on parade.	
NOMAIN	30.11.18		No training was carried out, the Saturday holiday being observed. An Officers V Sergeants Football match was played,result being a win for the Sergeants by 10 goals to 1.	

Secret   1st Batt. North Stafford Regiment

Operation Order No 36.

1. The Batn. with 72nd Bde. will move by march route to Blaveries[?] on Nov. 2nd. 1st Line Transport will accompany Batn.

2. The Batn. will parade ready to move off in column of route at 13.50 hours, head of Bn. passing Church will be at 0 on 00.40. 2nd Line Transport will be in rear of Batn. ready to move off at this hour.

   Dress – Full Marching Order.
   Box Respirators in Alert Position.
   Steel Helmets worn.
   Leather jerkins packed in packs – according to pattern.

3. All Blankets (rolled in tens) & Officers Kits will be stacked outside Quartermasters Stores by 11.00 hours. All Officers Mess material, Cooking Utensils Etc. will be stacked outside Q.M.S. by 13.00 hours.
   * All Officers Mess Kit surplus to one box per Company will be sent to Q.M.S. by 0900 hours. This will be stored in advance by the Quartermaster.
   * And all Officers Kit surplus to 40 lbs per Officer.
   As only 1 lorry is allotted for transport of blankets, No Officers Kit weighing more than 40 lbs & not more than 1 box (mess) per Coy. will be accepted for transport.

4. OC Coys will notify B.H.Q. when billeting of their Coys is completed in Blaveries[?].

5. Acknowledge.

Issued at 21.20 hours.   Date 1-11-18

(Sd) D C Butterworth Capt & Adjt
1st Batn North Staff Regt.

Copy No. 7

1st. Bn. Northern Staffords Regt.
OPERATION ORDER No. 56.

Ref. Sheet 51b. 1/40,000.
     51b.N. 1/20,000.

1. The Bn. will move by march route tomorrow, Novr. 11th. to Bellot in Squares V.38., 32, 30.
    Bn. will be formed up in column of route, facing west, west of Bn. Hd. qrs. Coy. at gate of Bn. Hd. qrs. mess (S.38.B.60.10), at 06.00 hours. Bn. Hd. qrs. Coy. will lead. Coys. will be in following order. "A". ...
    Dress. Fighting order. Steel helmets worn, bat respirators slung. Packs, pumps and S.A.A. (170) to be carried on Coys. limbers.
    DRAFT. The reinforcement draft of 85 other ranks will parade as a separate Coy. in rear of "D" Coy. they will be under command of 2/Lt. J.C. Porter assisted by 2/Lt. T. Lambert. Dress for all ranks will be Full Marching order. Steel helmets will be worn.

2. Officers Kits, Mess utensils - Orderly Room cords etc. will be stacked outside Bn. Hd. and Bn. Hd. qrs. by 06.00 hours. Transport Officer will arrange to collect.

3. Bearers of 72nd. Field Ambulance will report to 2nd. Field Ambulance at S.32.B.8.5. at 06.00 hours, 11th. Novr.

4. Watches will be synchronised with 2nd Larrace at Bn. Hd. qrs. to-night.

5. ACKNOWLEDGE.

Issued at 23.00 hours.   10 - 11 - 18.

                                        D.C. Butterworth
                                        Capt. & Adjt.
                                        1st. Bn. North. Staff. Regt.

Copies to:-
    1. Commanding Officer.   2. O.C. "A" Coy.
    3. O.C. "B" Coy.   4. O.C. "C" Coy.
    5. O.C. "D" Coy.   6. & 7. War Diary.
    8. Transport Officer.   9. Quarter-Master.
    10. R.S.M.   11. 2/Lt. J.C. Porter.
    12. Medical Officer.

S E C R E T.   1st. Bn North Staffordshire Regiment.

OPERATION ORDERS No 40.

Ref:Sheets 51 and 51.A. 1/40,000.

1. The Battalion will move by march route to MARESCHES to-morrow 17th inst.
   The Battalion will be formed up in column of route facing S.W. with the head of the column at H.22.a.2.3. ready to move off at 08.05 hours.
   Companies will march in following order:-
   B.H.Q. "B" "A" Coys. "C" "D".
   Markers will report to R.S.M. at Bn Hd qrs at 07.30 hours. They must be in possession of accurate states showing numbers on parade.

2. First Line Transport will accompany the Battalion and will march in rear.
   It will be formed up in the Transport Lines ready to move by 08.05 hours.

3. Dress.   Full marching order. Soft caps will be worn, leather jerkins will not be worn.

4. Lewis guns and magazines will be carried on First Line Transport.

5. Blankets(rolled in bans) will be stacked outside the Qr.Mr's. Stores by 07.00 hours.   Orderly room boxes, Officers' Valises, Mess Utensils,/etc., will be stacked outside respective Hd. qrs. by 07.15 hours. Transport Officer will arrange to collect.

6. Watches will be synchronised with Sgt. Baggage at Bn. Hd. qrs. by 07.15 hours tomorrow.

7. ACKNOWLEDGE.

Issued at 19.30 hours.   16 - 11 - 18.

                                    G.Robinson
                                    2/Lieut. & A/Adjt.
                                    1st. Bn. North Staffordshire Regt.

Copies to:-
   No. 1. Commanding Officer.   No. 2. & 3. War Diary.
    " 4. O.C. "A" Coy.   " 5. O.C. "B" Coy.
    " 6. O.C. "C" Coy.   " 7. O.C. "D" Coy.
    " 8. Transport Officer.   " 9. Quarter-Master.
    " 10. R.S.M.   " 11. Sgt. Baggage.

SECRET.   Copy. No...7......

1st. BN. NORTH STAFFORDSHIRE REGT.

OPERATION ORDER NO. 41.

Ref. Sheet. 51.A. 1/40,000.

1.   The Battalion will move by march route to the LOURCHES area tomorrow, 18th. inst.
        The Battalion will be formed up in column of route facing E. with the head of the column at L.25.d.0.9. ready to move off at 08.10 hours.
        Companies will march in following order:-
          Bn. Hd. Qr.s "A" "B" Drums "C" "D".
        Markers will report to R.S.M. at Bn. Hd. Qrs. at 07.55 hours. They will be in possession of accurate states showing numbers on parade.

2.   First Line Transport will march in rear of Battalion. It will be formed up facing S., head of column at L.25.d.05.90. ready to move off at 08.10 hours.

3.   Dress, as for today.

4.   Lewis guns and magazines will be carried on First Line Transport.

5.   Blankets (rolled in tens) will be stacked outside Qr. Mr's. Stores by 07.00 hours.
        Officers' valises, Mess utensils, Orderly Room boxes, etc., will be stacked outside various Hd. Qrs. by 07.00 hours.
        Transport Officer will arrange to collect.

6.   Sgt. Lappage will arrange to synchronise watches by 07.15 hrs. tomorrow.

7.   Advance parties constituted as follows, will report to 2/Lt. Goodwin at Bn. Hd. Qrs. Mess at 07.00 hours
          1. N.C.O. per Coy. and 1. N.C.O. for Bn. Hd. Qrs.
        They will bring with them bicycles lent to Coys. for this purpose yesterday.
        Transport Officer will send a mounted orderly with this party.

8.   ACKNOWLEDGE.

Issued at 23.15 hours.   17 - 11 - 18.

                                                2/Lt. & A/Adjt.
                                          1st. Bn. North Staffordshire Regt.

Copies to:-
   No. 1. Commanding Officer.   No. 2. O.C. "A" Coy.
    " 3. O.C. "B" Coy.   " 4. O.C. "C" Coy.
    " 5. O.C. "D" Coy.   " 6.& 7. War Diary.
    " 8. Transport Officer.   " 9. Quarter-Master.
    " 10. R.D.M.   " 11. Sgt. Lappage.

S.D.R. & C.   **1st. NORTH STAFFORDSHIRE REGT.**
Copy No. 7

OPERATION ORDER NO. 43.

Ref Sheet VALENCIENNES 1/100,000.

1. The Battalion will move by march route to the sCAILLON area tomorrow, 19th. inst.
   The Battalion will be formed up in column of route facing S.W. with the head of the column at the point where Coys. broke off today ready to move off at 09.30 hours.
   Coys. will march in the following order:-
   Bn. Hd. Qrs. "B" "C" Drums "D" "A".
   Markers will report to the R.S.M. at Bn. Hd. Qrs. at 09.10 hours, they will be in possession of accurate states showing number on parade.

2. First Line Transport will march in rear of the Battalion.
   It will be formed up ready in rear of the Battalion ready to move off by 09.30 hours.

3. DRESS, as for today. Ground sheets will be worn if wet.

4. Lewis guns and magazines will be carried on First Line Transport.

5. Dinners will be cooked on the march.

6. Blankets (rolled in twos) will be stacked at the Qr. Mr's Stores by 08.15 hours.
   Officers- valises, Mess utensils, Orderly Room boxes, etc., will be stacked outside respective Hd. Qrs. by 08.30 hours.
   Transport Officer will arrange to collect.

7. Sgt. Lappage will arrange to synchronise watches by 08.30 hours.

8. Advance party arrangements will be notified later.

9. ACKNOWLEDGE.

Issued at 19.45 hours.   18 - 11 - 18.

                                   [signature]
                                   2/Lieut. & A/Adjt.
                                   1st. Bn. North Staffordshire Regt.

Copies to:-
No. 1. Commanding Officer.   No. 3. O.C. "A" Coy.
 " 2. O.C. "B" Coy.   " 4. O.C. "C" Coy.
 " 5. O.C. "D" Coy.   " 6. & 7. War Diary.
 " 8. Transport Officer.   " 9. Quarter-Master.
 " 10. R.S.M.   " 11. Sgt. Lappage.

S E C R E T.   Copy No......

1st Bn North Staffordshire Regiment.

OPERATION ORDER No.45.

Ref sheet VALENCIENNES 1/100,000.

1. The Battalion will move by march route to the LANDAS Area to-morrow 25th inst.
    The Battalion will be formed up in column of route facing S, head of column at the turning opposite B.H.Q.Mess, ready to move off at 06.30 hours.
    Companies will march in the following order:-
    C. D. Drums .A .B. Bn Hd Qrs.
    Markers will report to the R.S.M. in the square at 06.10 hours. They will be in possession of accurate parade states.

2. First line Transport will march in rear of the Battalion. It will be formed up in rear of the column ready to move off at 06.30 hours.

3. DRESS. - Full marching Order, soft caps worn, leather jerkins not worn.

4. Lewis guns and magazines will be carried on First line Transport

5. Dinners will be cooked on the march.

6. Blankets (rolled in tens) will be stacked outside the Q.M.Store by 05.15 hours.
    Officers Valises, Mess utensils, Orderly Roomboxes etc will be stacked outside respective headquarters by 05.15 hours.
    Transport Officer will arrange to collect.

7. Sgt Lappage will arrange to synchronise watches by 05.30 hrs.

8. A C K N O W L E D G E.

                                    (Sgd) E.T.Pairson 2/Lt & A/Adjt,

                                         1st Bn North Staffordshire Regt.

COPIES TO.

    No.1. Commanding Officer   2&3 War Diary.
       4. O.C. "A" Coy   5.O.C. "B" Coy.
       6. O.C. "C" "   7.O.C. "D" "
       8. Transport Officer.   9. Quartermaster.
      10. R.S.M.   11. Sgt Lappage.

SECRET   Copy No. 3

1st Bn North Staffordshire Regiment.

OPERATION ORDER No. 44.

Reference Sheet 44 1/40,000.

1. The Battalion will move by march route to the NOMAIN Area tomorrow 26th inst.
   The Battalion starting point will be road junction H.14.d.8.0.
   Head of Companies will pass this point at the following times:-

   "D" Coy   11.10 hours
   "A" "   11.12   "
   "B" "   11.14   "
   "C" "   11.16   "
   B.H.Q.   11.18   "
   Transport   11.20   "

   The Drums will march at the head of "B" Coy.

2. DRESS.- Full marching order, soft caps worn, leather jerkins not worn.

3. Lewis guns and magazines will be carried on First line Transport.

4. Dinners will be cooked on the march.

5. Blankets of "A" & "C" Coys and B.H.Q. will be stacked at the Q.M. Stores by 09.00 hours. "B" & "D" Coys blankets will be stacked at H.14.d.8.0 at 09.15 hours. O.C. "B" Coy will leave 1NCO and 3 men in charge of these blankets until they are picked up by the lorries.
   Officers valises, Mess utensils etc will be stacked outside respective headquarters by 09.15 hours.
   Transport will arrange to collect.

6. Advance parties:-
   1 N.C.O. each from "A" & "C" Coys and B.H.Q. and a mounted orderly from Transport will report to 2/Lt. Goodwin at Orderly Room LANDAS at 08.00 hours.
   1 N.C.O. each from "B" & "D" Coys will make their own way to the Church NOMAIN meeting 2/Lt. Goodwin there at 08.45 hours.

7. Sergt. Lappage will arrange to synchronize watches by 09.15 hrs.

8. ACKNOWLEDGE.

Issued at   25/11/18.

                                    (Sgd.) E.T.Peirson. 2/Lieut. & A/Adjt.
                                           1st. Bn. North Staffordshire Regiment.

Copies to :-
   1. Commanding Officer.
   2. War Diary.
   3. War Diary.
   4. O.C., "A" Coy.
   5. O.C., "B" Coy.
   6. O.C., "C" Coy.
   7. O.C., "D" Coy.
   8. Transport Officer.
   9. Quartermaster.
   10. R.S.M.
   11. Sergt. Lappage.

Army Form C. 2118.

WAR DIARY
or
INTELLIGENCE SUMMARY.
(Erase heading not required.)

9846

CONFIDENTIAL

1st Bn NORTH STAFFORDSHIRE REGIMENT

WAR DIARY

Month of December 1918.

Army Form C. 2118.

WAR DIARY
or
INTELLIGENCE SUMMARY.
(Erase heading not required.)

Instructions regarding War Diaries and Intelligence Summaries are contained in F.S. Regs., Part II. and the Staff Manual respectively. Title pages will be prepared in manuscript.

Place	Date	Hour	Summary of Events and Information	Remarks and references to Appendices
NOMAIN	1/7/18		Church parade was held in the field at NOMAIN in the morning.	DCL
			Football match was played during the afternoon to decide on Battalion team. Capt. D.O. Bat. arrived, joined from leave, 2/Lieut. C. Dickson joined Battalion and was posted to "B" Coy.	
-do-	2/7/18		Company training was carried out before Debate was from 09.00 – 11.00 hours and Battalion drill from 11.00–12.00 hours. Football match was played during afternoon with 73rd Field Ambulance resulting in a win for the Battalion by 10 goals to Nil. Filtering party returned from NOMAIN as news was received that the Battalion would probably stay in NOMAIN for some longer.	DCL
-do-	3/7/18		Weather was very hot. Lectures were given to Company Commanders. During the afternoon "B" Coy beat "A" Coy by 4 goals to Nil in Football match.	JCL
-do-	4/7/18		Weather again interfered with training to a considerable extent. During the afternoon the Battalion beat the 8th E.W.Kent Regt at Football by 3 goals to Nil.	DCL

WAR DIARY
or
INTELLIGENCE SUMMARY.

(Erase heading not required.)

Army Form C. 2118.

Place	Date	Hour	Summary of Events and Information	Remarks and references to Appendices
NOMAIN	5/11/18		Training was carried out under Company arrangements during the morn-ing and Battalion parade was held at 11.00 hours. Capt.W.D.B.Oxley. M.C. is granted permission to wear badges of rank of Major pending his promotion in the London Gazette.	DCB
-do-	6/11/18		Training was carried out as for 5th inst, during the afternoon B.H.Q. Football team played "A" Coy in the semi-final. Hd.Qrs won by 1 goal to Nil. A Colour Party this day left for England to bring back from the depot at LICHFIELD CATHEDRAL the Regimental Colours at present hanging in LICHFIELD CATHEDRAL. The party was composed as follows:— 2/Lt.W.I.Harper M.C. (in charge), 2/Lt.W.S.Jaques, C.S.M.Yates, C.S.M.Tobson, Cpl.Meagher, Cpl.Cartledge.	DCB
-do-	7/11/18		No training was carried out, the afternoon being set aside for a holiday. A party of 50 Officers and 58 men were selected/next (?) day and men but selected men but selected men were detached from the Battalion at an informal parade lining the road from NOMAIN to TEMPLEUVE as a whole in glory as passed His Majesty the King, arrived at 11.30 hours. LILLE down which road His Majesty the King arrived at 11.30 hours. No.5 Platoon beat No.6 Platoon in semi-final by 4 goals to Nil.	DCB

Army Form C. 2118.

WAR DIARY
or
INTELLIGENCE SUMMARY.
(Erase heading not required.)

Instructions regarding War Diaries and Intelligence Summaries are contained in F.S. Regs., Part II. and the Staff Manual respectively. Title pages will be prepared in manuscript.

Place	Date	Hour	Summary of Events and Information	Remarks and references to Appendices
NOMAIN	8/1/18		Church Parade was held at 11.00 hours in Village school room.	DCB
-do-	9/1/18		Company training was carried out until 11.00 hours when Battalion	DCB
			parade was held until 11.45 hours. The Officers riding class met at	
			11.45 hours.	
-do-	10/1/18		Company training was carried out throughout the morning, weather very	DCB
			cold. Captains Murray and Lomax proceeded on leave to Paris. 2/Lieut	
			Dunk rejoined from leave.	
-do-	11/1/18		Company training was carried out until 11.00 hours, a Battalion	DCB
			parade being held at 11.45 hours. L/Cpl.Maturias.M.M. was despatched	
			to Corps Concentration Camp TOURNAI, for demobilisation as a miner	
			being the first man of the Battalion to be released.	
-do-	12/1/18		Training was interfered with by unfavourable weather.	DCB
-do-	13/1/18		Company training was carried out from 09.00 - 12.00 hours.	DCB
			Recreational training was interfered with by bad weather. 13 miners	
			were despatched to Concentration Camp for demobilisation.	
-do-	14/1/18		The Saturday holiday was observed. The final of the Inter-Platoon	DCB
			Football competition was played between No.5. Platoon and No.	

WAR DIARY
or
INTELLIGENCE SUMMARY.

(Erase heading not required.)

Army Form C. 2118.

Instructions regarding War Diaries and Intelligence Summaries are contained in F. S. Regs., Part II. and the Staff Manual respectively. Title pages will be prepared in manuscript.

Place	Date	Hour	Summary of Events and Information	Remarks and references to Appendices
NOMAIN	14/9/18		(Headquarters) Platoon. A first class and most keen game resulted in a draw 2 - 2, 30 minutes extra time being played without deciding the match. The band of the 9th Battn East Surrey Regt played during the match which was witnessed by a large and enthusiastic crowd of spectators.	See
-do-	15/9/18		Church Parade was held at 11.00 hours in the Village School room.	See
-do-	16/9/18		Three men of "C" Coy were wounded by a mine explosion. A lorry took a party of 35 Officers and men to TOURNAI.	See
-do-			Training was carried out by Companies from 09.00 - 12.00 hours. The final of the Inter-Platoon Football Competition was replayed, another keen game took place No.6. Platoon being the winners by 4 goals to 2.	
-do-	17/9/18		Training was carried out by Companies from 09.00 - 11.00 hours remainder of the day being devoted to cleaning up billets. The colour party rejoined having escorted the Regimental Colours from LICHFIELD CATHEDRAL. Colours were duly placed in R.H.Q. Mess.	See
-do-	18/9/18		The Battalion moved to TOURNAI marching off at 08.10 hours. The route followed was the ORCHIES - TOURNAI main road. (Copy of Operation Order No.4 attached).	See

Army Form C. 2118.

WAR DIARY
or
INTELLIGENCE SUMMARY.
(Erase heading not required.)

Instructions regarding War Diaries and Intelligence Summaries are contained in F. S. Regs., Part II. and the Staff Manual respectively. Title pages will be prepared in manuscript.

Place	Date	Hour	Summary of Events and Information	Remarks and references to Appendices
TOURNAI	18/12/18		The Battalion reached the Infantry Barracks, where the mens billets were situated, at about 12.30 hours, the Barracks were occupied by the three Battalions of the 72nd Infantry Bde, the Battalion occupied these & the main entrance - Barracks were discovered to be in a filthy condition and devoid for the most part of heating appliances, washing and latrine accommodation. 53 miners left for Concentration Camp.	DCB
-do-	19/12/18		The day was spent in cleaning up equipment and billets. The Commanding Officer inspected billets and a conference of Company Commanders was held to discuss the furnishment of the Barracks. Lieut. J.K. Bostock M.C., joined the Battalion and was posted to "D" Coy.	DCB
-do-	20/12/18		Company training was carried from 09.00 - 12.00 hours. The B.G.C. 72nd Infantry Bde Arthur Bate inspected the Billets during the afternoon. Major the Hon W. Littleton and Lieut. F.T. Robinson left the Battalion to join the 13th and 1/6th Battalions North Staffordshire Regiment respectively.	DCB
-do-	21/12/18		The day was observed as a whole holiday. A cross country run of 3 miles	DCB

WAR DIARY
or
INTELLIGENCE SUMMARY.
(Erase heading not required.)

Army Form C. 2118.

Instructions regarding War Diaries and Intelligence Summaries are contained in F. S. Regs., Part II. and the Staff Manual respectively. Title pages will be prepared in manuscript.

Place	Date	Hour	Summary of Events and Information	Remarks and references to Appendices
TOURNAI	21/12/18		was held at 10.30 hours. "A" Coy being the winners. "A" Coy beat "B" Coy 3 - 1 in an inter-Coy ny Football Match.	DCB
-do-	22/12/18		Church parade was held in the TOURNAI cinema, during the afternoon the Battalion played the Belgian team provided by the Union Sport- -ive Tournaisienne the game resulted in a draw of 3 goals all. The weather was bad. 16 miners were sent to Corps Concentration Camp this day.	DCB
-do-	23/12/18		Day spent in cleaning of Barracks &c. 34 men were sent to Corps Concentration Camp for demobilisation. Medals were presented by the Commanding Officer to No.5 Platoon and B.H.Q. Football team.	DCB
-do-	24/12/18		Day spent in preparing for Christmas festivities. Men received that men can proceed on leave and under certain circumstances if they obtain employment not return.	DCB
-do-	25/12/18		Church parade was held 10.30 hours. A B & D Companies Christmas Dinners were held in the Barracks at 13.00 hours were a great success, the rooms were tastefully decorated. "C" Coy Christmas	DCB

Army Form C. 2118.

WAR DIARY
or
INTELLIGENCE SUMMARY.
(Erase heading not required.)

Instructions regarding War Diaries and Intelligence Summaries are contained in F. S. Regs., Part II. and the Staff Manual respectively. Title pages will be prepared in manuscript.

Place	Date	Hour	Summary of Events and Information	Remarks and references to Appendices
TOURNAI	25/12/18		dinner was at 17.30 hours and was also a great success.During the morning a Six a side Football tournament was won by "B" Coy.	DCB
-do-	26/12/18		Day was observed as a holiday.Commanding Officer proceeded on leave and Major.E.D.R.Oxley.M.C. Assumed Command.	DCB
-do-	27/12/18		Training under Company arrangements was carried out during the morning,the weather proved too bad for recreational training to be carried out as arranged.	DCB
-do-	28/12/18		Day was observed as a holiday.A lecture was given on Dickens by G.S.O.3. 24th Division.	DCB
-do-	29/12/18		A Voluntary Church Parade was held during the morning in the Y.M.C.A. TOURNAI.	DCB
-do-	30/12/18		Training was carried out during the morning under Company arrangements,a lecture was given to the Brigade by Major Delaney on Boxing.	DCB
-do-	31/12/18		Training and education were carried out under Company arrangements, the afternoon lectured. The R.C. Inspected educational training and afterwards lectured the Officers of the Brigade on the educational scheme and it was decided to put the scheme on a basis by Platoons and make each	DCB

Army Form C. 2118.

WAR DIARY
or
INTELLIGENCE SUMMARY.

(Erase heading not required.)

Place	Date	Hour	Summary of Events and Information	Remarks and references to Appendices
TOURNAI	31/12/18		Platoon Commander responsible for the education of his Platoon and specialist subjects would be dealt with by qualified instructors.	

SECRET.   1st Bn North Staffordshire Regiment.   Copy No........
                 !-!-!-!-!-!-!-!-!-!-!-!-!-!-!-!-!   11

                       OPERATION ORDER NO 49.

       Ref sheet 44 1/40,000.

1.   The Battalion will move by march route to TOURNAI on 18th
inst.

2.   The Battalion will be formed up in column of route facing
South east, head of column at road junction at G.13.b.08.60,
ready to move at 08.10 hours.
           Order of march will be as follows:-
       "A" Coy, "B" Coy, Drums, "C" Coy, Bn Hd qrs,"D" Coy, First Line
Transport.
           Markers will report to R.S.M. at 07.50 hours at Bn Hd qrs.
           DRESS.- Full marching order less steel helmets and ~~box
respirators~~. (Canteens will be carried in the pack.) Leather jerkins carried

3.   (a) All kits of Officers not at present with the Battalion
will be sent to Quartermaster's Stores by 07.30 hours 18th inst.
           (b) All steel helmets and ~~box~~ box respirators of all ranks will
be stacked at Quartermaster's Stores before 16.00 hours today.
           Sgt Chisholm will arrange transport for (a) and (b).
           (c) All blankets will be rolled in tens and stacked at
Quartermaster's Stores by 07.30 hours 18th inst.
           (d) All kits of Officers with the Battalion, Mess utensils,
Orderly Room goods etc will be stacked outside Coy and Bn Hd qrs
by 06.30 hours 18th inst.
           Sgt Chisholm will arrange to collect.
           (e) All Lewis guns and magazines will be loaded on Company
and Bn Hd qr limbers today.

4.   Breakfasts will be at 06.00 hours on 18th inst, dinners will
be cooked on the march.

5.   Sgt Lappage will arrange to synchronise watches at 20.30
hours today.

6.   A C K N O W L E D G E.

       Issued at 12.30 hours   17th Decr 1918.

                              D C Butterworth
                                                Capt & A/Adjt,
                              1st Bn North Staffordshire Regiment.
                       !-!-!-!-!-!-!-!-!-!-!-!-!-!-!-!-!

Copies to:-
     No.1 Commanding Officer.   No.2 Major N.D.H.Oxley.M.C.
     " 3   O.C. "A" Coy.   " 4   O.C. "B" Coy.
     " 5   O.C. "C" Coy.   " 6   O.C. "D" Coy.
     " 7   Quartermaster.   " 8   R.S.M.
     " 9   Sgt Lappage.   "10   Sgt Chisholm.
           Nos 11 & 12 War Diary. ✓

Headquarters,

    72nd Infantry Bde.

                    Herewith copy of "War Diary" for month of December 1918.

                                    E. Dawson Pelly, Major,

                    Comdg 1st Bn North Staffordshire Regiment.

```
ORD PLY ROOM.
DATE 1.1.19
No. 1626
1ST NORTH
STAFFORDSHIRE REGT
```

WAR DIARY

For Month of

JANUARY 1919

Army Form C. 2118.

Instructions regarding War Diaries and Intelligence Summaries are contained in F. S. Regs., Part II. and the Staff Manual respectively. Title pages will be prepared in manuscript.

WAR DIARY
or
INTELLIGENCE SUMMARY.
(Erase heading not required.)

Place	Date	Hour	Summary of Events and Information	Remarks and references to Appendices
Tournai	1/1/19		Training and Educational Classes carried out under Company arrangements until 1230 hours. Lieut. K.E.H. Murray proceeded on leave to England. The Battalion football team played 10th [illegible] R.W.K. (Army Special) match being 1 goal each.	DCB
	2/1/19		Company training and Educational Classes during the morning. Weather bad. ~~[illegible]~~	DCB
	3/1/19		Company training was carried out during the morning. The Battalion Colours were shown to the men by platoons and short explanation of the Colours given. During the afternoon 'D' Coy. played 8th E. Surrey Regt. in Brigade knock-out competition beating them by 6 goals to 3.	DCB
	4/1/19		Day was observed as holiday. 'A' Coy. beat 'B' Coy by 7 goals to nil. in inter Coy. Football League. Bn Sergeants Mess was opened this day.	DCB
	5/1/19		Church Parade was held in Y.M.C.A. Tournai at 1100 hours. Weather very bad. Orders were received that all time serving soldiers with two or more years unbroken service would proceed on 28 days furlough in the near future.	DCB
	6/1/19		Training was carried out under Company arrangements during the morning. Weather was bad and games were interfered with.	DCB
	7/1/19		Training was carried out under Coy. arrangements during the morning. Weather was bad and games were interfered with. ~~A meeting was this day held and it was decided to give a [illegible] [illegible] committee [illegible] being elected [illegible].~~	DCB

(A9475) Wt W2358/P360 600,000 12/17 D. D. & L. Sch. 52a. Forms/C2118/15

WAR DIARY
or
INTELLIGENCE SUMMARY.

(Erase heading not required.)

Army Form C. 2118.

Instructions regarding War Diaries and Intelligence Summaries are contained in F. S. Regs., Part II. and the Staff Manual respectively. Title pages will be prepared in manuscript.

Place	Date	Hour	Summary of Events and Information	Remarks and references to Appendices
TOZIVRZI	8/1/19		[illegible handwritten entry]	App
"	9/1/19		[illegible]	App
"	10/1/19		[illegible]	App
"	11/1/19		[illegible]	App
"	12/1/19		[illegible]	App
"	13/1/19		[illegible]	App
"	14/1/19		[illegible]	App
"	15/1/19		[illegible]	App
"	16/1/19		[illegible]	App

Army Form C. 2118.

WAR DIARY
or
INTELLIGENCE SUMMARY.

(Erase heading not required.)

Instructions regarding War Diaries and Intelligence Summaries are contained in F. S. Regs., Part II. and the Staff Manual respectively. Title pages will be prepared in manuscript.

Place	Date	Hour	Summary of Events and Information	Remarks and references to Appendices
Tournai	17.1.19.		Battalion took over the duties of Bn. on outpost duty. Battalion resumed its training and education. "D" Coy. beat H.Q. Bn. at football by 3 goals to 2 in Bde Knock-out Tournament.	
"	18.1.19.		Day observed as a whole holiday. Major G.O.F. Oxley M.C. proceeded on leave of absence. 2nd Lieut. Inch rejoined from conducting duty. "B" Coy. beat "C" Coy. at football in the 18th Bde. R.F.A. team in Coys. Knock-out Competition.	
"	19.1.19.		Church Parade was held in Church at 1100 hours. During the afternoon "A" Coy. beat "D" Coy. in Bn. league match, result being a draw.	
"	20.1.19.		Battalion beat 15th Bn. Middlesex Regt. in Tug of War which was pulled off at 14.00 hrs. 12 men were sent to Concan Camp for Lewis Gun Coy. Instr. A.A. Bloc. proceeded to Concan Camp for Coy.	
"	21.1.19.		The whole of the Battalion were given this day as a holiday on account of the Battalion winning the Military Cross to Capt. E.F. Sharp, D.C.M. Petition was sent to Army Command. Camp for demob. etc. A meeting of future Battn. football and cricket was held to discuss the benefit of future Staff etc. Old Comrades Association.	
"	22.1.19.		Eleven men were despatched to Coys. Duncan Camp this day. 2nd Lieut. Sanderson proceeded also for conducting duty.	
"	23.1.19.		Bn. pulled 5th Bn. West Kent Regt. at Tug of War in Divisional Tug of War Contest at 0930 hours.	
"	24.1.19.		Large Working Party hut Divisional Train Heavy Motors in 24th Divisional Semi-Final Tug of War Competition. Lieut. J. Portock M.C. struck off strength on being detained in some on (compassionate grounds).	

WAR DIARY
or
INTELLIGENCE SUMMARY.

Army Form C. 2118.

Place	Date	Hour	Summary of Events and Information	Remarks and references to Appendices
FOZNY 221	25/1/19		Day observed as Whole Holiday. Battn.pulled 24th Divisional H.T. in Cairo Flotto Cup. B.N. in the final of Divisional Pulls, but lost to a heavy team. A cinema was given by the Sergeant's Mess on the night of 26th which proved a great success. 16 men sent to Depot.Camp.Boen.Faim. a day.	A.B.
"	26.1.19		Church Parade was held at 1100 hours. 14 men sent to Depot Boen Sec. Camp this day.	A.B.
"	27.1.19		Training carried out under Company arrangements during the morning. Fall of snow interfered with afternoon training. Inter-Company football match was held in the afternoon. 17 men & two N.C.Os. sent to Depot Boen.Camp.	A.B.
"	28.1.19		2nd Lieut.E.Rutherns proceeded for duty with L.Div.A.S.C. at Auberchicourt. 2nd Lieut.W.Ground proceeded to Corps Concert.Camp for conducting duty. 29 men sent to Depot Boen.Camp.Faim.	A.B.
"	29.1.19		Training under Coy. arrangements was carried out during the morning. In the afternoon Educational and Recreational training, the first of the latter being for football or other games naming. Men allowed to Corps Concert.Camp this day.	A.B.
"	30.1.19		7and- Frost still holding. Divisional Commander inspected Barracks.	A.B.
"	31.1.19		Training carried out on lectures was from 1015 to 1230 hours. Same and Educational Classes from 1015 to 1230 hours. Ration Strength of Battn.was NCOs 146 and Other Ranks of 6 5 available for duty. The weather has still too frosty for drill or operations of any description.	A.B.

[signature] Lieut.-Colonel,
Cmdg. 1st Bn. North Staffordshire Regt.

Army Form C. 2118.

WAR DIARY
or
INTELLIGENCE SUMMARY.
(Erase heading not required.)

1 N Stafford Rgt 9/8 48

War Diary
For
February 1919

Army Form C. 2118.

WAR DIARY
or
INTELLIGENCE SUMMARY.
(Erase heading not required.)

Place	Date	Hour	Summary of Events and Information	Remarks and references to Appendices
Tournai	1.2.19		Day observed as a holiday. Weather still very cold, a hard frost still holding. Recreational Training impossible, 13 men this day dispatched to 1st. C.C.C.	ack
"	2.2.19		Church parade was held in Y.M.C.A. at 10.00 hrs. 22 men were sent to C.C.C. this day for demobilization.	ack
"	3.2.19		Weather still very cold. Divnl. Boxing contest began at 14.00 hrs. at Cavalry Barracks. 10 men sent to 1st. C.C.C. for demobilization.	ack
"	4.2.19		Nothing to record.	ack
"	5.2.19		Nothing to record. Fall of snow prevented any recreational training being carried out.	ack
"	6.2.19		Battn. took over duties from 8th. Bn. Royal West Kent Regt. A photograph was this day taken of the Officers of the Battn. 25 men proceeded to 1st. C.C.C. fo demobilization. 2/Lieut. T. Lambert proceeded for conducting duty.	ack
"	7.2.19		28 men this day sent to 1st. C.C.C. for demobilization. Nothing further of event to report.	ack
"	8.2.19		7 men sent this day to C.C.C. for demobilization 2/Lieut. G.W. Brookes proceeded to 1st. C.C.C. for conducting duty, hard frost still holds & no recreational training possible.	ack
"	9.2.19		Lieut. G.W. Gibson & 7 men sent to 1st. C.C.C. this day for demob- ilization. Major G.D.R. Oxley M.C. rejoined from leave.	ack
"	10.2.19		C.S.M. Hobson & 1 man proceeded to C.C.C. for demobilization. A conference was held & owing to the depleted strength of the Bn. it was decided to reduce the Battn. to a Two Coy. basis, A & B would combine also C & D, and Coys. would be known as Nos. 1 & 2 Coys.	ack
"	11.2.19		Nothing to report. No men proceeded for demobilization.	ack

Army Form C. 2118.

WAR DIARY
or
INTELLIGENCE SUMMARY.

(Erase heading not required.)

Instructions regarding War Diaries and Intelligence Summaries are contained in F. S. Regs., Part II. and the Staff Manual respectively. Title pages will be prepared in manuscript.

Place	Date	Hour	Summary of Events and Information	Remarks and references to Appendices
Tournai	12.2.19		2/Lieut. E. T. Pierson proceeded on leave this day.	
"	13.2.19.		The Batn. is now constituted of 2 Companies only Nos. 1 & 2 Coys. Capt. R. W. Sharp M.C. Commands No. 1. Coy. & Capt. N.M. Fort Commands No. 2 Coy. 9 men sent to 1st. C.C.C. for demobilization.	
"	14.2.19		2 men sent this day to 1st. C.C.C. for demobilization.	
"	15.2.19		Day was observed as a holiday. 3 men sent this day to 1st. C.C.C.	
"	16.2.19		Lieut. & Q.M. H.A. Elsegood & 2/Lieut. J.W. Haworth rejoined from leave. 5 men proceeded to 1st. C.C.C. 2/Lieut. R. Souster proceeded to C.C.C. on conducting duty. Capt. K.F.M. Murray rejoined from leave	
"	17.2.19.		50 men proceeded for demobilization, 2/Lieut. A.A. Ridge proceeded to C.C.C. for conducting duty. The Batn. took over Brigade duties from 9th. Bn. East Surrey Regt.	
"	18.2.19		Capt. S.E. Steeley proceeded to 1st C.C.C. for demobilization.	
"	19.2.19		Nothing of interest to report.	
"	20.2.19		21 men proceeded to 1st. C.C.C. 2/Lieut. J.G. Cook proceeded to 1st. C.C.C. for conducting duty.	
"	21.2.19		4 men sent to 1st. C.C.C. 1st. Govrs. Commander presented Union Colours to 9th. Bn. East Surrey Rgt. & 8th. Bn. Royal West Kent Rgt.	
"	22.2.19		11 men sent to C.C.C. 2/Lieut. J.D. Mc. Laren to conducting duty 2/Lieut. W.R. Goodwin returned from conducting duty.	
"	23.2.19		2 men sent to 1st. C.C.C. for demobilization.	

Army Form C. 2118.

WAR DIARY
or
INTELLIGENCE SUMMARY.
(Erase heading not required.)

Place	Date	Hour	Summary of Events and Information	Remarks and references to Appendices
Tournai	24.2.19		Capt. R.W. Sharp M.C. & 2/Lieut. A Peacock proceeded to 1st.C.C.C. on conducting duty.	A
"	25.2.19		2/Lieut. H.G. Curtis & 2/Lieut. W.I. Harper M.C. rejoined from conducting duty.	B
"	26.2.19		Nothing to report.	B
"	27.2.19		6 men sent to 1st. C.C.C. for demobilization.	B
"	28.2.19		Final judging of Guard Mounting Competition took place No. 1 Coys guards were judged on 27th. inst. & No. 2 Coys. on 28th. Two guards per Company were judged. First Prize was awarded to No. 1 Coy. for a guard of 2 N.C.O's. & 6 men. The NCO i/c of the guard received a silver medal all other members bronze medals.	B

W.J. Slamer.
Lieut.-Colonel,
Cmdg. 1st Bn. North Staffordshire Regt.

Army Form C. 2118.

Appx 49

WAR DIARY
or
INTELLIGENCE SUMMARY.
(Erase heading not required.)

War Diary
for
March 1919

WAR DIARY
or
INTELLIGENCE SUMMARY.
(Erase heading not required.)

Army Form C. 2118.

Instructions regarding War Diaries and Intelligence Summaries are contained in F. S. Regs., Part II and the Staff Manual respectively. Title pages will be prepared in manuscript.

Place	Date	Hour	Summary of Events and Information	Remarks and references to Appendices
Journal	March 1st		2/Lieut. W.T. PETERSON returned from leave.	
"	2nd		2/Lieut. J. MACKIE proceeded to 1st. Corps. concentration camp for conducting duty. 2/Lieut. J. MILLER to leave. 2/Lieut. J. PORTER	
"	3rd		Capt. R.B. LAWTON returned from leave & commenced conducting duty.	
"	4th		Nothing of interest to report.	
"	5th		7 Officers & 31 other ranks of the 5th. Bn. West Surrey Regt. were this day taken on the strength of the Batn. all being eligible for demobilization. 5th Bn. West Surrey now a life Brigade to the 4th Army of Occupation.	
"	6th		An Officer's Revolver Competition in rapid & deliberate practices was held. Lieut. D. DICKSON won.	
"	7th		Nothing of interest to report.	
"	8th		2/Lieut. G.I. REID rejoined the Batn. from 73rd. Trench M. Battery.	
"	9th		2/Lieut. G.W. BROOKS & 2 men proceeded to 1st. C.R.C. for demob.	
"	10th		Capt. K.F.M. MURRAY proceeded to reporting pool for duty.	
"	11th		Nothing of interest to report.	
"	12th		Nothing of interest to report.	
"	13th		2/Lieut. F.M. DUNN proceeded to leave.	
"	14th		3 men proceeded to 1st. I.B.D. pool demobilization	
"			2/Lieut's RIDER & SOUSTER returned from leave. The Mobilization Stores of the Batn. were inspected by A.D.O.S. 1st. Corps. preparatory to the movement of same to England.	

(10560) Wt.W5300/P715 750,000 3/18 E.S.&L. Forms/C118/6

Army Form C. 2118.

WAR DIARY
or
INTELLIGENCE SUMMARY.

(Erase heading not required.)

Instructions regarding War Diaries and Intelligence Summaries are contained in F. S. Regs., Part II. and the Staff Manual respectively. Title pages will be prepared in manuscript.

Place	Date	Hour	Summary of Events and Information	Remarks and references to Appendices
Tournai	March 15th		Major S.B.R. OXLEY, M.C. proceeded to England to attend a course at HARROW & is struck off the strength of the Battalion from this date. 2/Lieut. J.G. COOK rejoined from conducting duty. Capt. K.M. ROFT returned from leave.	
"	16th		Capt. E.L. WITTMAN, Lt. W.T. WEBB, 2/Lt. E. SOUSTER, 2/Lt. R.G. CLARKS, 2/Lt. D. DICKSON & 20 men proceeded to 1st I.C.C. for demobilization.	
"	17th		A Regimental Dinner was held as a farewell to Officers who will soon be leaving the Battn.	
"	18th		Nothing of interest to report.	
"	19th		Nothing of interest to report.	
"	20th		Orders received that the Battn. would move to CAMPHIN on 21st. 2/Lt. D.J.C. CRUICKSHANK & 2/Lt. R.R. HUGHES rejoined from leave & sick leave respectively.	
Tournai Camphin	21st		Battn. moved by march route into CAMPHIN & was billeted in the Chateau de Luchin (see OPERATION ORDER No. to attached). Various for 1st. line transport not parked at BUISIEX.	
Camphin	22nd		Capt. R.W. STAPF, M.C. returned from conducting duty, 34 other ranks of the Band joined the Battn. from the 5th. Battn. in IRELAND.	
"	23rd		Day spent in settling down into billets.	
"	24th		Nothing of interest to report.	
"	25th		Nothing of interest to report.	
"	26th		Nothing of interest to report.	
"	27th		2/Lieut. A. PEACOCK returned from conducting duty.	

Army Form C. 2118.

WAR DIARY
or
INTELLIGENCE SUMMARY.
(Erase heading not required.)

Place	Date	Hour	Summary of Events and Information	Remarks and references to Appendices
Boulogne	March 28th		A draft of 80 obtainable personnel proceeded to join 10th. Battalion of this Regt. DUNKIRK. Capt. R.J. STAAF M.C. & 2/Lieut's GOWEN & MACKIE conducted this draft to DUNKIRK.	ref.
"	29th		Nothing of interest to report.	ref.
"	30th		2/Lieut's. CRUIKSHANK, R.H. HUGHES, A.L. RIDGE, & A. PEACOCK proceeded to 1st. G.C.T. with 29 men for demobilization. 2/Lt. F.M. DUNK rejoined from leave.	ref.
"	31st		Nothing of interest to report.	ref.

(Sgd) Skinner
Lieut.-Colonel,
Cmdg. 1st Bn. North Staffordshire Regt.

1/6th BATTALION NORTH STAFFORDSHIRE REGT.   Copy No.

OPERATION ORDER NO 46

Ref: BELOTTE and PART of FRANCE Sheet No 37 1/40,000.

(1) Battalion will move by march route tomorrow 21st inst. to CAMPHIN (N 31B).
    The battalion will be formed up in close column of Companies on the
    Barrack Square ready to move off at 13.30 hrs. Dinners will be at 12.00
    hrs.
    Dress:- Full marching order. Leather jerkins will be carried in the pack.
    Steel helmets will be carried and goffered worn.
    If the weather is inclement ground sheets will be worn.

(2) A colour party composed as under will as end as R.S.M's Mess at 13.15 hrs
    to bring the coloured. Colour party will march between Nos. 1 & 2 Coys.
    Colour party will be as under:-
              2nd Lieut. R.H. Warner Kings
              2nd Lt. W.E. Jaques
              Sgt Harrison M.R.   No 2 Coy
              4 Corporals to be detailed by R.S.M.

(3) An advance party consisting of the following Officers and NCO's will
    rendezvous at Battalion Orderly Room at 08.45 hrs tomorrow and proceed to
    CAMPHIN under the command of 2/Lt E.T. Pedrsen.
              1 Corporal and 1 N.C.O. per Coy
              1 N.C.O. for L.M. Stores
              1 N.C.O.   " Orderly Room
              1 N.C.O.   " Battalion H.Q.
              1 Servant from B.H.Q. Mess

(4) All Officers kits and Mess goods will be stacked outside Company and
    Battalion H.Q. and Orderly Room roads outside Orderly Room at 09.00 hrs.
    Transport Officer will arrange transport thereof. Any more goods which
    arrive on waggons at 09.00 hrs will be stacked outside messes as early as
    possible afterwards and will be transported to CAMPHIN with the mess
    goods as under above.
    Each Company will detail 1 N.C.O. and 5 men to assist in H.Q. at 08.30 hrs
    as loading parties.
    Mens blankets will be rolled in 10's and stacked in the barracks by 08.45
    hrs.

(5) R.S.M. will detail a guard of 1 N.C.O. and 5 men who will march with
    advance transport to CAMPHIN and who will then mount 1st line transport
    coming by rail. O.C. Coys will arrange for rations for this Guard.

(6) Tea will be cooked on two cookers going direct to CAMPHIN and will be
    ready for issue at 14.30 hrs.

(7) CPL Foss will arrange to synchronise watches tomorrow morning.

(8) ACKNOWLEDGE.

              Issued at 14.45 hrs.
              Date   20/2/40
              (Sd) N.G. Butterworth Capt & A/Adjt.
              1st/6th North Staffordshire Regiment.
Copies to:-
    (1) Commanding Officer
    (3) O.C. Coys.   (2) O.C. H.Q. Coy
    (5) Quartermaster   (4) Transport Officer
    (8) R.S.M.   (6) & (7) War Diary
                                      (9) Town Major Tournai

HEADQUARTERS

72nd Infantry Brigade.

Herewith War Diary for the month of March 1919.

Please acknowledge receipt.

W. D. Stamer.
Lieut. Col.
Comdg. 1st Bn. North Staffordshire Regiment.

2/4/19.

ORDERLY ROOM
DATE 2. 4. 19
No. M630/2
1ST NORTH
STAFFORDSHIRE REGT

Army Form C. 2118.

WAR DIARY
or
INTELLIGENCE SUMMARY.
(Erase heading not required.)

War Diary
April 1919

Instructions regarding War Diaries and Intelligence Summaries are contained in F. S. Regs., Part II. and the Staff Manual respectively. Title pages will be prepared in manuscript.

Place	Date	Hour	Summary of Events and Information	Remarks and references to Appendices

ORDERLY ROOM.
DATE 2/5/19
No. 192/13
1ST NORTH STAFFORDSHIRE REGT

Army Form C. 2118.

WAR DIARY
or
INTELLIGENCE SUMMARY.
(Erase heading not required.)

Place	Date	Hour	Summary of Events and Information	Remarks and references to Appendices
Camphin	1/4/19		Capt. R. D. Sharp, M.C. & 2/Lieut. Cowden returned from Conducting Duty	
"	2/4/19		Nothing of interest to report.	
"	3/4/19		Lt. Lieut. H. W. Every returned from Conducting Duty.	
"	4/4/19		A draft of 36 Other Ranks proceeded to join 243rd. P.O.W. Coy., DUNKIRK, 2/Lieuts J.G. Cook & T. Lambert conducted this party.	
"	5/4/19		Nothing of interest to report.	
"	6/4/19		Church parade was held at 10.15 hrs.	
"	7/4/19		Nothing of interest to report.	
"	8/4/19		Nothing of interest to report.	
"	9/4/19		3 men sent to 5th. C.C. for demobilization including C.S.M. Austin, D.C.M. S.M. also proceeded for furlough on re-enlistment.	
"	10/4/19		2/Lieut. W. Cowden proceeded on leave.	
"	11/4/19		2/Lieut. J.C. Porter conducted a draft of 5 N.C.O's. & 39 men to join 243rd. P.O.W. Coy. DUNKIRK this day.	
"	12/4/19		Capt. W.H. Lester 2/Lieuts J.G. Cook & J. Mackie proceeded to England for duty	

WAR DIARY
or
INTELLIGENCE SUMMARY.
(Erase heading not required.)

Army Form C. 2118.

Place	Date	Hour	Summary of Events and Information	Remarks and references to Appendices
Campher	13/4/19		The Battn. beat the 8th. Battn. Queen's Regt. in the 1st. round of the Cadre Football Competition by 10 goals to 1.	
"	14/4/19		A party of Officers & N.C.O's proceeded by lorry to LENS & BULLY GRENAY & an interesting though very wet day was spent in the area occupied by the Battn. during the period May, October 1918.	
"	15/4/19		Nothing of interest to report.	
"	16/4/19		Capt. R. W. Sharp, M.C. 2/Lt. W.L. Harper, M.M. Lieut. J.W. Haworth 2/Lieut's T. Sherratt & J. Lambert proceeded to 5th. C.C. for Demobilization.	
"	17/4/19		Nothing of interest to report.	
"	18/4/19		Nothing of interest to report.	
"	19/4/19		Nothing of interest to report.	
"	20/4/19		Church parade was held in the village of CAMPHIN.	
"	21/4/19		Capt. G.W. Loxax proceeded to No 5. C.C. SWAIN for demobilization.	
"	22/4/19		2/Lieut J.L. Higinbotham proceeded to England independently for demobilization	
"	23/4/19		Nothing of interest to report.	
"	24/4/19		2/Lieut. W. W. Goodwin proceeded to England to attend Educational Course.	
"	25/4/19		Lieut. C.C.Holmes conducted a draft of 1 W.O.C. & 24 men to join No 3. P.O.W.	

Army Form C. 2118.

WAR DIARY
or
INTELLIGENCE SUMMARY.
(Erase heading not required.)

Instructions regarding War Diaries and Intelligence Summaries are contained in F. S. Regs., Part II. and the Staff Manual respectively. Title pages will be prepared in manuscript.

Place	Date	Hour	Summary of Events and Information	Remarks and references to Appendices
Cambrai	26/4/19		Nothing of interest to Report.	ACA
"	27/4/19		2/Lieut. A. Cowden returned from leave. Lieut. Pearson admitted to 51 C.C.S.	ACA
"	28/4/19		Nothing of interest to report.	ACA
"	29/4/19		The Battn. played 24th Bn. M.G.C. in the third round of the Cadre Football competition but were beaten after a hard game by 1 goal to nil.	ACA
"	30/4/19		2/Lieut. A. Cowden proceeded to join No. 3 Regt. S. Repots. Coys : 30/5/11/5.	ACA

W. Skrine.
Lieut.-Colonel,
Cmdg. 1st Bn. North Staffordshire Regt.

Army Form C. 2118.

WAR DIARY
or
INTELLIGENCE SUMMARY.
(Erase heading not required.)

1 N Staff R¹
Vol 51

War Diary
May 1919

ORDERLY ROOM.
DATE 1. 6. 19
No. M 11845
1ST NORTH
STAFFORDSHIRE REGT

Army Form C. 2118.

WAR DIARY
or
INTELLIGENCE SUMMARY.
(Erase heading not required.)

Instructions regarding War Diaries and Intelligence Summaries are contained in F. S. Regs., Part II. and the Staff Manual respectively. Title pages will be prepared in manuscript.

Place	Date	Hour	Summary of Events and Information	Remarks and references to Appendices
Camphin	1919 1st/2/19		3 men proceeded to No. 5 C.C. SOMAIN for demobilization.	A & B
do	2nd		Lieut. C. C. Holmes rejoined from conducting duty.	A & B
do	3rd		Nothing of interest to report.	A & B
do	4th		Nothing of interest to report.	A & B
do	5th		Lieut. & Qr. Mr. Flesgood rejoined from Hospital, 2/Lieut. W. E. Jaques proceeded on leave.	
do	6th		Nothing of interest to report.	A & B
do	7th		Nothing of interest to report.	A & B
do	8th		Nothing of interest to report.	
do	9th		Lieut. & Qr. Mr. Flesgood proceeded on leave.	A & B
do	10th		Regimental Sports were held at CAMPHIN, the weather was very fine & competition for events was keen.	A & B
do	11th		2/Lieut. J. G. Porter proceeded to join 107 Prisoners of War Coy. DUNKIRK, Church parade was held in CAMPHIN.	A & B
do	12th		Information received this day that the Battalion would proceed home on 15th inst.	A & B
do	13th		Date of entraining changed to 16th inst.	A & B

Army Form C. 2118.

INTELLIGENCE SUMMARY.
(Erase heading not required).

Instructions regarding War Diaries and Intelligence Summaries are contained in F. S. Regs. Part II. and the Staff Manual respectively. Title pages will be prepared in manuscript.

Place	Date	Hour	Summary of Events and Information	Remarks and references to Appendices
Étaples	May 1919 15th		7 O.R's. proceeded to join No 3 Prisoners of War Coy TROUVILLE.	ref
do	16th		Lieut. C. C. Holmes and 8 O.R's. proceeded to No 5 C. C. SQUAIN for Demob'y.	ref
do	17th		Nothing of interest to report. Hope to UK present	ref
do	18th		Nothing of interest to report.	ref
do	19th		A/R.S.M. Pryor proceeded to England for 28 days furlough.	ref
do	20th		Nothing of interest to report.	ref
do	21st		2/Lieut W. E. Jaques proceeded to England for duty.	ref
do	22nd		Nothing of interest to report.	ref
do	23rd		Nothing of interest to report.	ref
do	24th		Nothing of interest to report.	ref
do	25th		Nothing of interest to report.	ref
do	26th		Nothing of interest to report.	ref
do	27th		Lieut. & Qr. Mr. H. A. Elsegood rejoined from leave.	ref
do	28th		Nothing of interest to report.	ref
do	29th		Nothing of interest to report.	ref
do	30th		News received that Battalion will proceed to England on June 2nd.	ref
do	31st		Nothing of interest to report.	ref

(sd) Stowe
Lieut.-Colonel
Cmdg. 1st Bn. North Staffordshire Regt.

29TH DIVISION
72ND INFY BDE

1ST BN NTH STAFFS

NOV 1915 - MAY 1919

From 6 Div 17 BDE